Also by Tom Schaudel

Playing with Fire: Whining and Dining on the Gold Coast

A SECOND HELPING

HELPING

Whining and Dining on Long Island

Tom Schaudel

A SECOND HELPING
WHINING AND DINING ON LONG ISLAND

iUniverse books may be ordered through booksellers or by contacting:

iUniverse
1663 Liberty Drive
Bloomington, IN 47403
www.iuniverse.com
844-349-9409

ISBN: 978-1-6632-4011-8 (sc)
ISBN: 978-1-6632-3388-2 (e)

Library of Congress Control Number: 2022909555

Print information available on the last page.

iUniverse rev. date: 08/04/2022

CONTENTS

TESTIMONIALS

I've had the pleasure of reading *A Second Helping* and offer the following comments:

Tom Schaudel, Long Island's true celebrity chef, has done it again. Not satisfied with exposing his worst customers in his bestselling *Playing with Fire: Whining And Dining on the Gold Coast*, he has gone back for *A Second Helping*, one of the funniest and wittiest books I've read in years.

You should buy and read this book because you may see yourself in these stories, you may see your family or friends on these pages, and you will never again be an a-hole in a restaurant. The late Anthony Bourdain's *Kitchen Confidential* was an eye-opener; Schaudel's *A Second Helping* is a gut-buster.
—Nelson DeMille, best-selling author

Tom is a master storyteller. It seems there will never be a shortage of the witless, and Tom is there to capture it all!
—Jim Douglass, DJ, 103.1 MAX-FM

Tom Schaudel is a good friend, an accomplished chef, an all-around great guy, and a stand-up comic. His stories about the restaurant industry are so engaging and hilarious because you know they are true. You can't make this stuff up!

—Kareem Massoud, winemaker, Paumanok Vineyards

Tom continues to set high standards on the Long Island culinary scene. With his many years of experience, we can always count on him for advice. It's amazing that he still has the passion, drive, and energy. And of course, we can depend on him for one of his many restaurant stories for a laugh. Tom, a good friend of many years in the kitchen and on the golf course, still contributes. Long Island can't wait to see what's next.

—Bill Holden, chef and owner, Market Bistro

Having grown up with Tom in our small town of Carle Place, Long Island, and being one of the few who followed his path into the outrageous world of restaurants, I have been entertained by Tom and his idiosyncratic approach over the years. Tom has always been able to keep his fascination for food and wine with a thirst to keep it real, playful, and upbeat. His ability to tell it like it is defies the *customer is always right* theory. Tom Schaudel is a hoot. No one can argue his logic when it comes to the rationale of his abstract sense of sanity in those get-real moments. Cheers to Tom for bringing his anecdotes to the world!

—Michael Vai, restaurateur, Fire+Wine, VAI's, EVO and ASH

Tom, recognizing your potential, I gave you an opportunity to prove yourself years ago, and you certainly have outdone yourself. Renowned chef, creator of unique dishes, fantastic storyteller, and now master of the written word. Your rendition of today's Long Island dining public is superb.

—Dr. Emilie Sair, English professor,
high school principal, retired

Tom Schaudel is a true Renaissance man in every way: a highly acclaimed, passionate, award-winning chef; successful restaurateur and businessman; talented musician, singer, and performer; writer; TV and radio personality; philanthropist; avid golfer; kung fu expert; political satirist—and I've just scratched the surface. He's funny to the point of pain, and he's a really nice guy. Tom's hilarious stories of customers driving him and the waitstaff crazy first started more than twenty years ago in my *Great Restaurants of Long Island* magazine. The series was called *Tom's Top Ten,* but it was number one in popularity, and readers looked forward to it every year. I'm thrilled it has now grown into a second book and I can't wait to read it.

—Morris Sendor, publisher and owner, *Great Restaurants of Long Island* magazine

Besides being renowned for his excellent culinary skills and acclaimed restaurants, Tom Schaudel is also a gifted writer and this book, *A Second Helping*, is a glorious sequel to his first book, *Playing with Fire.*

Virtually every sentence in this book is funny to me. He has the insightful ability to creatively capture the foibles of the human condition and show them in a way that outlines their nonsensical absurdities while also showcasing them in a way that makes the insanity of the participants obvious and humorous. This can perhaps be called satirical wisdom. Most participants and situations are relatively harmless, but there are certainly some doozies.

This satirical wisdom is food for the soul for all those who find themselves agonizingly tolerating the sense of entitlement, ignorance, and inflexibility of others.

In an odd way, the stories in this book, and the way they are depicted, seem to scratch an itch that is rarely reached by anything else. It's all in the delivery. You hear of those books that once you start reading them, you won't be able to put them down. Well, you'll want to carve out some time to sit down with this gem because it is an absolutely rewarding read.

—Steve Vai, guitar virtuoso, Sony recording artist

For Harley and Hawke.
Grandkids are your reward for not killing your children.

FOREWORD

Here's the thing about eating out: You don't get to haggle. Like it or not, when you order a dish, you're agreeing to pay the price listed on the menu. But surprise, surprise: When the check arrives, some people like to raise a stink. They feel entitled to all kinds of extras: extra attention, food and drinks, discounts, gift cards … world domination.

If you've already read Tom Schaudel's first book, *Playing with Fire: Whining and Dining on the Gold Coast*, you'll know precisely what I'm talking about. Well, Tom is back, and his latest collection of anecdotes, *A Second Helping: Whining and Dining on Long Island*, introduces a new cast of characters with new complaints and new shenanigans.

You might wonder, as I once did, why do Tom's restaurants seem to attract all of Long Island's schemers, operators, manipulators, complainers, and crackpots? I mean, this kind of stuff must be going on everywhere, right? I'm pretty sure it is. But whereas other restaurateurs may write it off, Tom writes it up.

One reason Tom may have so many stories is because he's been involved with so many restaurants—places with names like Tease, Lemongrass, Coolfish, Passionfish, Starfish, and Kingfish. Although Tom was briefly involved in a roadhouse debacle called Eli's *(which you'll read about in the upcoming pages)*, most of his restaurants have been high-end spots.

Don't imagine for a moment, though, that the well-heeled clientele is any more refined than the folks you'll find at your local diner. Early in the book, you'll witness a free-for-all between two generations in the tastefully appointed dining room of a North Fork Italian restaurant, a place that offers no shelter from free-flying f-bombs.

Tom bears no ill will toward the entitled who both eat and act out at his restaurants, even calling this anthology of their exploits a, *love letter to Long Island.* He seems to relish dancing back and forth across the slippery line between, *"The customer is always right"* and *"You've got to be kidding me!"*

That may explain the mischievous glint in his eyes. Tom is a guy who stands out in a crowd. He's big and solidly built, with his stark white beard and unruly mane contrasting with dark, heavy eyebrows. Usually, you'll find him wearing a chef's jacket and checkered pants, his forehead obscured by a colorful bandana. He looks less like a chef than a pirate—one with a lightning wit and velvety Russell Crowe voice.

It was a voice I came to know over the years I worked as a restaurant critic and reporter for Long Island's *Newsday.* Whenever I needed a snappy soundbite or two, I knew I could always count on Tom. There came a point where I had to ration my use of him as a source.

Reporting on his openings and closings kept me busy enough. It became headline news when Tom launched his swankiest spot, Jewel. Before its opening, he described, *fountains, lights, waterfalls, flying monkeys, and dancing pigs.* That's not to mention the glass-walled wine cellar, open kitchen, and an impish sideshow of a men's room that became a destination in itself. Step up to a urinal, and you are bombarded with flashing neon lights and a soundtrack with voices commenting on the proceedings. Crude? Of course. But funny? Big-time. And quintessentially Tom.

For all the years I'd known Tom, we had never met face-to-face until the night of my retirement party in 2015. Unbeknownst to me, he had been invited by my editor as the evening's surprise.

Here, I must digress. Back then, restaurant critics kept their identities secret, to avoid getting special treatment that could color a review. Even though Tom's restaurants were at a higher price point than my beat, I always closely guarded my anonymity.

My party was winding down when my editor suggested a game. She asked all the women in the room to stand in the front of the restaurant. Then out steps Tom as she asks him, "Can you pick out Joan Reminick?" He never got to answer because my hand flew up to my mouth, and I rushed over to give him a big hug, ruining the game.

I later came to know Tom from another perspective, when he hired me as a restaurant consultant. What fun it was, helping him to revitalize and launch dining spots. I was always ready to nitpick *("Do you really want to send out a plate where everything is brown?"),* and he was always open to criticism. Not that he followed every recommendation I made. I don't think you'll see my suggestion of a vegan ceviche on his menus any time soon.

But if Tom doesn't have the passion for something, he's not going to fake it. He doesn't shy away from controversy. In fact, he dives into it head-first. Reading this book may induce a few cringes, but it's also sure to spark a barrage of chortles, guffaws, and all-out belly laughs.

Tom is a true Long Island original who serves up comic schtick as gleefully as he does his iconic finale: a giant bag made of chocolate, filled with gelato, bananas, strawberries, caramel and fudge. This book, like that dessert, is generous, indulgent, and over-the-top. And also like the dessert, it's well worth paying full price for.

Joan Reminick, *Newsday* restaurant critic, retired

ACKNOWLEDGMENTS

There are many people to thank who contributed mightily to this endeavor. I'm quite certain I'll forget some, and I apologize in advance and tell you that it's my memory and not their contributions that has been diminished.

This couldn't have happened without …

Ellie Go and the team at iUniverse Publishing for coordinating the project

The editing team at iUniverse publishing for the cleansing and shining up the content.

Courtney Schaudel, my daughter, for helping me navigate through the crazy world of restaurants and for always being there with a glass of wine while explaining to me where I screwed up.

Jean Koh, whose pre-editing, patience, and admonishment, reminding me, *"Your grandkids will read this someday,"* saved me from my excesses and greatly improved the finished product.

Joan Reminick, for her honesty and friendship, for writing the Foreword, and for her sage advice and counsel in helping me avoid some disastrous literary decisions.

Ed Chernoff, dear friend, business partner, and the most generous and understanding person there could ever be.

Nelson DeMille, for his friendship, kind words, and generosity of spirit.

Jim Douglass, DJ at 103.1 MAX-FM, for our segment twice every Friday of, *Customers Behaving Badly,* and a million laughs.

Stu Schrager, for producing my radio show, *Playing with Fire*, and for fervently believing in the project.

Steve Vai, who inadvertently gave me the book's title, for providing the background music for many hours of typing and reminding me how much practice time I managed to avoid.

Rosalie and Morris Sendor, who graciously published my initial writings in their *Great Restaurants of Long Island* magazine. I'll be forever grateful.

Ann May, my sister, for her loyalty and diligence.

Diane Flynn, whose memory, sense of humor, and general shenanigans were instrumental in the retelling of these tales.

Dr. Emilie Sair, my ninth-grade English teacher, whose dedication to educating her students was second to none, who made me make up a year's worth of work I had refused to do at the time, and for sparking the love of writing inside me that I enjoy to this day; a very belated thank-you.

Art Smulyan, my high school guidance counselor, whose suggestion, *"Why don't you study mortuary science?"* sent me on the express train to cooking school.

Bill Holden, dear friend, chef extraordinaire and golf buddy, for the food, the fun, and the pre-tee-off therapy sessions.

Santon "Sandy" Curti, lifelong friend, mentor, partner, and father figure. I love and miss you.

The Massoud family of Paumanok Vineyards, whose platinum standards and winemaking skills have allowed me to believe that I know how to make the stuff, and who have given me untold *Come to Jesus* moments in the tasting room—and the occasional morning-after headache.

And finally …

Louis Ellis III (a.k.a. Shorty), for my initial introduction to cooking, consumption, and criminality, and his immortal words, *"If you don't start taking these motherfucking tempitudes (Shorty speak, for temperatures) and this cooking shit mo' serious-like, I'm going to beat yo' little honkey ass to a motherfucking lump." (Shorty speak, for pulp)*. Thank you, my friend. I did.

WARNING!

This book contains adult language and an occasional sexual reference, so its chances of garnering a G rating are remote. I promise that none of it was gratuitous and was necessary to the retelling of these vignettes to stay as close to the original events as possible. As a result, I feel that it's my responsibility to warn various segments of the population.

If you are currently a malnourished rock star tour manager, an expert on lobster procreation, in need of a toupee, an aspiring counterfeiter, in possession of elevated olfactory abilities, a coupon collector, someone who has given birth to the nine year-old Antichrist, an amateur porn star, sporting a 35 USGA handicap, a foie gras fraudster, campaigning for the presidency of your local Elks Club, a foul-mouthed octogenarian, in possession of a document listing more than forty-seven of your favorite allergies, a fiancée on the verge of a public proposal, a person having lead singer's disease on karaoke night, a self-appointed traffic cop, an elite Yelper with questionable grammar skills, have an accent of any kind, a D-list celebrity with a sense of entitlement on a par with Hunter Biden, a Democrat, a Republican, or a politically correct advocate yearning to be offended, you may want to stop right here, close the book, and not subject yourself to any further abuse. But if you find humor in the absurdities that occur as we navigate ourselves through an increasingly crazy restaurant world, well then, this just may be what the doctor ordered.

T. S.

AUTHOR'S NOTE

These stories have been compiled over a period of fifty plus years and there is some material that will feel dated. I've worked in, owned, consulted on, and had partnerships with, many restaurants over the years, and these tales were originally written when they occurred for either publication in a magazine or as a nod to a less-than-perfect memory. You will see references to political events, famous folks, time frames, and restaurants that no longer exist but were relevant at the time these happenings occurred and were essential to their retelling. It was unavoidable, so enjoy them for what they are, or were, because I believe humor to be timeless.

INTRODUCTION

This book, believe it or not, is a love letter to Long Island. Having been born, grown up, resided, and worked here for nearly six decades, I feel qualified to pass on some insight as to what it's like to be in the restaurant business on what I believe to be a unique piece of geography. Long Island is the largest and most populous island on the U.S. mainland. It stretches 118 miles long east to west, is 23 miles at its widest point north to south and is bordered by the Atlantic Ocean to the south and east, Long Island Sound to the north, and the East River to the west. There are four counties on Long Island—Kings, also known as Brooklyn; Queens; Nassau; and Suffolk—with a combined population of over seven million. The thing is, when folks talk about Long Island, they are in essence talking about Nassau and Suffolk because Brooklyn and Queens are technically part of New York City. So, for the purposes of this book, when I refer to Long Island, I'm specifically referring to those two counties. They stretch from the Queens County line at mid-island, past the Hamptons and the North Fork to the Atlantic Ocean, and they have a combined population of a little more than three million people. That number is important to keep in mind as you read on.

For those who don't know of me or my previous book, a quick bit of background is in order. In 1968, I lied my way into a dishwasher's job at a local steakhouse. I was fifteen years old at the time and legally one couldn't work until one was sixteen. Not that anyone really cared but I decided to err on the side of caution, hence the fib. I was an aspiring musician at that time with as much aspiration as a fifteen-year-old could muster, practicing guitar several hours a day and dreaming of a career playing on stage, basking in the adoration of fans, having unlimited access to all manner of mind-altering chemicals, an overweight bank account, and an underweight underwear model. Scraping dried ketchup and uneaten grizzle from a few hundred dinner plates on a six night-a-week schedule will certainly motivate you to take your career ambitions more seriously and it drove me to practice even harder for fear of spending the next twenty years at that particular position. I was miserable, but at least I had spending money. My epiphany arrived in the person of a man named Shorty, a five-foot, three-inch, African American man who was a heavily muscled, illiterate, severely alcoholic, profane, gun-toting maniac. He was hired after the original chef left. Shorty hadn't been there two days when three of the cooks and one prep person quit out of fear for their lives. Because I showed up every day, a trait uncommon in dishwashing circles, and the fact that I had taken two years of high school Spanish convinced Shorty to *promote* me to prep man and head translator.

I was torn—happy to not be washing dishes, but terrified of this psychopath.

He told me, "Boy, I'm gonna teach yo' ass everything I know."

I thought, *God help me.*

And he did. Not God—Shorty. God couldn't possibly have been paying attention.

I could write an entire book on Shorty, recounting the three years that we spent an inseparable amount of time together, but that's a tale for another day. He taught me plenty when he wasn't inducing a heart attack. Some of it was good, most of it was terrible, but as I reflect on it today, I probably gained more knowledge from the bad than the good which has kept me from making some very poor decisions through the years. It was an unlikely friendship for certain, but it was a real friendship, nonetheless. I grew to love Shorty and, in his own inimitable way, I'm sure the feeling was mutual. What Shorty did at that time though, through no fault of his own, was show me the parallel experience between food and music. You had a medium with which to express yourself, the stage being the kitchen, a fan base of customers, a sense of applause when people liked what you created, unlimited access to mind-altering chemicals, a steady flow of money, and an occasional waitress. Because everyone eats several times a day there were many more job opportunities in food than there were in music. I grew to be completely seduced by the life and have spent the last fifty plus years weaving a slew of bad habits into a restaurant career.

I was sixteen years old when my path became clear and I have Shorty to thank, or hate, for that depending on the day you ask me. There were other mentors who have had an influence on my life, my cooking, and my time in the restaurant business, but none were more seminal than Shorty. Kung Fu masters will tell you that when the student is ready, the teacher appears. That was probably the case with Shorty, and I'll be forever grateful for knowing him. I've heard it said that people come into your life for a reason, a season, or a lifetime, and each of them will leave their own indelible mark on your personal evolution. Shorty certainly made the most out of the reason and the season, being the universe's most unlikely sage, but I would have never survived a lifetime with him, so the brevity of his visit was a kindness, whether intended or not, and he'll forever remain in my thoughts, my heart, and my craw.

That nugget of spiritual philosophy brings me back to the more than three million folks who live here on Long Island. In

2008, I wrote a book called *Playing with Fire*, chronicling my one hundred worst or wackiest customers. One hundred out of three million is a miniscule number, as a percentage of the whole, but these folks stood head and shoulders above their peers in their ability to turn the simple act of dining out into the Battle of Little Bighorn. What is it that turns these seemingly normal people into culinary IEDs? Well, how about allergies, gluten issues, sauce on the side, chop my salad, vegetarians, vegetarians who eat meat, vegans, vegans who eat lobster, pescatarians, pescatarians who don't eat fish, lactose intolerance, identity theft, and credit card fraud, just to name a few? Then add in a laundry list of other neuroses, both real and imagined, and you will have some idea of what life can be like cooking in a restaurant on Long Island. We seem to vibrate at different levels than the rest of the world, and I'll be damned if I know why. When I was younger, I would become annoyed or sometimes angry at the myriad special requests, instructions, and restrictions we would receive with what felt like every other dinner order. As I aged and matured, I softened a bit and was able to see the humor in the antics. To paraphrase Alan Funt of *Candid Camera* fame, people being themselves can be hilarious, and I started to memorialize some of these special folks in an article series for the *Great Restaurants of Long Island* magazine. That series gave birth to my first book and seeing that there seems to be no shortage of talent out there, here is *A Second Helping*.

I tell these tales for two reasons. First and most importantly I think they are funny, admittedly at levels from mildly amusing to side-splitting, and I'm never one to pass up a good laugh. Heaven knows that with the state the world seems to perpetually be in, we could all use one. The second reason is a bit more complex. I believe all the restaurant angst that these customers cause simply boils down to attention. They attach whatever the reason *du jour* is to whatever the requests are, but in the end it's always about attention. By giving them that attention and scratching that itch, maybe, just maybe, someone will recognize their behavior, think for a moment, and with a little luck and humility, modify it. I have more than a bit of caution in my optimism. There seems to be little to no consideration for those restaurant workers who must deal with the requests, attitudes, and behaviors of the overly entitled. A little patience and grace would go a long way especially when tossing a proverbial monkey wrench into the gear box of a restaurant operation. It would help to make the restaurant experience a pleasant one for all involved. And shouldn't that be the goal?

That said, I'd like to thank the good people of Long Island for the support over all these years. You're the reason my dreams were realized, and I was able to accomplish goals beyond anything I'd have thought possible. And in conclusion, I once again want to give a heartfelt thanks to the most difficult, fusspot, hilarious, and certifiably crazy group of folks a restaurant person could endure. I've lost a few hairs, had countless laughs, and had many tales to tell. You have colored my life in ways I would have never imagined and although the reasons aren't quite clear and the seasons have been many, it looks like we're destined to spend a lifetime together. So, let's raise our glasses, smile, and toast to a most unusual relationship.

Fresh herbs,
Tom

∾⃝∽

CUSTOMERS

C ustomers, whether you love 'em or hate 'em are obviously the lifeblood of the restaurant industry. I've served north of two million people over the course of my career, and I can honestly say I've appreciated every one of them. Some more than others, I'd have to admit, but I'm grateful for them all. I really am. No, really, I am. Early on, I did notice though that some of my customers were a bit different from the others. Let's call them *special* because the traits and behaviors exhibited by these folks truly were. So special were they that I thought not documenting the antics would be a disservice to them, me, and the world at large. So here is my contribution to humankind in the hope of making the world a slightly better place—a kinder, gentler, more understanding place. It is an ambitious goal, no doubt, with the ultimate achievement always in question, but what cannot be questioned is the passion and commitment these folks have shown in their pursuit of turning the simple act of dining out into a blood sport, effecting the career change of more than one disillusioned restaurant employee, and ultimately landing me on a therapist's couch. What also can't be questioned is the fact that dealing with them day-to-day makes you a better restaurateur, a better raconteur, and a better provocateur, and although there's tremendous value in that, the psychic income derived from the constant entertainment provided by these tortured souls is priceless.

QUIET, PLEASE

We'd recently experienced the first outbreak of gang violence at one of my restaurants, Amano. You may be wondering, was it the Bloods and the Cripps? No. It would be reasonable to assume that it could have been a long, simmering dispute between the Hell's Angels and the Pagans. It wasn't. Was it the Yankees and the Red Sox, the Marines and the Taliban, me and my ex-wife? That would be no, no, and no. This skirmish happened to be the direct result of a two-generation gap that was a divide too far to bridge. The entertaining little psychodrama unfolded on a very busy summer Saturday night. Kerry, the hostess, happened to be working at the front desk that fateful evening. Kerry is a very sweet, intelligent, and mannerly young lady whose upbringing on the heretofore sleepy North Fork did nothing to prepare her for what was about to transpire. A party of twelve generation Xers came in for a 7:00 reservation at about 6:00 and set about reducing my liquor inventory by half, killing time at the bar while waiting for their table to be ready. They were a pleasant and fun group of couples that had the look young parents have when their babysitters have temporarily liberated them from their children. One hour and a few cocktails later they were seated in the dining room. As they were settling in, a party of six belonging to, as Tom Brokaw termed it, *The Greatest Generation* arrived for their reservation. The older party were seated in the dining room as soon as they arrived, foregoing what would have been a welcomed warm-up at the bar. Amano's dining room seats about sixty people, so these two tables represented a third of the entire room. Because it's an older structure and has hardwood floors and lots of glass, Amano's dining room can get loud on busy nights. It was very crowded that evening and although the two parties accounted for about thirty percent of the crowd, they accounted for eighty percent of the noise. There were two reasons for this. The younger table had already had a few and that always leads people to ramp up the volume. Combine that with a large group of twelve, sitting at a rectangular table and trying to converse with one another at approximately the same time, and you can get awfully close to the definition of mayhem. There seemed to be a slightly different problem at the older table: hearing loss. The group at the older table was having a problem conversing in normal tones, so in order to compensate for diminished audio levels, they found themselves screaming at each other, making their own unique contribution to the already cacophonous volume in the room.

Some of the other customers were starting to become a little annoyed with the younger party and several tables complained politely to Kerry. Kerry approached the younger table and said, "Excuse me. We've had some other tables complain about the noise in here so I was wondering if we could keep it down just a little bit?"

One of the young men asked, "Who's complaining?" That is never a good sign.

Kerry said, "Well, it doesn't really matter but it's been a little loud in here and we just need to bring it down a bit, if that's okay."

The man replied, "I want to know who is doing the complaining."

Kerry asked, "Why?"

The man said, "Because I want to send their table a bottle of wine."

Kerry replied, "That's very nice of you, sir, but there were four or five tables that mentioned the noise."

He said, "Get them all a bottle of whatever they're drinking and tell them we're sorry. We're just having a good time."

Kerry, "You really want me to buy all those tables wine?"

The man then told her, "Absolutely, and tell them that we apologize."

I've had the noise problem before, as you can imagine, but this was a first for me. This extremely classy guy restored my faith in the intoxicated and set an example for all to follow going forward.

Kerry told all the offended parties that the gentleman at the table of twelve would like to buy them a bottle of wine, their choice, and that they apologized for making so much noise. Four out of the five tables that complained accepted the man's generosity and ordered the wine. The older table did not.

The speaker of the older group, a well-dressed, petite woman of about five feet two inches, with the Presbyterian visage of a younger, prettier Barbara Bush, said, "No, thank you. We don't drink. Just tell them to keep it down; we can't hear ourselves think."

Kerry relayed the four *"Thank-yous"* and the one *"Keep it down"* to the gentleman at the younger table.

He raised his glass in a collective cheer to the dining room and said, "Sorry if we offended anyone. Good luck."

Everyone cheered him back except for the older table, where someone said, "Keep it down over there." And down it went.

The younger gentleman said to the older table, "Come on, ease up. We're just having fun."

Someone at the older table replied, "Well, we're not having fun. We're trying to have dinner here and it's too noisy to eat. Keep it down."

The younger man shrugged and said, "Sorry."

They did try to keep it down for a while, but it just wasn't to be. It seems that free wine brings people together and the other tables in the room were getting into the party with the twelve-top, thanking them for the wine, laughing, carrying on, and ratcheting up the noise level even higher. One of the men at the older table, seemingly at the end of his wits, placed his thumb and middle finger in his mouth and let out a whistle that had to have had every dog within two miles sprinting for home. The whole dining room fell silent. Someone—it may have been the whistler—shouted, *"Shut up!"*

One of the younger men responded, "You know what? Lighten up."

Apparently, the phrase, *"You know what? Lighten up"* was the trigger that sent Barbara Bush off the rails.

She got up, marched halfway to the twelve-top and screamed at the top of her lungs, "Fuck you!"

Let me tell you why this bothers me. First, that kind of language in a restaurant is extremely inappropriate and having the sentiment expressed by an octogenarian who's a dead ringer for the wife of our forty-first president leaves me in a state of confusion as to whether to laugh or cry. The second reason is that in the lexicon of cursing, *"Fuck you"* shows a complete lack of imagination. There are many other interesting and colorful ways to express yourself through the wonders of profanity in a more thought-provoking manner. I much prefer using phrases that include a member of one's family or a specifically illicit sex act. It shows an elevated level of creativity, and it usually achieves the desired response in half the time. The conveniently brief, albeit ignorant, phrase *"Fuck you"* always sets me to pondering; *"Does he or she want me to fuck myself? Who exactly is supposed to be doing the fucking? Am I fucking them, or are they fucking me? Do I say 'Yes, please' or 'No, thank you' after considering who issued the invitation?"* And perhaps the most perplexing question of all: *"Is that a complete sentence?"* I think *"Fuck you"* is highly over-rated, highly over-used, and highly over-reacted to.

So, this woman screamed, "Fuck you!"

One of the men at the younger table said, "Hey, don't talk like that in front of my wife."

One of the men at the older table responded, "Don't *you* talk to *my* wife like that."

Barbara Bush, elaborating on her initial point, screamed, "Oh, yeah, fuck you!"

One of the wives at the younger table then decided to weigh in. "Fuck you too, lady!"

One of the men at the older table then shouted, "Watch your mouth!"—another curious phrase, if you think about it.

Five or six "*Fuck you*s" later, upon realizing that she had lost control of the dining room, Kerry ran in to try to quell the impending riot and appeal for calm. The manager came running to her aid and positioned herself resolutely between the warring factions. As an experienced referee in the restaurant business, she took the matter in hand and told everyone to shut up.

Barbara Bush said, "I want them thrown out."

That's rich. I have a dead-sober woman in full-blown Tourette's, screaming profanities through the dining room, demanding the eviction of a party of twelve fun people who are spending money like drunken Congressmen. I don't think so.

The manager told her, "Ma'am, you've got to get hold of yourself. They haven't done anything wrong. We asked them to keep it down, and they did. They even offered to buy you a bottle of wine."

"We don't drink!" she exclaimed.

The manager then said, "Well, I'm not asking them to leave."

Barbara responded with yet another, "Fuck you," to the manager and then announced that their table would be leaving. They got up to go, with the manager still standing guard between the two tables. As they went past the hostess stand, where a visibly shaken Kerry had resumed her post, Barbara Bush said to her, "We're leaving, and we're never coming back to this fucking restaurant again. You can go fuck yourself. In fact, all you people can go fuck yourselves. You're all a bunch of fucking assholes! Fuck you!"

Kerry stood there stunned. This alien life form in the body of what appeared to be a cute little grandma had just given her some valuable hostess experience, which, if it doesn't kill you, will make you strong as hell. I must admit that in the end, I was comforted by the fact that when the word *fuck* is whirling around the restaurant, my staff is professional enough not to react to it and, more importantly, that the woman promised never to come back.

I just pray she's fucking serious.

HAPPY HOUR

I've often wondered about the origin of language and how things got to be called what they are. I'm not sure if it's a Puritanical hangover, political correctness, denial, an unwillingness to face the truth, or a combination of all the above, but we have made some awfully flawed calls in naming certain things over the years. I'll give you some examples.

Cafeteria Food: Rarely.
Unalienable Rights: Would seem to mean that you can pretty much do whatever you want if you haven't listed Mars as your primary residence.
Government Worker: Ever seen one?
Adult Male: I don't believe it's happened yet.
Catfish: All right, pick one.
Political Leadership: I can't even go there.

Even single words like *asteroid* and *hemorrhoid* lead me to believe that there were some pranksters in the Funk and Wagnall's office. An *aster*oid is up in the *hem*isphere and a *hem*orrhoid is, well, on your *ass*. Seems to me someone with a seriously warped sense of humor switched them around. But my all-time favorite must be *facial tissue*. Has anyone ever handed you a wad of toilet paper and said, *"Here, wipe that smile off your face?"* It seems that regardless of what these things are or are not, we just can't seem to tell ourselves the truth. This brings me to maybe the greatest white lie of all, *Happy Hour.* Let's, for a moment, examine this Godzilla of all misnomers. First, it's never an hour; it's an hour and a half or two hours, and even if you try to hold it to an hour, there's always one or two professional happy hour patrons who know enough, or are shameless enough, to order three or four cocktails at one minute until the deadline, extending the happiness indefinitely. I realize that some people get off work at a time that just happens to coincide with reduced-priced drinks. Good for them but there is a segment of the population that goes out solely for happy hour, and they're never happy. Do you know why? It's because eventually happy hour must end.

"Can't we get one more?"

"It's not 7:00 yet."

"My watch says it's five to."

There are three other groups involved in this fiasco and each one is unhappy for a different reason. There's the the bartender. You can probably imagine why he's not happy. Tips are calculated based on the total amount of the check. Therein lies the problem. He's working twice as hard for half the money. Who of you would be willing to take that cut? And on top of that he must deal with the effects of certain customers slamming as many drinks as possible in the allotted time limit. The second group is the regular restaurant goers. They're unhappy for two reasons. The first is that they may have missed it and are required to pay full price and the second is that they must suffer the effects of a somewhat elevated noise level that is the direct result of the collective caterwauling in the aftermath of what seemed to be a good idea at the time. The third group are the restaurant owners. We are extremely unhappy. It's painful to see things given away. You work your whole career to try to prevent bartenders from putting friends and family on scholarship and then you voluntarily sanction behavior you've pledged your entire career to prevent. It's a soul twister. I've never seen a happy hour at a car dealership, or Macy's, or a jewelry store. Could you imagine the scene with happy hour priced diamonds? Half of Long Island would look like the Kardashians. I would like to suggest renaming the thing and giving it an element of honesty. Let's face it head-on, show some courage, and call a spade a spade. How about the, *I Wanna Get Shit-Faced Hour*, or the, *Let's Drink as Much as We Can Because We Have Only an Hour, Hour,* or better yet, because it's essentially become an entitlement program, maybe we could give it one of those flowery government program names that try to describe the damned thing like the, *Community Tension and Dignity Relief, While Repeatedly Saying the Same Thing Over and Over Again Hour.* I'll be taking suggestions.

What am I getting at? Well, it seems we have ourselves a couple of happy hour regulars hell-bent on draining the happy out of the hour and I use the word *draining* literally. This couple comes in for happy hour which, I should let you know, is served at the bar. Let me explain what a *the bar* means in case anyone may have not grasped it: a *the bar* means … at the bar. It does not mean in the dining room, it does not mean on the patio, and it does not mean for a catered house party, all of which we have been asked to indulge. So, like half-priced pizza night, happy hour is one of those fun little promotions that is served at the bar. A couple, whom I'll refer to as Fred and Ethel, were seated in the dining room by the window. A casual glance outside rewards Ethel, by way of a hand-painted plywood masterpiece of a sign, announcing to all who drive by, *Happy Hour, Half-Priced Drinks at the Bar.*

Ethel said to Fred, "They have half-priced drinks at the bar."

Fred said to Ethel, "Really?"

Ethel said to Fred, "Yes."

The server walked up to the table and asked, "Can I get you anything from the bar?"

Ethel said to the server, "Are the drinks really half price?"

The server replied to Ethel, "Yes, they are but only at the bar."

Ethel said to the server, "We can't have them in the dining room?"

The server said, "I'm afraid not. You must buy them at the bar to get the happy hour price."

Ethel said, "Okay, we'll just take some menus."

The server asked, "Nothing to drink?"

Ethel said, "No, we're fine."

The server fetched two menus, returned to the table, placed them down, and headed to the kitchen. After a brief conference, Fred got up and proceeded to the bar. Upon his arrival, he flagged down the bartender and ordered one Sam Adams and one Amstel Light. Fred, not being an experienced server, bobbed and weaved slowly back to his table with the two beers and the two glasses.

The server returned to the table to take the dinner order and noticed the two beers. The server said to Fred and Ethel, "I see you changed your minds on the drinks."

Fred said to the server, "We thought we'd take advantage of the happy hour price and get them ourselves."

The server said to Fred, "Alright then, are you ready to order?"

They gave the server their order and after guzzling their beers, Fred went back to the bar for another round. He managed a second successful trip back to the table and as he was settling in the server delivered their meals. As she set them down, she saw the second round and said, "I'll take these empties for you."

Appearing startled, Ethel yelled to the server, "No, no don't take them! Oh, sorry for yelling. just leave them there."

"Okay …"

The couple finished their meal and as the server went to clear the table, she saw a curious thing. All four beer bottles were lying on their sides, on the table, between pieces of silverware to keep them from rolling. The server naturally assumed that there were four *dead soldiers* and tried to remove the bottles from the table.

Ethel grabbed the server's wrist and shouted, "No, don't take those bottles! Sorry, I didn't mean to shout but I want you to leave the bottles here."

The server said to Ethel, "Then why did you put them down? I figured you wanted me to clear them from the table."

Ethel replied, "No, we lay them down so all the beer that's on the sides of the bottle will drain down to the bottom and when we pour them out, we'll get more beer than if we stand them upside down."

The server asked, "This is a proven theory? You've done this before?"

Ethel, while pouring the beer bottles into the glass and showing her all six milliliters of salvaged beer, said, "All the time."

There's absolutely nothing happy about happy hour.

"HARRY, KEEP THE CHANGE"

Politicians have categorically stated that we don't torture in the United States. Oh, yeah? I would like to personally invite some of them and, if need be, a team of UN observers to take a hard look at the goings-on at Amano on half price pizza night. First, some background. The East End of Long Island, in the winter, is the best possible place to be a restaurant patron. Being the off-season, restaurant owners have devised all kinds of bright ideas to increase business during this slow period. I have witnessed deals from the well-thought-out and soberly executed to flat-out prostitution, and in the spirit of full disclosure I have participated in both. Cash flow or credit card flow is essential to winter survival. There is also the boredom that comes from one hundred and twenty slow days in a row, allowing a Jack Nicholson–type madness to slowly filter into one's psyche. So, in order to stay both solvent and sane, we run, *Specials.* Specials, being the operative word, attract special people and parts of that special group are people who get extremely excited over the fact that there is a deal. I'm convinced that, to this group of folks, the terms of the deal are irrelevant; it's the deal itself that motivates, details be damned. These same people, coincidentally, seem to have a zealot's respect for a buck and tend to guard it at all costs, no pun intended. Thrift, when taken to the extreme, becomes cheap and cheap, when taken to the extreme, becomes dogma. The truly cheap are as nutty as any committed religious fanatic. I remember the story of one four-foot, eleven-inch, extremely cheap restaurant owner who, as he was being robbed of $673.47 in cash and eight Cryovac-ed, sixteen-ounce New York strip steaks, at gunpoint at 2:00 a.m. in the basement of his restaurant, where if he was shot no one would have found him for hours, latching himself onto the leg of the fleeing bandit and after several valiant attempts at severing the perpetrator's Achilles tendon with his incisors, screamed, "You can have the steaks, you fucking scumbag, but not my money." This courageous or pathologically disturbed individual, depending on one's perspective, wasn't parting with the cash without a fight, common sense notwithstanding. What I find most amusing is that although he was willing to buy the robber and his family the steaks, he was also willing to die for $673.47. A conflicted soul, no doubt.

And that goes to the heart of my cheap and religiously zealous observations. There's a passion there that can't be denied. My partner at Amano, Adam, is a great restaurant guy. Smart, savvy and experienced, he decided he wasn't going to sit around all winter waiting for someone to show up, so he decided to offer some *Specials,* to entice customers on the weekdays. It's a good idea and, all in all, it worked out well. We kept the rear ends in the seats during the off-season and that was a good thing. But I must tell you there are occasionally some unintended consequences attached to almost anything you try in the promotion of your restaurant. The one lesson that I have learned, and learned well, is that you get the market that you target, sometimes in spades. We had been doing a promotion with WHLI radio and giving out some twenty-five-dollar gift certificates. It says, in bold print on the front of the document, assuming one can read, *Not to be combined with any other offer.* On Thursday nights we offer half-priced pizzas at the bar. Let me define, once more, what a*t the bar* means: *"At the bar* means … *at the bar.* It doesn't mean in the dining room, it doesn't mean on the patio, and it certainly doesn't mean twenty to go for the local Little League, all of which we've experienced. We serve them a*t the bar.* Check it out. A gentleman walked in and saw that the bar was full. He was craving a half-priced pizza, more likely the price than the pie.

He asked, "Can I get the half-priced pizza in the dining room?"

The bartender said, "Actually sir, we only serve the half-priced pizzas at the bar."

The man then started the speech we've all heard a thousand times. "But I'm a good customer. Why can't I have it in the dining room? The bar is full."

The bartender replied, "I'm sorry, it's house policy. I'm sure a seat will become available soon."

He said, "But I'm a good customer. I can't believe this."

The bartender again said, "I'm sorry, sir. It shouldn't be more than a few minutes."

The man proceeded to cruise the bar like a bluefish eyeing a school of mackerel. Looking … searching … waiting … yearning for that half-priced pizza. And then bingo! A couple got up to settle their check. I swear he was in the seat before they were done paying. They were looking at him as though he was possessed but as focused as he was, I'm sure he didn't notice. He proceeded with ordering his pizza and confirmed his thrift-cred by ordering his Coke with ice on the side. The reason for this, I'm assuming, is so you get an extra ounce of soda in the glass that's not displaced by the ice. The only other explanation would be an exposed nerve, in which case you would be in a dentist's chair instead of on a barstool looking to tear into a fifty percent discount. I believe that if you ordered every soda in your life with ice on the side, you could cumulatively save enough money to buy a couple of full-priced pizzas and although that may have a certain level of appeal for the skinflints among us, it's hardly a sum worth sacrificing your dignity for. Anyway, he got his half-priced pizza and his soda filled to the top with ice on the side, and he ordered a second pie.

He said, "The second one is half-priced also, isn't it?"

The bartender replied, "Sure is."

The man had his second pie and asked for the check. The bartender tallied up the two pizzas, the soda with ice on the side, and the fifty percent discount. He came up with a grand total of $17.32. The man picked up the check folder, added, readded, and re-readded just to make sure we didn't overcharge him and placed not one but two twenty-five-dollar gift certificates in the folder. The bartender took the folder and on his way to the register to process the bill he noticed the two gift certificates and said, "Sir, I think you gave me two gift certificates."

The man said, "That's right."

The bartender replied, "One will cover the bill, sir."

The man said, "I know. I'll just take the change."

This *good customer* as he put it, spent $17.32 for $34.64 worth of food and he wanted to pay for it with two $25.00 gift certificates and get $32.68 change, thereby receiving roughly twice the amount of money from us that we got from him. I guess sometimes a customer can be so good that you would pay *him* to come in. I just haven't found that customer yet.

I DO ... DON'T I?

Don't you just hate it when you ask someone to marry you and they say, *"No?"* It tends to put a damper on the ensuing celebration. My proposal experience in the restaurants runs about eighty percent yes and twenty percent no. You would think that the yes's would be a higher percentage, but that's not the case. We have had some momentous failures in the *"Will you marry me?"* department. And I find it especially noteworthy because, being a rather insecure individual, I would think you would want to be reasonably certain of a positive response if you are going to kneel down in a crowded restaurant and literally beg someone to put up with you for as long as they can stand it, using champagne to muddy up the decision process and a diamond as a bribe, in front of two hundred people who have a pretty good idea of what you are about to get yourself into. And still, two out of ten say no. There's nothing worse than the future nuptials going down in a ball of flames in front of an audience. Why not do it in private so if things don't turn out quite like they do in the movies, you can retain a shred of dignity and head for the nearest singles bar to drown out the rejection? It's a certain breed of cat who feels the need to expose themselves to such a calamitous outcome and there's more than a hint of exhibitionism in that kind of a proposal. I feel that these are the same guys who feel the need to jog half naked along Main Street, and the same guys who paint letters on their bare chests and go to sporting events in the winter feeling the need to educate the rest of us as to spelling of the word *Jets*. These are the guys who show up at the local bagel store in a pair of painted-on, nylon bicycle shorts, proudly displaying their various shortcomings while the rest of us are eating lunch.

Different strokes, I guess, but here's one of our greatest hits: We once had a guy take the suite in our boutique hotel, order a very expensive bottle of champagne and a tasting menu, reserve the private wine cellar for two, had us fashion a plate cover to hide the diamond ring that was to be substituted for dessert, and arrange for an after-dinner, in-room couple's massage. You have to admire the effort. He seemed a little nervous and uptight. We set about flawlessly executing this highly choreographed proposal, which went swimmingly until the dessert course. Out comes the server, down goes the plate, off comes the cover, and there sits the diamond. Hoping to morph from boyfriend to fiancé, our hero gets down on one knee on a very hard stone floor, stares straight into her eyes, and asks, "Will you marry me?"

Not quite the loving answer the question begged, the girlfriend let out a gastric response to the volume of food she had just consumed, covered her face with her hands, and started ten minutes of uncontrollable bawling. Completely in the dark about what was going on in the cellar, the rest of the staff decided to go down, *en masse*, to congratulate the happy couple. Needless to say, it didn't work out very well. The crew bounded down the stairs and all at once said, "Congra ... uh-oh," while staring at the two weeping lovers. Not to sound overly harsh but you put people in a very uncomfortable situation when you don't complete your fiancée research. No one quite knows how to handle a hacked marriage proposal. Should I charge him for his dinner? If they don't stay the night, should we give him his deposit back? And how about the masseuse? Could you have a little consideration for the rest of us, for heaven's sake? Now that you have some history and statistical data, here's a case where the victim of a blown restaurant proposal had absolutely nothing to do with the blowing of the proposal.

File this under collateral damage: A gentleman called the restaurant and said he was coming in on Saturday night with his girlfriend and he was going to ask her to marry him. He said that he ordered some roses for the table and asked if we would put them out for him before he got there.

We said, "Of course."

He said to put the reservation under the name *James*. We did so.

A day later, another party called up and reserved a table of three for the same night and under the same name, *James*. One of the servers caught it right away and told the hostess to make sure that the roses went to the correct table: the deuce *James*, not the three-top *James*. The hostess, who'd been married so many times that she still had rice in her hair and, as a result, tended to be a tad cynical about young love, passed the job of placing the roses on the table to the coffee girl. Why? you ask. I have no idea. I can only surmise that she did it to give us a much better shot at screwing it up, which of course is what we did. The coffee girl placed the roses directly on the three-top, diagonally across the dining room from the correct, glaringly flower-less deuce. The three-top arrived first: a man, his wife, and his mother-in-law. They were led through the dining room by the hostess who brought them to the rose-laden table, to the shock and surprise of the man's wife, and of course her mother.

The wife said, "I can't believe you had roses put on the table. That's so sweet. These are beautiful. Are they for me or Mom?"

This is a no-win position for anyone who's ever been a guy. You need to choose between two dead-ends and do it quickly. If he keeps quiet about it, he must sweat the outcome for a couple of hours, hoping the seemingly innocent mistake will go uncorrected. That makes it awfully hard to enjoy dinner. But if he says, *"I didn't buy you flowers,"* he risks hearing what an insensitive asshole he's always been and is reminded of every transgression his testosterone-fueled antics have visited upon her for the length of their union, with the affirmatively nodding support of his mother-in-law.

Resigning himself to a prayer and a package of Tums, he chose plan *A,* and let her think the flowers were for her. I've been a guy for a long time and, frankly, that's a rookie mistake. You've got to know that you can't possibly pull it off. There are too many people involved and too many ways for it to go sideways. Better to come clean, take your medicine and that nostalgic trip down memory lane, listening with rapt attention to the dates, times, places, and the color of the shirt you were wearing at the time of your every screw-up in the last twenty-seven years. Then apologize profusely for being an idiot, swear with as much sincerity as you can muster that you will try harder to think more like a woman in the future, and then try to get through dessert before Mom-in-law decides to lend her voice. The worst part is that even though you've done nothing wrong, sometimes the cosmos will stick it to you for no apparent reason, and what's even more unfair is that you know that you'll never be able to even the score. Not once in the history of humankind has a coffee girl ever mistakenly put a fishing rod, with a bow on it, on the wrong table as a man, his wife, and his father sit down to eat. So, you see, this is a problem unique to us guys and if these exhibitionist proposers didn't exhibit themselves so much, the state of marital relations, at least from the guy's perspective, would be much better served for both the pre- and the post-proposers.

Meanwhile, back at the proposal, the man realized that with some male ingenuity, some conniving, and a little luck, he just might be able to salvage the rest of his evening. He excused himself from the table and pulled my manager, Diane, aside.

He said, "I have a situation here. Those aren't my flowers, but my wife doesn't realize it yet so I'm wondering if I can buy those flowers from you and then you can just leave them there and save me the cost of a divorce lawyer."

Diane said, "Oh, no. The girl put them on the wrong table. Those flowers are for that table over there. I'm so sorry."

The man asked, "Whose flowers are they?"

Diane replied, "They're for a couple who are getting engaged tonight, hopefully."

The man replied, "Tell him I'll buy the roses from him. Tell him I'm desperate and will pay him anything he wants."

Diane said, "I'm sorry, I can't."

The *James* two top arrived at a flower-less table. The excited, soon-to-be fiancé was bewildered and started to get that feeling you get when you feel that nothing is going to go the way you feel it should go. His girlfriend saw that there were no flowers on the table, but she wasn't upset because she was not aware that anything was amiss. He excused himself from the table and flagged down Diane to tell her that his roses were missing.

Diane said, "We were keeping them fresh for you," and she made a mad dash for the other table. She removed the roses from the first table saying, "Excuse me, these are on the wrong table," and whisked them diagonally across the room to the rightful owner, much to the surprise of his prospective fiancée, and much to the chagrin of two extremely disappointed women at table number one. Not to mention one haplessly innocent, anxiety-ridden victim whose stay of execution had just been lifted by governing forces well beyond his control.

Here's the wrap-up. Two young people pledged their undying love for each other and sealed the promise with champagne, roses, a romantic dinner, and a ring. Things were a bit more subdued at the other table. The evening's remaining conversation was terse at best. The two women spent the rest of their night staring diagonally across the dining room at the roses and wondering what might have been, and I'm sure the gentleman has a new appreciation for the serendipity of karma. When they finally finished their dinner, the man at the three-top pulled Diane aside and asked, "Could you do me a favor?"

Diane said, "Sure."

The man said, "Could you go over there and tell that man that he just ruined my dinner, my night, and possibly my marriage? Oh, and make sure you tell him that I couldn't be happier that she said yes."

REACH OUT AND TOUCH SOMEONE

Some people just have that certain look. You develop radar after so many years of doing this and it serves as a self-protection mechanism to allow you to ready yourself for impending trouble. You sort of feel it coming. We had a couple walk in one night for dinner. He was a slick kind of guy—lots of jewelry, a winter tan, whitened teeth, fancy car. His date that night looked like a recently retired lady wrestler; pretty or maybe you would say attractive, but big, brassy, and loud with a look that said, *"I bet I can kick your ass."* They sat at the power/romantic table number eight, the scene of some fabulous high jinks in the past.

Diane was pregnant at the time. Like most of us, she needed to make a living and wound up working deep into her pregnancy. You can only imagine how tough being on your feet in the latter part of your pregnancy can be and combine that with trying to drag what is essentially two of you around a crowded dining room floor delivering food, drinks, and psychiatric counseling to a few hundred people a day, not to mention an internal chemical combo that would frighten Keith Richards. It can get to a girl. The fated meeting of these two behemoths must have been in the stars because they took an instant dislike to each other. Maybe in a previous life they had some unresolved lesbian relationship or dated each other's boyfriend but whatever it was, you just knew it wasn't going to click.

Diane approaches the table and asks, "Can I get you anything from the bar?"

The woman says, "No, we just want to sit here and look at each other."

Well then, game on.

Diane replies, "Fine. Call me when you can't stand it any longer and I'll bring you a drink."

The man interjects and says, "We'll have two Cosmos, light cranberry."

Diane writes down the order and heads for the bar, struggling to get through the crowded dining room. Exhausted from working with the extra weight, she gets to the bar and asks the bartender for two Cosmos and says, "Did you see that woman at table eight?"

The bartender asks, "You mean the Fabulous Moolah?" The two of them were cracking up.

Diane says, "She looks like Sylvester Stallone with boobs and a blonde wig, and she has quite an attitude."

The bartender says, "Yeah, I'm sure the Cosmo will chill her out."

Diane replies, "She needs to be clubbed like a baby seal."

Diane brings the drinks back to the table and the happy couple seemed to have fallen under the spell of table eight. They are getting, how you say, cozy, and they resented the interruption.

Diane ignores the drama and asks, "Are you ready to order?"

"Do we look like we're ready to order? We'll call you when we're ready."

Diane mutters as she waddles away from the table, "Yeah well, check out time is eleven, Toots."

They call Diane over ten minutes later and say, "We're ready to order."

Diane asks, "What would you like?"

They give her their order and when they were finished, they asked, "Could we get two more Cosmos?" Then they went back into the clinch they were in before they ordered. Diane leaves the table and struggles through an increasingly crowded dining room as she heads for the bar.

She puts in the dinner order and asks the bartender, "Can I have two more Cosmos for the Amazon and her pet?"

He loses it. "She's getting to you, huh?"

"They're both ridiculous, and nasty. I don't have the patience for this."

"Maybe you should quit working until after the baby's born. You're starting to look like Humpy Dumpty."

Diane retorts, "Maybe you should just shut the fuck up and make the Cosmos."

Diane delivers the two Cosmos to the table, and the woman says, "What took so long?"

Diane answers, "Obviously the place is packed, and the service bar is crowded. Sorry."

The woman then says, "You probably shouldn't be working in that … you know, that condition."

Diane shoots back, "What condition is that?"

The woman says, "Your … pregnant condition. You seem to be having a hard time getting around the room."

Diane can be extremely funny and has a killer sense of humor but there is nothing funny about late-term pregnancy and she has just gotten her second fat crack in less than five minutes. She somehow manages to control herself and get away from the table without killing anyone—something several very hormonal women have been acquitted of in England, I understand—and duck-walks through the dining room back to the bar. It would have been an interesting altercation had they thrown down and I would have been hard-pressed to predict a winner. They were in the same weight class, although one was two feet taller, and with the weight being the same and the height advantage in her favor, it's tempting to pick the wrestler. But having once been married to an extremely uncomfortable, late term, pregnant woman, I'd have bet on the hormones—heavily.

Diane picks up and delivers their food. As she puts it down, the woman says, "Can we get two more Cosmos? And I'd like to get them before we finish our dinners. Think you can manage that?"

Diane sarcastically replies, "Oh, I think we can help you with that." She goes bouncing back to the bar. I guess she wasn't fast enough because here's what happened. The woman, who I'm assuming is a quick eater, took out her cell phone and dialed the number of the restaurant.

The hostess picks up the phone and says, "Coolfish."

The woman says, as she's waving her arms, "Look in the back of the dining room. You see me here? I'm in your restaurant, in the back. See me waving back here?"

The hostess turns around to see this six-foot, two-inch blonde bombshell waving frantically and asks, "What can I do for you?"

The woman sat back down, and I swear this is what she said. "Tell *fatso* to hurry up with the Cosmos."

Upon the word for word relaying of the message and after five seconds of thoughtful consideration, Diane had to be physically restrained.

PAYING ONE'S DUES ... OR IS THAT DON'TS???

Before I left the Jedediah Hawkins Inn, we had a regular customer who qualifies as one of my favorites. I'll call her Gretchen because I can't use her real name. Gretchen used to come for dinner about once every two weeks. She always came alone, and she always wore a hat. The hat thing is critical because for those of you who have not read any of my past ravings, I subscribe to the belief that anyone who wears a hat, smokes a pipe, or sports a bow tie is a potential wack-job. Refer to my book *Playing with Fire* for the full explanation of how I came to feel this way, if you must know but, trust me, it's never failed to pan out.

I'll describe Gretchen for you in a *Nutshell,* pun intended. She was a diminutive soul of about five-foot nothing, with large eyes, a small nose, a pleasant smile, and dark curly hair. She had more hair than height, the management of which I guess could drive one crazy, so rather than trying to groom such an unwieldy coif, Gretchen instead chose to stuff thirty pounds of locks into the proverbial one-pound hat. She never did manage to get it all up in there, so there were always bunches of hair hanging out and down around her face. The hair that did manage to stay up in the hat strained it to the breaking point, making the entire thing look like a Jiffy Pop pan in full bloom, which is how I and my less-than-mature crew referred to it. To complete her look, Gretchen always seemed to find clothes that didn't match. I think she was aiming for the retro-hippie, Earth Mother thing, but it just looked like she got dressed in a hurry, in the dark. She always came to dinner by herself and due to the lack of company she was always very talkative. The two biggest problems we had with her were getting her seated and then keeping her seated. She would stand there talking to the hostesses for as long as they would indulge her. Then if they tried to seat her, she would find the manager or bartender and talk to them. Once you got her to her seat, the only way to keep her in it was food or duct tape. When she wasn't chewing, she was talking to anyone who would listen. She would wander around the dining room searching for a kindred spirit or a sympathetic ear for one of her nonstop diatribes. Whenever Gretchen would wander around the dining room between courses, annoying the other guests, Eileen the manager, would commandeer her to the office and talk with her until her food was ready. Every time she ate there, we knew it would be an interesting and entertaining evening, and one that had the potential to be an all-nighter. Most of Gretchen's antics were of the harmless sort, mildly amusing to mildly annoying, and it was fun to have her around because you never knew what she would pull but toward the end, she started to show signs of being seriously screwed up.

She arrived one night in a taxi. They pulled up next to the open patio, Gretchen got out, and in her uniquely Gretchen way, she tried to convince the driver to have dinner with her, nearly yanking him through the passenger window. Outweighing her by two hundred pounds worked to the cabbie's advantage as Gretchen had her feet on the door of the cab, her full five-foot frame including the Jiffy Pop hat stretched and straining, parallel to the ground, yanking on the poor man's sleeve and saying, "Come … have … dinner … with … me! I'll … buy!"

Eileen went out and convinced her to release the cabbie, which Gretchen did reluctantly when the cabbie agreed to accept a *to-go* dinner, to be provided by us, paid for by Gretchen, and given to him upon his retrieving her at the completion of her meal. Gretchen came in and talked for an hour with Eileen, Mary Ellen the hostess, and Evan the bartender. Then she sat down for dinner, gave everyone in the dining room her take on war in the Middle East, went back to the office to chat again with Eileen about weather patterns and how they affect grapes, and then thankfully ran out of gas three and a half hours later. She ordered a full, three-course dinner for the cab driver and asked for the bill and a glass of water. All that talking had apparently dried her out, and we were thrilled to have her mouth occupied even if I was just for a few seconds. We gave her a rather large glass. Pam brought her a check for $146.72. Gretchen looked at her bill, placed three different credit cards in the folder, and handed it back to Pam. Pam took the folder to the service station, opened it, and saw that there were three cards.

She called Gretchen over and said, "Gretchen, you gave me three cards."

Gretchen said, "Yeah, I know."

"Why three?"

"I want to pay the bill."

"Which card do you want me to use?"

"All three."

"You want me to use all three?"

"Yes, all three."

Pam asked, "So you want me to divide the checks equally between these three cards?"

If it were anyone else Pam might not have asked the question and just gone ahead and split it in three but having considerable Gretchen experience, she took the more prudent path and inquired.

Gretchen thought a moment and said, "No. Put $46.72 on the Amex, $82.00 on the Visa, and $18.00 on the Mastercard."

"Huh?"

Gretchen then said, "Yeah, that'll do it," and called for the cab. The cab came shortly thereafter. She said one of her forty-minute good-byes, got in the taxi, handed a perfect stranger $75.00 worth of take-out food and went home. Three days later, she came in and repeated the exact same drill with two exceptions. She chose not to assault the taxi driver and her method of payment was a bit more traditional. She got her bill and asked Pam if she could split it on three credit cards again, but it was a Friday, and Pam was busy, so she said no.

Gretchen left the unpaid bill on the table and wandered back to the office. As she walked up to Eileen, she opened her purse. Eileen told me that she must have had thirty credit cards and a thousand dollars in assorted bills stuffed in a ball and hanging out of her pocketbook.

Eileen said, "Gretchen, be careful with your money. You're going to lose it."

After pushing a wad of hair back into the Jiffy Pop hat, she asked Eileen, "How much are your gift certificates?"

Eileen asked, "What do you mean, how much are they?"

Gretchen replied, "I want to buy a gift certificate, so I need to know how much they are."

Eileen, with a forefinger in each eye, patiently explained, "You can buy one for any amount you want. You want one for fifty dollars, you can buy one for fifty, or one hundred, or five hundred, or just twenty. Whatever number you want, you can have."

Gretchen considered this a moment and then asked, "So what if I wanted to buy one for forty-five dollars?"

Trying to believe what she was hearing, Eileen said, "No problem, Gretch. I'll give you one for forty-five dollars."

"Okay, I'll take one for forty-five dollars."

"Great. Whom do you want me to make it out to?"

"Make it out to?"

Eileen said, "Yeah, we usually make it out to the person you're giving it to."

Gretchen, "Oh, okay. Make it out to me."

"To you."

"Yeah, to me."

"No … Gretchen, we usually make it out to the person who's going to *use* the certificate."

"Yeah, that would be me."

"You."

"Yes, me."

Amused, Eileen asked, "You're buying yourself a gift certificate for a dinner here?"

"Yeah."

"Okay, you go, girl."

Eileen came in the back to tell me what happened and said, "Gretchen just bought herself a gift certificate made out to her." She lost it, laughing.

I said, "You mean crazy Gretchen? Wow, I hope it's not supposed to be a surprise."

Gretchen left the office with her brand-spanking-new Jedediah Hawkins Inn gift certificate in its brand-new envelope and, being cognizant of the one-year expiration policy, laid that baby on Pam for payment of her forty-two-dollar check and said, "The rest is for you."

I HAVE A COMPLAINT … ACTUALLY, MAKE THAT A PROTEST

Here's what turned out to be one of the most unique situations that I have ever encountered without fully encountering the situation. As far as threats go—and I've received my share—this stands out as one of my personal bests and it came on every restaurant worker's favorite holiday, Mother's Day. Sometimes seemingly unconnected events can link together to form a completely new entity that takes on a life of its own. What made this so unique and so hysterical, was that it brought together the winning of a contest, a gift certificate, a biracial couple, a hamburger, two types of chicken, the Better Business Bureau, a credit card, Mother's Day, Coca-Cola, a price-fix brunch special, and the NAACP. Quite the combo platter, I'd say, and I'll be happy to explain it all but first a word about Mother's Day.

We all love our mothers; that's a given. But some people love their mothers so much that they take them out for dinner once a year. Conventional wisdom dictates that if you endeavor to improve at something you must practice because, after all, practice makes perfect, right? Well, that axiom also applies to eating out. Mother's Day brings us, along with a serious amount of volume, the most inexperienced diners that we have all year. They obviously do not practice enough and they're very easy to spot. Their single most identifying characteristic is the wearing of a corsage. When I see one of those things and the only time you ever see one is on Mother's Day, I shudder. And sometimes you'll see multiple corsages on the same table. It's horrifying. Three or more generations of corsage-wearing, price-fixing, Jell-O–craving restaurant patrons at the same table will scare the pants off the most battle-hardened of servers.

So, there we were on Mother's Day awaiting the Normandy-like invasion when this biracial couple walked in, she being African American, he being white, or whatever hyphenated title white guys are given these days. It's tough to keep up and before anyone gets their politically correct panties in a bunch and starts any unfounded racism accusation, I'll let you know that the only reason I mentioned it was because it's germane to the story, as you will soon see. And for those who may be a little squeamish about the mentioning of such things, you'll be glad to know that even in lunacy, there's diversity. It started off normally with a request for two Coca-Colas. This should have been seen as a warning shot over the bow because although there was no identifying corsage, the experienced diner always says, *"I'll have a Coke,"* whereas the rookie says, *"I'll have a Coca Cola."* Don't misconstrue this as quibbling, because it isn't. There's a difference and the server should have picked up on it and prepared herself. She did not. We did a price-fix brunch on Mother's Day that was three courses and included a glass of wine or a champagne drink.

They perused the menu for a long time and when the server went to take their order, the man asked, "We don't drink, so are our Coca-Colas included instead?"

The server said, "I think we can do that for you. Are you ready to order?"

"Yes."

The woman said, "I'm going to have the gnocchi."

"Great."

The man said, "I'll have a hamburger, medium rare."

The waitress said, "Um, sir, we don't have a hamburger on the menu."

He said, "I know. Just make one for me."

"Sir, I can't do that."

"Why not?"

"Well, it's because we don't have hamburgers. We don't have chopped meat, buns, pickles ..."

He said, "That's ludicrous. Every restaurant I've ever eaten in has hamburgers."

That was, I'm convinced, an accurate statement.

He then told her, "Forget it. Give me back the menu." He looked at it for several minutes and asked, "You only have two kinds of chicken?"

"Yes, sir."

"Well, I don't eat fish, so what am I supposed to do?"

She told him, "Have one of the chickens."

"I don't like the way you're serving the chickens and I don't believe you only have two chicken dishes on your menu. Every restaurant I go to has more than two chicken dishes on the menu." Don't you think a restaurant called Coolfish is an odd choice for someone who doesn't eat fish? The name's a dead giveaway.

He continued. "You know what? Forget it. I'll have the gnocchi and bring us two more Coca-Colas."

They had their salads, their gnocchi, six more Coca-Colas, and their desserts. The server brought them a check for $100.37 and left it on the table in a folder. The couple, seeing that we had charged them for six of their eight Coca Colas, went berserk.

The man asked, "What's this charge for?"

The server, "Six Cokes."

The woman chimed in, "I thought drinks were included with the brunch."

The server replied, "A drink is included; you had eight. We charged you for six."

The woman then said, "That's ridiculous. Alcohol costs more than soda so why do we have to pay for our sodas?"

Without getting into the economics of the whole deal, how about being just a little grateful about two free anything's instead of feeling entitled to something that's not really yours to begin with, and saying, *"Thank you."*

Allow me to illustrate the flaw in the logic with an analogy from another business. Let's say Best Buy had a sale on a fifty-six-inch flat screen TVs for five hundred dollars. Let's also say that you have a fifty-six-inch flat screen TV already mounted on the wall in your living room and you don't need another one. How far do you think you would get with the salesman if you said, *"You know what? I'd like the fifty-six-inch flat screen, but I just happen to have one already, so since the washers, dryers, BBQ grills, laptops, and toaster ovens all cost less than the flat screen, I'll take one of each instead."*

See the problem? We are the only business in the world where the persons who are getting shit for free get to dictate the terms of the largesse. It's sort of absurd.

As an aside, I must mention that I have a relationship with KJOY radio station. As a promotion, I was giving away some autographed books and doing some cooking demos and there was a prize of a one-hundred-dollar gift certificate. Apparently, the winner—and I mean winner—had graced us with a visit on Mother's Day. He presented the $100.00, KJOY certificate for the partial payment of his $100.37 bill, and to cover the remaining thirty-seven cents, he included a credit card. When the server went to ring in the credit card the machine informed her that even it knew the amount wasn't worth the effort, and to come back with a more appropriate sum. It turned out that one dollar was the required minimum to cover the costs of a transaction that probably bounces several times, back and forth, between New York and Bombay, and after suffering through the Coca-Cola crisis we felt compelled to warn him of the up charge. Unhappy, but nevertheless unwilling to cough up the cash, he agreed to run the card for one dollar, forcing himself to eat to eat the extra sixty-three cents, further pissing him off. They paid the bill and went to the bar to file their grievances with someone in charge.

The funny thing is no one's in charge on Mother's Day because everyone's too busy. I was running around like the proverbial headless chicken—our third chicken preparation, as it turned out—and had unknowingly walked by them several times while they were telling the bartender that the place sucked, we were a clip joint, and they were never coming back. I didn't hear them, and I'm grateful in a way because when I'm that busy I don't trust myself to respond well. The man told the bartender, "When I get home, I'm writing a letter to the Better Business Bureau. This is an outrage. You'll hear from me."

Then, completing the two-pronged assault, his wife comes out with what was to be the first of the two greatest lines I've ever heard: "And I'm calling the NAACP."

I'm sure that the people at the NAACP are some fine folks and they've done some very difficult and important work during their history but I'm not sure they have any interest in Cokes, burgers, chicken, or credit card machines. I can't see the NAACP leading a massive protest, or Al Sharpton cartwheeling through the halls of Congress, calling for the closing of a restaurant because the only available chicken items were grilled with faro and citrus glaze or sautéed with a red onion and preserved tomato relish. I found out later that the woman was mad because, as told to the bartender, she felt that I walked by and ignored them. The truth is that I never noticed them because I had Mother's Day to deal with and was very busy. There were what seemed to be five hundred people standing in the bar waiting to be seated so we were in constant motion.

She said, "Your boss, the owner—that guy with the rag on his head—he walked by us three times and didn't even acknowledge our presence. Who the hell does he think he is?" Then she announced the best one I've heard to date, and that's saying something. She said, "We are paying customers, do you hear me? Paying customers!!"

Coming from someone whose out-of-pocket expense totaled one dollar, that is quite a statement, my friends. Quite a statement.

SHAKEN WAITRESS SYNDROME

What is it about the shape of a table that is so important? I don't get it. I eat out every night that I'm not working, and not once have I ever said to anyone in a restaurant, *"I can't sit here. I don't like the shape of the table."* Did you know that when they were trying to end the Vietnam War and decided to have what were hilariously labeled the Paris Peace Accords, the leaders from several nations, while wringing their hands and drinking their lattes, argued for six weeks over the shape of the table and who would sit where? These were the best and the brightest among us, as they would have us believe. Well, this collection of forward-thinking, overeducated geniuses, who assigned themselves the unenviable task of getting everyone to calm down, stop the carnage, get the capitalists and communists to sing, *Kumbaya,* rebuild a shattered country, restore law and order to the American college campuses, relocate the boat people, negotiate a withdrawal that would allow all parties concerned to save a little face, free the POW's, account for the MIA's, and throw out Richard Nixon—all while agonizing over what to name the capital city of that newly conjoined country—simply couldn't decide on the shape of the table. If there weren't so many lives at stake, you would burst out laughing. I remember having had this vision of twelve well-dressed State Department types of different nationalities goose-stepping around a table in France to some obscure Edith Piaf tune and then breaking into a mad scramble for eleven chairs as the music cut off. I tell you this to illustrate the profound effect that the shape of a table can have on the outcome of world events. If it's important enough to suspend the cessation of a war, regardless of how many people are dying, then who am I to deny a person's right to choose a preferred table shape? That said, one does have to limit oneself to the generally accepted, restaurant tested and approved configurations. A room full of trapezoid tables, no matter how nattily turned out, would look ridiculous and would probably not lend themselves to the emergency slamming together of two or more to accommodate a twelve-top. I feel compelled to stick with the more traditional square, rectangle, round, and oval. It's a fairly diverse choice for those to whom such things matter and you would think it would reasonably satisfy the fussiest of furniture shopping restaurant patrons.

You would be wrong. Recently, we've had a growing movement of customers clamoring for a new restaurant table shape called, *the horseshoe.* It's just what it sounds like, and its two most annoying qualities are its penchant for taking up the maximum amount of square footage for a minimum number of guests and, as a result, tripling the degree of difficulty for the server to get around the table to serve. The profile of the horseshoe table aficionado is someone who believes one hundred and ten percent to be the minimum service requirement allowed but nevertheless creates a situation in which the server doesn't have a prayer of succeeding, leading to unbridled bitching, the usual litany of threats, and an occasional act of random violence.

One night, a member of the *horseshoe* club came for dinner. Upon discovering she was to be seated at an oval, she decided that the oval was unacceptable and said so. "I can't sit here; this isn't going to work."

"What's the problem?"

"I don't like the shape of the table."

"What's the problem with the shape?" the hostess asked.

She replied, "The table is an oval, and it's too long. How am I going to talk with someone at the other end?"

The hostess said, "I don't have another table that can accommodate twelve people. I only have the oval."

"Well, it's not going to work. Why can't we make it shaped like a horseshoe? Then we can sit on both sides and in the middle."

"Because there's not enough room, and the waitress won't be able to serve you."

"I don't care. I want to be able to talk to my guests, and I'm not sitting at an oval."

Okay, have it your way.

We set about trying to give her what she wanted, which can sometimes be the purest form of revenge, but this was a crowded Friday night and aside from being a major pain in the ass from a labor standpoint, it was very tight and uncomfortable. The funny part is that for her, it was all about control, the result was much worse for having a conversation, a service nightmare— and if, God forbid, someone had to get up from the table to go to the bathroom, half the table had to get up with them. She got her *horseshoe,* but I suspect she realized it wasn't such a brilliant idea after all, watching her server Courtney, struggling every time she brought something to the table. As Courtney was making one of her thirty-seven trips to the *horseshoe* replenishing empty, s*auce on the side,* containers, she caught her foot on the table, stumbled, and knocked over a glass of red wine. The wine, which was three quarters empty, went over but didn't really splash; it was more of a controlled fall to the middle of the table, as told to me by no less than four reliable witnesses. The only person who jumped up and screamed as the Pinot Noir bit the dust was—you guessed it—the *horseshoe* lady, and she was the farthest from the splash zone. Not one to waste a good crisis and guided by what I'm sure was a wealth of experience, she set about examining every square inch of her clothing. She did a full-frontal search, enlisting the help of her tablemates all the while excoriating Courtney and calling her names. Courtney was apologizing profusely while trying to assess the damage.

Finally, after five minutes of careful analysis, the woman spotted a stain. "Look! Look at this! The blouse is ruined. Look: there's a stain on it."

Courtney ran to get some club soda, the universal restaurant stain remover, but when she returned and offered to clean the woman's blouse, she couldn't find the stain. Neither could anyone else, except for the woman's daughter, who apparently was lucky enough to inherit her mother's X-ray vision. These two were carrying on like banshees, screaming and cursing at Courtney.

"You're an idiot!"

"What the hell's wrong with you?"

"How can you be so incompetent?"

"You're going to pay for this blouse."

You had to hear it, and the best part is out of thirteen people, including Courtney, only two could see the stain. It wasn't there.

They started again. "You don't realize what you've done. That was my favorite blouse. It was one of a kind."

Here it comes.

If there's one absolute in my business, it's that if one of my servers spills something on an article of clothing, I guarantee you I'll be informed that that particular piece of clothing was one of a kind; an irreplaceable gift, hand sewn by Vera Wang, using a mother of pearl needle with silk farmed from virgin moths in Bora Bora, and buttons made from a rhinoceros horn that the rhinoceros was so honored to be sacrificing, he committed suicide for the privilege. The restoration of the item is usually somewhere in the thousands. No one is ever just wearing a blouse. Courtney later said that it looked like it came off the rack at Target, but who knows?

She approached the woman and said, "I don't see anything. I think we're okay here."

The woman grabbed Courtney by the shoulders, started shaking her violently, and screamed, "What's wrong with you? Are you an idiot! Are you?"

It's a hard question to answer. How do you disprove a negative?

Courtney ignored the question and said to her, "Get your hands off me right now or I'm going to shake you back!"

The woman stopped shaking Courtney, which in some circles is referred to as assault, and said, "You're going to pay for this. I'm sending you a bill for this blouse!"

Yeah, yeah. Send a bill. Blah, blah, blah.

About a week later I got an email from her requesting $20.95 for a dry-cleaning bill. Normally I'm happy to pay for something that we did and, frankly, sometimes I'll even pay for something we didn't do, like someone spilling wine on themselves, but I just couldn't bring myself to do it. The woman must have had some sauce on her fingers because, ironically, when she was shaking Courtney, she transferred some of the sauce to Courtney's shirt. That kind of makes us even, no? Or maybe I'm just some kind of an idiot.

HALF-ASSED

Here's one I nearly forgot about, or maybe I was trying to block it out. Either way, here goes. I briefly—and I mean briefly—had a restaurant in an unnamed town on Long Island. It was my first foray into a downscale, high-volume restaurant. It had been a diner for years and it was located on a main road in what was a very busy location. At first, I thought I wanted to make it into an upscale diner like the Fog City Diner in San Francisco or the Buckhead Diner in Atlanta but because we have a diner culture here on Long Island, with very definite ideas of what a diner is and what it serves, I wasn't sure it would play. Plus, I don't know how many of you have ever cooked five hundred orders of eggs in fifteen minutes on a twenty-four-inch griddle, sharing that surface with a Mt. Everest–sized pile of home fries, but that will very quickly suck the wind out of your Sunday morning sails. I bagged the diner.

My second thought, in a spectacularly misguided series of bad ideas, was to do a family-style Italian restaurant because there were only about eight thousand of those on Long Island at the time. My financial partner, pulling rank and completing the questionable idea troika, nixed my dreams of unlimited plates of linguini and bad Rat Pack CDs and, being a dentist, decided that we were going into the barbeque business—along with hamburgers, pasta, salads, soup, shrimp, prime rib, lamb chops, meat (both loaf and balls), lasagna, lobster, sushi, curry, flanken, General Tso's chicken, bratwurst, knockwurst, weisswurst, liverwurst, macaroni and cheese, baba ghanoush, bubbles and squeak, fried rice, sauerbraten, Rueben sandwiches, tiramisu, lime green Jell-O with a banana suspended in the middle, doughnuts, takeout, and drive-through. I think that the combination of his years in dental school and relative inexperience in the restaurant business led him to the conclusion that anything that could potentially get stuck in a tooth should be on the menu. What we collectively knew about barbeque would have filled one of those little plastic cups that hold the coleslaw accompanying the stuff that the people who do know about barbeque, serve. How knowing that, never for one moment, deterred us from pressing on is one of the great mysteries of my life. Mike and I were a dangerous pair. He is one of the most engaged, enthusiastic, energetic, and fun guys that you could ever be involved with and when he gets an idea in his head or a project to work on, he is full speed ahead, twenty-four seven, one hundred miles an hour, right into the wall. We dove into the barbeque thing with the zeal of a newly minted environmentalist.

What I did know about barbeque was that we needed smoke, so I set out to find the Ferrari of all smokers. Mike wanted a fun, casual atmosphere with great music. He set out to find the best sound system available. We both found what we were searching for and to this day, I'm sure we were the only two restaurant guys who ever managed to spend the same amount of money on the sound system as we did on the cooking equipment. I spent a lot of time trying to figure out how to work Pink Floyd into the smoking process to see if I couldn't justify the expense and at the same time improve kitchen morale, but it never quite worked out. We were completely out of control. We hung a Harley over the bar. We ordered a wood-burning grill, a custom cooking line, and a seventy-five-gallon steam-jacketed kettle just for the beans. Mike had a beautiful take-out window, a brand-new bar, and a designer interior. As we got closer to opening, I started to get insecure about the barbeque thing. I was wondering if it would travel—as a cuisine, that is—out of the South and up to Long Island. I was also wondering if I could produce killer barbeque, considering my Carle Place roots wouldn't inspire any confidence in those who relish the genre. My last and probably most beguiling question was, *"Should we be a restaurant that's smoking pork butts in what was a predominantly Jewish neighborhood?"* These were perfectly legitimate questions that unfortunately should have been asked a lot sooner. I must have been becoming a pain in the ass because a week before we were scheduled to open, Mike sent me to Chicago to get me out of his hair. Eating at places like Charlie Trotters, Tru, and Spiaggia did nothing to quell my fears, and I retuned ready to open but scared to death. I'm still not sure whose idea it was to open on a Friday night, but I remain convinced it wasn't mine. Any worries that the neighborhood wouldn't warm to barbeque went right up the kitchen vent. Here are the numbers: three cooks including me on the hot line, two people in the pantry, two dishwashers, one bartender, two hostesses, one manager, five servers, two bussers, two runners, and one dentist. We did five hundred covers that first Friday. Five hundred covers and after many years of reflection, I can honestly report that we may have gotten twenty of them right. No, my friends, this was not what you would label one of my more stellar performances. I don't think I'd done five hundred covers in my entire career up to that point. I was hoping for and prepared to do two hundred. Yup, it was ugly. I was still there at 2:00 a.m. trying to get ready for the next day, which I'd heard could be even busier than a Friday. Butchering with tears in your eyes can be hazardous to your fingers and as I was considering that, I had an idea. I thought for the briefest of moments that if I cut myself badly, on purpose, two things could happen. First, although everyone would probably believe I did it on purpose after watching me seamlessly annihilate five hundred dinners, there would be a certain amount of residual doubt that would allow some room for sympathy. And more importantly, after stitching the wound and asking a few probing questions, perhaps the doctor would admit me for a twenty-four-hour observation period by professionals trained to deal with broken humanity, thereby allowing me to shove the potential six hundred Saturday customers off to someone else. Because opening a vein isn't the most sought-after method of scoring a night off, I believed that those who mattered would be convinced it was an accident. I never did muster the courage to slash myself, but I was very tempted.

Here's a culinary fact for the uninitiated: just because you can make ice cream out of fatted duck livers or decorate razor clams with chorizo foam, does not mean you can cook a hamburger. Hamburgers are a colossal pain in the ass and an art form all at the same time. My biggest problem turned out to be the hamburgers. How much of a problem, you ask? Consider this: The supporting cast for a hamburger consists of rolls, French fries, pickles, onions, mushrooms, lettuce, tomatoes, bacon, cheddar, Swiss, American, mozzarella, ketchup, and occasionally mustard or some other obscure condiment. Then throw in black and blue, rare, medium rare, medium, medium well, well done, and *"Burn the shit out of it,"* and you have the culinary equivalent of the theory of relativity. There's no end to the fun a customer can have at the expense of the cook. We were doing an average of two hundred hamburgers a day with roughly fifty different cooking and garnish combinations. That's like, algebra. Needless to say, the Ronald McDonald act was wearing thin, and I was becoming increasingly and visibly unbolted. I'd had it with the hamburger hell and hired a new chef in the anticipation of going back to Montauk and opening our other restaurant for the season. The only question was whether I would be able to hang on to my sanity long enough to make it. I soon got an answer.

One relatively quiet lunch, I was on the line when a server came in and said, "Chef-o, I have two ladies out there who want to split a hamburger. Is that a problem?"

I said, "No, I'll just cut it in half."

She replied, "Well, I don't think that's going to work."

"Why not?"

"One woman wants hers cooked medium rare, and the other one wants hers cooked medium."

"Are you kidding?"

"Sorry. What do you want me to tell them?"

"Tell them the hamburger is fifteen dollars for God's sake. How much am I supposed to endure for fifteen dollars? Tell them it's ridiculous and I'm not doing it."

She said, "Okay, I'll tell them, but I'm leaving out the *endure* and the *ridiculous* parts. I'll just tell them we can't do it."

"Fine."

Five minutes later, the waitress came back into the kitchen and ordered one hamburger, medium rare.

I ask, "Is that the burger for those two ladies?"

"Yes."

"They're all right with having it medium rare?"

She said, "I told them we couldn't do it and they just said, 'Whatever, make it medium rare.'"

"Okay, cool."

I cooked the burger, cut it in half, garnished it, and sent it out.

Two minutes later the waitress came back in the kitchen with one half of the burger and said, "Okay there, genius. This lady wants more fire on her half of the burger. I'd say medium ought to do it."

I began to cry.

PANTOMIME

Those of you who have read my writings over the years know that I believe it's perfectly acceptable to fire a customer. Let me explain to those who have not. A bad customer is very much like a bad employee, and they share similar traits. I'll give you a few examples. Neither one can seem to arrive on time for their scheduled shift or for their reservation, neither one has a good attitude with the other people who work in the restaurant, both have been known to demonstrate a talent for larceny and, worst of all, both show a blatant contempt for management. So why would you not tolerate that behavior from an employee and yet take it from a customer? It makes no sense, short of masochism, to subject oneself to people hell-bent on ruining your vibe. We try to operate under the notion that, *the customer is always right,* and in most of the cases that's true but, *always,* is an absolute that I'm not willing to accept. Not only is the customer not always right, sometimes they are willfully wrong. Please understand that we take complaints very seriously and in the case of a legitimate complaint, I will do whatever it takes to make the situation right. We derive our income by making the guests happy and I'm happy to fix any legitimate problem— notice the word, *legitimate.* But if you're going to fabricate a crisis as a substitute for boredom or the inability to get a life, I'm out. And after fifty years of doing this, I can recognize the difference almost immediately.

The two basic reasons I believe people do the *crisis/scene,* thing in restaurants is that they live a somewhat privileged existence, insulated emotionally and financially from everyday hardships and have to create them to find out how they feel, or they flat out need attention. I am not qualified to analyze, diagnose, and cure reason number one, but I feel the least I can do is accommodate reason number two.

I've often wondered about the spouses of these characters and how they not only handle their chosen one's neuroses but also put up with them daily without the benefit of a support group. I soon got an answer. We have a woman who frequents the restaurant on a regular basis with the sole intention, I believe, of reducing my partner to tears. This woman is a platinum pain in the ass. There's no other literary way to describe her. She has never sat at a table she's liked, has never enjoyed a meal she's eaten, and has never had good service. I'm beginning to suspect that it may not be us. One night a while back, she came in with her husband and her two children. Why they let people like this breed is beyond my comprehension. Apparently, the nanny was either on a vacation or a valium drip, so the kids and Mom were spending quality time together.

She waltzes in on a very busy Saturday night and announces that she has arrived. Being fresh out of trumpets, the only fanfare we could muster was, *"Hello, Mrs. So and So."*

She asks Adam, "Is my table ready?"

Adam responds, "Not yet. We were slammed and we'll need a few more minutes. Can I get you a drink at the bar?"

"No. I want to sit down. The kids are hungry," she tells him.

The kids are in the middle of their own mini-Summer Olympics, running amok through the bar. Mr. So and So stands passively by the hostess stand, not saying a word.

Mrs. So and So says to Adam, "How long are we going to have to wait?"

Adam replies, "A few more minutes. I have some tables paying their checks as we speak."

She asks, "Which one is going to be our table?"

Adam tells her, "That one over by the window." It seemed innocent enough, but I'm reasonably sure Adam will never again tell a customer where they are to be seated. After another couple of minutes, she walks through the dining room to the table that Adam pointed out to her. The six occupants are finishing their coffee and having a pleasant after-dinner chat.

As Mrs. So and So arrives at the table and the six guests look up, trying to figure out if they know her.

She says to them, "How much longer are you going to be?"

One of the startled guests asks the relevant question. "Excuse me, what did you say?"

Undeterred, she says, "I want to know how much longer this gabfest is going to go on. This is our table and, obviously, we can't sit until you leave, so I'd appreciate it if you hurry up."

Someone calls for a manager. Adam sees the woman at the table and knows nothing good can be happening.

He gets to the table and says to Mrs. So and So, "What are you doing over here?"

One of the guests says, "She's asking us to leave."

Adam is shocked. "She's what!?"

The guest says, "She just said that it was her table and she asked us to leave so she could sit down."

Adam says to Mrs. So and So, "Are you out of your mind? Why are you bothering these people? Go back to the bar and I'll talk to you when I get there."

Mrs. So and So says, "You said it was our table!"

Adam replies, "It's the table I was planning to seat you at. You don't own it. Get away from these people."

Mrs. So and So says, "I'm not waiting!"

Adam tells her, "Fine, then you can leave."

The woman goes back to the bar, appearing to be very agitated, talking excitedly to her husband and pointing at Adam. Someone once said that there wouldn't be any wars if the women weren't watching, meaning that a man's machismo red lines when a woman's attention is piqued, or her honor is sullied. The husband looks directly at Adam as he's shaking his head up and down while listening to her rant. She finishes and turns her head, so they are both staring across the room at Adam. The husband peels off and starts walking toward him. Adam's a big guy, as is her husband, and the last thing you want to see on a busy night is two big guys rolling around the floor over some woman's misguided indignation. Adam braces himself for trouble.

As the man approaches Adam, he says, "I'd like to I have a word with you."

Adam says, "Before you say anything and before this gets heated, I just want you to know that your wife was over there asking these people to leave. I tried telling her very nicely that she can't do that. She started to give me a hard time and I snapped at her, so for that I apologize. I could have maybe handled it better, but I can't allow her to do that."

The man looks quickly at the ceiling and then back at Adam and says, "Look buddy, no one knows what a nightmare this woman is better than me, but I have to go home with her. So, I need you to do me a favor, okay? I need you to step outside and make it look like I'm yelling at you. I'm going to move my head around, wave my arms, stomp my feet, move my lips, and not make a sound. I need you to stand by the window out there so she can see us, and I need you to pretend I'm scolding you. Look at the ground, shake your head up and down a couple of times, and do whatever you can think of. Help me out and I promise I'll have her out of here in no time."

A bewildered but thoroughly amused Adam says, "Sure, no problem."

The two men step outside and give a stellar performance. As they come back inside, the husband announces rather loudly, "That's it. We're out of here. Let's go."

She gathers the children and as she walks past Adam, she says, "This is the last time you'll ever see us here," and races out the door after the kids.

The husband hangs back a second as the door is closing behind her. He turns to Adam and says, "Thanks, man. I appreciate it more than you know."

Adam replies, "Sure, no problem at all."

Three weeks later she called for a reservation. We happened to be fully booked that night. Coincidence?

MARRIED ... AND FILING FOR SEPARATION

What is it about celebrity that breeds such false or misplaced respect? I've been fortunate or unfortunate depending on who we're talking about, to have had a lot of interaction with famous and semi-famous people. In the restaurant business it goes with the turf. I have found these people to be pretty much like the rest of the population in that some are very cool, some are marginally cool, some are not so cool, and some are not even close to cool. The big difference is that they're not treated like everyone else, by everyone else. It seems that the minute you've been on television, the big screen, a stage, or have starred in your own homemade porn video, you become a larger than life figure whose presence, thoughts, and opinions can bring a sense of excitement to otherwise stable adults. I was once seated next to Madonna in Nobu, in South Beach some years ago, and my dinner companion couldn't speak for an hour. She kept shifting her head and eyes in quick, not-so-subtle jerks to the left, making muffled, high-pitched noises through her nose. I remember thinking that she couldn't tolerate wasabi before I realized what was going on. Another time, my friend Ellen dumped a whole bottle of Helen Turley Zinfandel in my lap upon the surprise arrival of Hugh Jackman. What is it about these people that cause such reactions from grown men and women? I can understand children getting excited over seeing their heroes' playing sports or music because they're kids. If I'd met John Lennon in 1964, there's a better than even chance I'd have fainted, but in my defense, I was eleven. And why are we so interested in what they have to say? Intelligent people—journalists, no less—ask twenty-year-old, heroin-addled musicians their thoughts on questions such as, *"In your opinion, what effects do you think that genetically altered corn is having on sub-Saharan Africa?"* or *"Do you believe that Hugo Chavez's incarceration of opposition journalists and the takeover of his country's news outlets had any effect on his successful reelection?"* It's as hard to watch as the Academy Awards. Can you possibly sit through one more gag-inducing acceptance speech while someone resembling a pin cushion, wearing thirty different colored ribbons, blathers on? *"Our industry is so wonderful; we're so talented; we're so caring; we're all beautiful, intelligent, concerned, engaged and involved; and we love the homeless, windmills, the rain forest, club-footed ex-nuns, and soy milk."* Okay then, fine, I challenge you to house one, build one, save one, fix one, or one drink one … just one. These folks pretend for a living, and though there's an undeniable amount of value there, they're certainly not critical to the survival of the planet. One other thing: Can someone tell me why, if there's so much self-professed talent in Hollywood, we were subjected to remakes of *Get Smart* and *Bewitched*? Even Paris Hilton, whose sole accomplishment was removing her thong on a home video without strangling herself and not only is she sought out for her commentary but also was given her own show, presumably because she has so much more to offer than moaning.

So, I'm assuming that they assume that we need their guidance and here's why. I was dragged kicking and screaming to a Sheryl Crow concert some years back. No reflection on Sheryl or her music; it's just not my genre. Sheryl comes out and decides she needs to not only entertain but educate her adoring fans as well with this thoughtfully considered, articulately delivered, pearl of wisdom: *"War isn't cool, man. People die, man. People die!"* It almost broke my heart. Here I was praying that they would institute a *senior* draft so I wouldn't miss out on all the fun the brave young soldiers were having in Iraq without me, and Sheryl blows the whole thing by telling us—twice, just to make sure we understood—that people die. There we were, collectively delivered from our ignorance in one enlightening moment, which would have been fine had she just stopped there. Forty-five minutes of disjointed, rambling, ill informed, oil, money, Halliburton, tolerance, fear and loathing bullshit later, we were treated to a remake of a Bob Dylan song. And you wonder why I'm cynical? Just sing, or act, or do whatever it is you do. It's really all we need from you. Can you imagine if every Saturday night at seven o'clock, I stopped dinner service, shut off the music, and gave a forty-minute talk on politics or world events in the middle of the dining room? Is that any less ludicrous?

After reading that, you can imagine my feelings when a seldom-recognized, D-list celebrity came into the restaurant and told us that she would like to throw a party and have us cater it. I was thrilled—to cater it, that is. This woman, apparently lacking a grasp on reality, had all the diva of a Whitney Houston with all the name recognition of Arnold Stang. Undeterred, she set about making the most of her status by letting us know just how rich and famous she was and how lucky we were to be doing her party while negotiating the swag that she and her Hollywood cronies were so accustomed to. She intimated that the crowd would glitter, and our business and reputation would be greatly enhanced by her presence, and that should be of certain value to us, and that gratitude should be repaid with some form of financial compensation. What I'm trying to say is that she expected a whole lot of stuff for free. I thought these people made a lot of money. We threw in the cappuccinos and left her with a *"take it or leave it."* She took it and then spent the next few weeks making our lives difficult with endless requests, demands, and hissy fits. She insisted on doing an à la carte menu for the guests, which is unusual and difficult for a large party. We wanted to give them a limited, price-per-person menu, but she insisted that her guests were used to getting whatever it was that they wanted, so that was out of the question.

Party day arrived with the celebrity showing up in a bridal dress, which goes a long way in explaining the *-zilla* part of her personality, in a stretch limousine. We didn't know it was a wedding. She had a cake with her that I'm assuming she had stopped and picked up on the way, like all pampered celebrities apparently do, because it was still in the box with the name of the bakery and the address emblazoned across the top. She wanted to know if there was a service charge for the cake. There was. Forty-seven people celebrated the nuptials in fine Hollywood form, dancing, drinking and à la carte–ly eating their way through the afternoon. As the party was winding down, Bridezilla takes one of the servers aside and asks, "Do you have my bill ready?"

The server answers, "I'll have Adam make it up for you."

Bridezilla says, "Great, but tell him I need to talk with him first."

The server tells Adam that Bridezilla needs a word with him before he gives her the bill.

As Adam approaches Bridezilla, she asks, "How much is the bill?" Adam tells her. Bridezilla then says, "Okay, here's what I need you to do. I need you to make out separate checks."

Adam says, "What?"

Bridezilla says, "Separate checks. I need you to give me separate checks."

Adam says, "You want me to give you forty-seven separate checks?"

She says, "Yes."

He says, "I can't do that."

She asks, "Why not?"

He responds, "Because it's ridiculous. How am I supposed figure out who drank or ate what? We ran a bar tab, and no one is wearing a name tag with their food order on it."

She asks, "So you won't do that for me?"

Adam replies, "Absolutely not."

She then says, "Well, then, I don't know how you're going to get paid, because I don't have any money."

Adam asks, "Why would you throw a party for yourself—a wedding, no less—and not bring money for the bill?"

Bridezilla says, "Because I was going to give each guest a check."

Adam asks, "You were expecting your guests to pay for your party?"

Bridezilla says, "Yeah."

Adam says, "Well, I guess you'll have to start collecting."

Bridezilla responds, "You want me to go to each guest and ask them for money?"

Adam says, "That's what you were asking me to do. Besides, what other choice do you have?"

Bridezilla notes, "That's embarrassing."

Adam says, "Yeah, I imagine it is."

I guess it wasn't embarrassing enough to pay the bill. The collection took the better part of an hour, and she finally came up with the required funds to settle up, gave Adam the money, and left. Watch those show business types, my friends. They can be heavy on the show and light on the business.

TURN-ABOUT IS FAIR PLAY

What would this book be without another reservation story? For the life of me, I can't seem to figure out why people make securing a reservation so difficult. It's not that hard. You call, request a time, tell them the amount of people, leave a phone number, and hang up. Then you go to the restaurant at the allotted time, eat dinner, pay, and go home. It seems simple enough. If only it were so. I have another question. Why can't they sit in the first seat that's offered? Is it something tangible that identifies the perfect spot? Some folks just can't bring themselves to commit, to the restaurant, the seat, or the menu item. But really, what's the deal? Is it too many choices? I can't begin to tell you how many laughs I've shared watching people parade around a dining room looking for the perfect seat. Most of the time, the seats are the same. I've often said that it reminds me of walking a Labrador I once had that couldn't possibly relieve himself until every square acre of Westbury had been thoroughly sniffed. But the most amusing thing happens when people need to alter or change a reservation they've made and have no idea where they've made it, what time it was for, what name it was made under, or where they were even going. It's called getting caught, and it can be a whole lot of fun. Check out this, *hand in the cookie jar,* moment.

The telephone rings at Jewel, Courtney picks up the receiver and says, "Hello, Jewel. Can I help you?"

Without any salutation, a woman on the line rudely says, "How the hell do you expect me to eat at 9:30?"

Courtney says, "Can I help you?"

The woman gets nastier. "I have a reservation on Saturday night at 9:30. How the hell do you expect me to eat at 9:30? I need to change it to an earlier time. I can't eat at 9:30!"

Courtney says, "I don't expect you to do anything and I'm sorry, but we don't have anything open earlier. What would you like me to do?"

The woman then says, "Then I'm cancelling my reservation!!"

Courtney responds, "Okay, ma'am. That was Saturday night at 9:30, correct?"

The woman says, "Yes."

Courtney asks, "What was the name?"

The woman, "The name? Um … I … um, I don't know."

Courtney says, "We appreciate the call, but I can't cancel a reservation without the name."

The woman says, "Well, I need to cancel it because I don't want it to count as a no-show on Open Table."

An explanation is called for here. If you have too many no-shows on Open Table, which is a central station computer reservation system, they won't let you use it anymore under that name, and that's the reason for the *A.K.A.'s* and secret identities, which to my endless amusement, turns more people into Maxwell Smart than 007. Open Table is the reservation jihadist's, terrorist underground.

Courtney says, "I can't cancel it without the name, obviously, so I don't know what to do for you."

The woman then says, "All right. It could be under Tina, Alice, Goodman, Smith, or Reilly. Try those."

Courtney says, "Why don't we start with the name that got you kicked off Open Table in the first place?"

The woman says, "That's not funny."

Some people don't know how funny they really are.

Courtney soon replies, "Sorry, none of those names are here."

Exasperated, the woman says, "Try Rachel!" Then as Courtney is searching in vain for Rachel, the woman decides to punish us for being busy while at the same time admitting to making multiple reservations. "You know, I have a more reasonable reservation at another restaurant since you obviously can't accommodate us."

Courtney, still looking for Rachel, says, "That's great. I'm glad you got the time slot you wanted."

She tells Courtney, "And it's at one of *your* other restaurants," with an emphasis on, *your.*

Courtney asks, "Really? Where? At Coolfish?"

The woman, in that tone, says, "Nooo, Rothman's."

Courtney tells her, "We don't own Rothman's."

The woman says, "Yes, you do. I'm very tapped into the restaurant scene here on Long Island."

Courtney then says, "I'm telling you we don't own Rothman's. Ma'am, do you think you're talking to Blackstone or Insignia?"

The woman answers, "Um, why? Who is this?"

Courtney replies, "Ma'am, you're talking to Jewel."

The woman says, "Jewel? This is Jewel?"

Courtney says, "Yes, ma'am, this is Jewel."

Then in a complete one-eighty, like the sweetest woman ever, she says, "Oh, oh, Jewel … Okay, I'd like to make reservations on Saturday the twenty-eighth for four people at 7:30."

Courtney, stifling a guffaw, says, "I'm sorry, ma'am. All we have left is 10:00."

Click.

FOGGING OR BLOGGING

I've already stated that I think anonymous blogging is a problem and I was heartened to hear that they have a service now for internet users that helps to protect your reputation. Hopefully it will give pause to the late-night Hemmingway's spinning after-dinner fiction in their underwear. But I seriously doubt it, because I don't believe these folks can help themselves, and the funny thing is it's the same few people doing all the writing. My best guess is that they are driven by the id. They desperately want to matter, and it seems they have this chaotic, simmering pot of imagined slights that can only be rectified by a need to punish, without so much as a head-fake toward the demands of veracity. That's as close as I can get to a clinical definition. And by the way, it's cowardly. You had the chance to present your case before you left the restaurant, but that takes the spin angle out of it. Creative writing takes time and some thought. I'll give you some examples of recent masterpieces, grammar and all, and then I'll tell you what really happened.

Example #1:

i wanted to book this place for a party of 25 people and called 3 times before i got some rude woman to call me back. after promising to email me prices and menus i waited for emails that never came. i guess 25 people for dinner was not enough to warrant their interest. after that i swore i would never go back for dinner but i was invited by good friends and i could not refuse. the management staff was rude to my kids and they obviously were not welcome on a friday night. they are 13 years of age and were dancing on the dance floor with other patrons. they were harassed and made to feel unwelcome despite that i spents a few hundred dollars on drinks for the adults and food for everyone. a few of the waiters and other staff expressed concern for the way we were treated by management and said that many others complained of similar treatment. if the food was good i could understand their attitude but for average food and expensive drinks courtesy should really be uppermost. anyway i will never go back there again. many places offer better food and treatment.

Yes sir, the first thing we tell our management and hostesses to do is to be as rude as you possibly can, and to never answer the phone when someone is trying to book a party. The second most important element of training is to make sure the customers don't mistake the rudeness for special treatment and to let them know that everyone else is treated just as rudely. The first distortion in every bullshit tirade is the word *rude*, the second is food quality, and the third is the word, *expensive*. This guy got to *rude* quicker than most. I respect the fact that he refrained from posting his, *I've eaten all over the world,* resume and just got to it. He must be one of those no-nonsense fellows. Read one hundred of these and those four words—rude, food quality, and expensive—will appear in at least ninety. Don't get me wrong; I'm not saying that some folks don't have legitimate complaints. They certainly do, and we do everything we can to correct them, but that's not what we're talking about, is it? Here's what really happened.

After dinner, this guy was out on the patio having a few apparently, *expensive* cocktails with his wife and friends. His two daughters, ages thirteen and I'm guessing eleven, were inside dancing on the dance floor along with some of the customers. This is in the bar area, which serves alcohol, at 11:30 at night. We said nothing. The two kids decided to expand the dance floor to the raised platform area where people were still eating. We politely asked them to stay on the dance floor. We're not rude to children; we all have them. The two girls went outside for a bit, and when they came back and started dancing again, they were shoeless. The manager went over and told them that if they wanted to stay on the floor, they had to wear shoes. Broken glass is a safety hazard. I will challenge any other restaurateur to a glass-breaking contest. My busboys and dishwashers can't stand to see a glass in one piece and if any of you think you can beat my staff in the broken glass department, I'm willing to make a substantial wager. Anyway, we were concerned about the safety of the girls and asked them, politely, to put their shoes on. The girls went back outside and told Papa Bear what happened.

In he came and told the bartender, "I want to know where the guy is who was being rude to my kids?"

The bartender stated the obvious. "Sir, no one was rude to your kids. These people eating here were annoyed because they were running up and down the platform disturbing them. I asked them to please stay on the dance floor. We asked them to put shoes on so they wouldn't get hurt, and it is a bar, and it's almost midnight. They're not supposed to be in here unsupervised."

I guess when you have a cigar planted in your puss for the better part of an hour the smoke clouds your vision.

He said, "That's bullshit. You don't have to be rude to my kids."

I spared you the back-and-forth that the child had with the bartender but for a thirteen-year-old, she had quite an attitude.

Papa Bear said, "That's it! Give me a check. We're getting out of here."

He paid the check—I think he said it was a couple of hundred dollars—and collected his wife and the girls. They left through the front door. As they were walking out, the thirteen-year-old turned around and low danced, bending slightly backward and limbo-like, flipping the bartender the bird with both hands while singing, "Bad employee, bad employee, bad employee, bad employee."

A couple of things: First, why would we be rude to someone who was trying to book a party for twenty-five people, especially after supposedly missing the first three opportunities? Second, why would you spend an extra two hours drinking *expensive* drinks and smoking cigars in a restaurant that you were dragged to against your will? Third, when have multiple members of a restaurant staff ever come over to your table to chat about what a rude management team they have? And fourth, what parent leaves two preteens in a bar full of drinking adults unsupervised?

A couple more observations. Number one, your writing skills could use a little work. It's lacking creativity. I'm certainly no expert, but you need to spend a little less time on the rude thing and a little more on nuanced offenses such as cold food, poor lighting, forgetful waitresses, blown reservation times, and the like. It would color it up tremendously. Number two, I realize that in this economy, money can be tight, but the price of dinner does not include babysitting fees. Perhaps you should consider restaurants that more fit your budget and would watch the little ones at the same time. The Zagat Guide could be very helpful in that pursuit, and they also welcome feedback from folks like you who have the time and the inclination to do so. Number three, get a grip on your kid. We all had a pretty good laugh about the style with which she gave the bartender the finger, but really, a thirteen giving the finger to an adult? You have a budding Courtney Love on your hands there. Good luck to you. And number four, don't say you'll never come back if you don't mean it. It's cruel to tease people that way. I'm getting too old to have my hopes shattered like my glassware.

Example #2:

I went to Jewel with a group of friends last month(girls night out for a birthday). The restaurant has a great ambience but thats the best part of it. We asked the waitress if she could remove the cheese that was on a table right behind me, the odor was extremely strong. She asked the chef who said no. We said half joking then at least let us try it. The chef came over and slapped a small sliver of cheese in front of me and walked away not saying a word. We should have all got up and left after that rude incident but didn't. The food was OK, very expensive for what we ordered, some of us even shared. It came to over $60pp with 1 drink each($15 per drink) and we shared some entrees and only got 3 desserts for 7 of us. I won't be going back

Here's what really happened. The girls came in and were seated at a six-top near the cheese display. The ringleader said to her server, "The cheese stinks. Could you get someone to move it?"

The server said, "Okay, I'll ask."

The server came into the kitchen and said, "Those ladies on table forty-six are saying that the cheese stinks."

I said, "Well, if that's true, the cheese is doing its job; it's supposed to stink. Otherwise, they'd call it milk."

She said, "Chef, they want you to move it."

I responded, "They want me to move the cheese? That's a great name for a book. You don't suspect they've read it, do you?"

Annoyed, she asked, "Could you just move it?"

Me, "No, I can't move it. Where would you have me put it? Just move them to another table on the other side of the room, out of nose-shot."

She went back to the table and told them, "I can't move the cheese, but we'll be happy to move you to another table, over there, away from it."

The ringleader said, "We don't want to move over there. We like this table. We'd like you to simply move the cheese."

Okay, here's the deal. It's a cheese *station*. Cheese, garnishes, fruit, honey, plates, bread, knives, gloves, oils—get the picture? You can't simply move it. You can simply move six women to another table, provided one's olfactory discomfort is paramount to busting someone else's truffles, so to speak. It wasn't.

The waitress came back in to inform me, "They said that they didn't want to move, and if you don't move the cheese, they are going to leave."

As far as threats go, I've heard worse. The part that got me was that we had a perfectly reasonable solution; we simply didn't have reasonable people. What can you do?

I told her, "Look, I'll move their table, but I'm not walking into a hostage situation over cheese. This is ludicrous. If they want to leave, there's nothing we can do. I guess they'll have to leave." I shrugged my shoulders and went back to work, and they decided to stay.

The ringleader then said to the server, "All right, we're staying, but that cheese smell is disgusting. Tell the chef that if we have to sit here and smell this cheese, the least he can do is give me a free piece."

When was the last time you said, *"Wow, that smells like shit. Let me taste it."*

I could see that this was becoming a power game and sometimes it's fun to see just how far people will take it. She issued an idle threat, and I didn't react to it, so now with her friends watching, she had to save face and make me *do* something. We were very busy that night and I was in the weeds but decided to play along. I ran out to the cheese station, cut a piece of cave-aged Cardona, one of my favorites and not terribly stinky, and delivered it personally to the offended party. I placed it down in front of her, we all laughed, and I scurried back to the line to finish service. That was the end of it. We all laughed … really.

When I read her post, I was honestly shocked, and after thinking about posts I've read in the past for all sorts of restaurants, I started to wonder about the truth of all of them. It's a certain type of person who will write something about your restaurant to punish you for whatever perceived offense they endured, and that's what that is: punishment. But people take it to another level when they out and out lie about what happened. I'm no lawyer, but it seems to me that it gets perilously close to slander. A couple of things: I guess we just have to live with this as the cost of doing business, much like no-shows, and compensate by exposing it as best we can. It's also a little sad that some folks derive value by demanding a menial task out of others just to watch them do it. The cheese smell wasn't bad enough to move the table, just bad enough to use an excuse to watch me to perform a trick for her like I was her own personal cocker spaniel. It's sad when you think about it—vacuums being filled and all. A couple of other things: First, the grammar. For heaven's sake, edit yourself. If you had Dr. Emilie Sair for your ninth-grade English teacher, as I did, you'd still be there. You can only hope nobody read it. Second, very few people who aren't married to you will be willing to perform tasks for your entertainment because for us, there's precious little reward. Third, congratulations; it took a while for you to get to the rude thing, the food quality, and the expensive part, but it came in just under the wire and elevated a poorly written post into something truly mediocre. And fourth, for all the yapping about the stinky cheese and never coming back, guess who showed up for lunch two weeks later? Yup.

ART DEALER OR ART CARNEY

The only people who annoy me more than vegetarians are the folks who are always trying to get something for nothing. Okay, I know a couple of very cool vegetarians who've adopted that way of eating because they think it's healthier and it makes them feel better about not killing their fellow inhabitants. I get that, although I have a couple of SEAL Team Six squirrels that have been assaulting my compound of late and I wouldn't mind taking those little bastards out if they weren't so gamey. I prefer quiet vegetarians who don't feel the need to announce their vegetarian-ness like its proof of a more highly evolved spirit; they're plants, dude, not divinity. You know the vegetarians I'm talking about. They're always making comments while passing the filet mignon on a buffet table, and it's always some overly dramatic diatribe about eating something with a face, the mother of the deceased, and capital murder. I just can't take the sanctimony. Here's a recent exchange I had with a couple on the East End.

I said, "You should come by and check out Amano sometime."

The gentleman said, "Yeah, we'll do that. What kind of restaurant is it?"

I told him, "A Tuscan-style restaurant with a country feel."

The woman asked, "Do you have anything on your menu for vegetarians?"

What kind of question is that? Have you ever been in one restaurant in your life that didn't have salad, vegetables, pasta, potatoes, or fish?

I stated the obvious. "We have salads, vegetables, pasta, potatoes, and fish."

Humorless and annoyed, she said, "I don't eat fish. I'm a vegetarian."

I said, "Oh, in that case we have salads, vegetables, pasta, and potatoes."

She then asked, "So you don't really have anything for vegetarians?"

I asked, "You don't eat salad, vegetables, pasta, or potatoes?"

Still humorless and more annoyed, she replied, "Yes, I eat vegetables. I was asking if there was anything on the menu strictly for vegetarians—menu selections for vegetarians."

I asked her, "You mean items that only vegetarians are allowed to have?"

Her husband chuckled; it wasn't improving her mood. "No, I mean items created for vegetarians in mind."

I said, "Nope, but we will make you all manner of vegetables, wood-fired pizza, or pasta. You don't have a gluten allergy, do you?"

She said, "No, but I don't understand why restaurants don't offer more vegetarian options."

I told her, "We really don't get that many calls for it. Most folks are satisfied knowing they can get all the veggies they want, and we almost always have a meatless pizza special to go with the along with the classic tomato and basil."

She replied, "Well, there are more of us than you think. You should start paying more attention."

Egging her on a little, I said, "It's a fad. I'm sure it'll pass." Then I asked her, "You don't eat any meat or fish at all, even for the protein? I couldn't do without fish, and I can't even imagine giving up meat altogether. I don't eat it very often, but I sure like to have it available when I'm in the mood, and I like the stranger preparations like salumi and sausages."

She said, "No, I don't eat anything with a face."

It's a line I've heard one hundred times. Then, with what is invariably the vegetarian one-two punch, she says, "If you saw how sausages were made, you'd never eat them."

I said, "I don't think about it. If I thought about how things are made, I wouldn't be able to look at my brother."

Her husband spit his wine. She, on the other hand, never cracked a smile. How can you take yourself that seriously? That's precisely why vegetarians annoy the shit out of me … but not quite as much as cheapskates.

The only redeeming quality about some cheapskates is that they can be brilliant in their pursuit of free stuff. It drives them to places where we mortals dare not tread. You need courage to be cheap. Since stepping out of the Age of Aquarius and into the twenty-first century, we now employ gift cards instead of gift certificates. As I've said in the past, I prefer paper to plastic because they're easier to lose, thereby making them harder to redeem and lowering my food costs to manageable levels. I haven't used paper in some years now, and although the redemption rate has risen with the plastic cards, those same plastic cards make the fake gift certificates, printed on paper, impossible to miss. It seems there are still a few intrepid souls out there, with remedial printing skills, who are willing to risk it all for a free dinner.

Here's what happened. A guy came into Coolfish for dinner, with his wife. He had a gift certificate, and it was a lulu. I've had fake gift certificates before and described one of the better ones as a fourth-grade art project. It said, *gift certificate for four,* and had different colored swirls and polka dots. It was clearly put together with care and if it wasn't for the fact that it looked nothing like one of our gift certificates, the server might have honored it. It was on an 8.5×11 sheet of plain white paper. Squarely in the middle was a picture of me and under the photo, in the newspaper cut-out letters that are favored by serial killers everywhere, it said, *"Give Harry Two Dinners on Me: T. S."* I swear to you, that was it. Wouldn't you love to see this fellow turn to counterfeiting? I can imagine him putting Obama on the twenty-dollar bill and being completely confounded as to how they caught him.

The manager calls me, describes the thing, and tells me the guy is swearing it's legit. Then the manager asks me, "What should I do?"

We were rolling. I mean, what do you do? That kind of courage must be duly rewarded. How can you not?

I said, "Honor it."

The manager said, "You're kidding, right?"

"No, I'm not. Honor it." And we did.

Truth be told, there's a teeny-tiny chance that I told someone I'd donate a dinner, in a wine-induced haze, and rather than come and pick the damned thing up, they decided to get all Picasso with themselves and create their own. I think the chance of that being the case is rather remote—not the wine part, the gift certificate part—and I believe that didn't happen. I like wine, so I shudder to think how many more I could have potentially authorized, but there aren't that many requests for donations, so I'm fairly confident that if it was legit, it was a one-off. Why did I honor it, you ask? Well, I did it for three reasons. Number one, I find certain levels of mischief to be fun. If no one is getting hurt, I will happily jump on board. Number two, something inside me just wants to reward such a ballsy move. Number three, for the fun of it and the story to tell.

THERE'S NO NEED FOR ARGUMENT, THERE'S NO ARGUMENT AT ALL (VAN MORRISON, "DOMINO")

As I get older, I'm undergoing a sort of metamorphosis. I guess it's the inevitable slowdown that one experiences as the years advance. I'm fighting it, kicking and screaming, but as my friend Charles says, *"Life is a partnership with Mother Nature and she's the senior partner."* Turning sixty was a revelation in that, number one, I made it! There were more than a few betting I wouldn't. And number two, that day, everything started to ache.

Maybe it's all in my mind but it sure feels like it's everywhere else, and while bitching about it to a buddy, he said to me, "Man, you're making way more out of this than you should. You're not old; you're simply entering middle age."

I asked him, "Middle age? How many 120-year-olds do you see running around town? Middle age, my ass. I'm old, dude. Old, done, out to pasture, headed for that great kitchen in the sky."

He said, "You are one depressing bastard. Cheer up. You're healthy, you eat and drink for a living, and you have most of your hair. You don't look a day over fifty-eight. Is it really that traumatic?"

I said, "No, I guess not, and I've been seriously considering the bright side and trying my damnedest to be positive. But consider this: Everything's in play now—social security, fifty-five and older condo association dances, the Villages, Phillips' milk of magnesia, shuffleboard, and bingo. What's there to be depressed about?"

He says, "I can't listen to this. You're an idiot. There's nothing good at all, nothing, about entering this stage of your life?"

I thought for a moment and said, "Honestly, I'm a bit more relaxed—mellower, if you will. I don't know if it's maturity or exhaustion, but it doesn't really matter; the result is the same.

Where I would sometimes let myself get angry with customers or employees, now, most times anyway, I laugh and shrug it off. I used to be a little feistier, but I've since learned that if you don't swallow the argument bait, there are more fun ways to remedy the situation and to show people how ridiculous their actions are."

My friend said, "Yeah, you're a regular Dr. Phil."

Here are a couple of examples, if you'll indulge me.

Every year for Christmas for the last twenty-eight years that we've been divorced, my dear friend and beloved ex-wife has bought me at least one sweater, and in good years when she's not pissed off at me, as many as three. The fact that I have never worn a sweater in my life has never once occurred to her in one of her sweater-buying frenzies on Black Friday, at Old Navy. About three years ago, I broached the subject on Christmas morning.

"Di, can I ask you a question?

She says, "Of course."

I ask her, "How long have we known each other?"

She answers, "Since we were fifteen."

I then ask, "Have you ever seen me in a sweater?"

She says, "Actually, I don't recall."

I tell her, "I know it's the thought that counts, and I don't want to seem ungrateful, but I don't wear sweaters. Never did."

Diane says, "Why don't you try one on and wear it for a day? It'll look nice on you."

"I don't like them, and I don't want to try to like them. The gift is a nice gesture, but it's a waste of money. I'm not going to wear them."

She then asks, "What have you done with all the sweaters I've bought you over the years?"

I tell her, "I gave them to the guys in the kitchen."

She asks, "You gave them away?"

I reply, "Yeah, I don't wear sweaters. What can I tell you?"

Diane says, "You're such an asshole. You gave all those sweaters away?"

"Yes. You work at the restaurant. You didn't notice any of the guys leaving with sweaters down to their knees? No one in the kitchen is over five feet six."

Diane says, "I can't believe you gave all those sweaters away. You would look good in those. I don't understand why you won't try wearing them. It's not like you have any fashion sense."

I reply, "Why, if you're going to spend the time and money for a gift, can't you buy me something I like, or at least something I can use?"

"Like what? A Porsche?"

I said, "I'd be happy with toothpaste. At least I'd use it. How about an onion? Do you know how many onions I go through in a year? How about a bag of onions? I'd feel less silly walking out of your house on Christmas morning with a bag of Vidalia's than I would sporting one of those sweaters."

Diane tells me, "You're such an asshole, Tommy."

I replied, "Merry Christmas."

The following year, I got three sweaters, Old Navy, extra-large.

I opened the box and said, "A sweater! How did you know?" I thought my daughter would wet her pants.

Diane said, "Oh, shut up and wear it. It'll look good on you."

Here's the mellower, nonconfrontational, nonargumentative me. Last year, I decided to buy my beloved ex-wife a gift she couldn't possibly use under any circumstances and then spend all of Christmas morning explaining to her what a great idea it was. I went to Dick's Sporting Goods. As I entered the store, a young stoner apparently trying to earn some holiday cash for weed, said, "Can I help you find something, sir?"

I said, "Nah, I'm looking to buy a football helmet, but I'll find them myself."

He said, "You sure? I'll be happy to help you find something, dude."

Then I had an inspiration. I said, "On second thought, you know what? Maybe you *can* help me. Do you sell athletic supporters?"

He said, "Oh, wow, dude. Athletic supporters? I don't think we have those."

I said, "The sign on the building says Dick's. That would indicate to me that you have athletic supporters."

He said, "Man, I don't think so. I've never seen them here."

Giving up, I said, "Maybe I should just go look."

He said, "Sorry, man."

It turns out Dick's does have athletic supporters and I found them in the section with the balls. I picked out a high-speed model that not only supplied support but had a hard cup for protection as well—two completely useless options in one Christmas gift. I found myself humming Jingle Bells on the way home.

Diane opened the gift on Christmas morning and, after looking at it from every conceivable angle, asked, "What the hell is it?"

I said, "It's an athletic supporter."

Diane said, "An athletic supporter? What am I supposed to do with that?"

Me, "Wear it. It'll look good on you. It even has a cup for added protection in case you find yourself on a boy's bicycle or playing catcher in a pick-up baseball game."

Diane replied, "You're such an asshole, Tommy."

Now, I may very well be an asshole, but as you're about to learn, I'm not an argumentative asshole.

A very nice, unassuming woman made a lunch reservation for fifteen. It looked like an office lunch or a going-away party. It was fifteen women having a nice time together. I was in one of the other rooms tasting some Burgundies with a supplier. Tough job, I know.

My daughter came in and said, "Dad, that lady who booked the fifteen-top brought in a huge sheet cake."

I asked, "Had she spoken to anyone about it?"

Courtney said, "No, she just walked in with it. How do you want me to handle it?"

I told her, "Explain to the woman that there's a cake-cutting fee of three dollars per person." Courtney said, "Got it," and left for the table.

Two minutes and two sips later, Courtney returns with, *the look,* on her face and said, "She's not wild about the cake-cutting fee. She refuses to pay it and told me that for three dollars per person, she'll cut the cake herself."

Just to be clear, the cake-cutting fee isn't merely for cutting the cake. We have to cut the cake, serve the cake, plate the cake, provide the silverware, wash the plate, wash the silverware, stack the plates, sort the silverware, pay the server, pay the dishwasher, pay the rent, and pay the electric bill. The privilege of serving free food holds relatively little appeal. I told Courtney to explain to her about the plates and silverware and all and hoped that reason would prevail. If it did, I wouldn't be writing this, would I?

The woman said to Courtney, "Your boss has quite an attitude. I'm not paying the fee. I'll cut the cake and we'll use the forks we already have."

Courtney relayed the message. "Now she says they'll use the forks they already have, and by the way, she doesn't like your attitude."

I asked, "Are you kidding me? She brings a cake that's larger than the soccer field that they installed in Guantanamo, into a restaurant that serves dessert mind you, refuses to pay for having it served, and she doesn't like my attitude?"

We were both laughing very hard by this point when the new and improved, nonconfrontational, nonargumentative Tommy said, "Okay, let her have it."

Courtney said, "What? Don't charge her?"

Me, "Nope, don't charge her. Let her cut her own cake and use the forks they already have. Oh, and I'm assuming she doesn't need plates either because they would fall under the cake-cutting fee. I'm not going to argue about it, but I don't want to see any extra plates brought to the table. Let them use the ones they already have."

Out came the cake and it was placed in the middle of the table of fifteen. The woman stood up to cut the cake and asked the server, "Can we get some plates over here?"

The server told her, "I'm sorry, but the plates are part of the cake-cutting package, and you told us that you didn't want that. I'll get you plates, but I'll have to charge you for them."

She said, "Fine, we'll do without them."

I don't know if you've ever seen fifteen grown women standing over an occasion cake, forks in hand and digging in, with whipped cream from their eyebrows to their chins. It was a beautiful sight, I must say, and it kind of reminded me of ants at a picnic.

As I walked by, she said, "This is ridiculous. I can't believe this."

You can't believe it? You engineered it! We gave you exactly what you asked for. Who brings their own dessert into a restaurant without even a phone call to see if it's okay? Next time you come, why not bring the entrees and a hibachi as well, and tailgate your ass into a free meal? You'll get no argument from me—and no plates either.

DI-RECTILE DYSFUNCTION

For the most part, Long Island is an affluent, educated, and socially comfortable place to live. I'm fully aware that that is not the case for every Long Islander, but let's for a moment assume that it is the case for the people who eat out at expensive restaurants on a regular basis. I think that should be enough of a caveat to satisfy even the most sensitive of us so as not to offend anyone for any reason. But the one thing that the affluent and the not-so affluent folks both have now, thank God, are navigation apps. Before that, we never had the person with the one name like Magellan, or a truly unfortunate albeit memorable name like Cabeza de Vaca, to set the standard for getting from here to there—a talent that seemed to elude some of our fellow Long Islanders for the longest time. We could never seem to find where we were going, satellites notwithstanding. Speaking of Cabeza de Vaca for a moment, who would follow a guy whose name, literally translated means, *Head of a Cow?* Cows don't really go anywhere; they just stand there and chew. If I'm going to go exploring, I want to follow a guy with a name like Cabeza de Homing Pigeon. At least I know at some point I'll be returning. Maybe I'm just more aware of the points on a compass, but I've been all over the world and have never had a problem finding the place to which I was traveling. I've eaten in almost every restaurant in the United States, or at least it feels like I have, and I have never had a problem getting there. Have I been lost occasionally? Absolutely, but with a quick call for directions or an on-the-fly look at a map, it was a fairly easy process to find your way, providing that you wanted to be there and assuming that arguing about the directions isn't more important than listening to them. I realize that the well-adjusted among us must be scratching their heads but hear me well: there are some folks out there who are so mad about whatever they're mad about that even a succinct recitation of directions is cause for a confrontation. Why? I don't know. I'd have to consult a professional, but I've devised some fun responses to the hopelessly lost because I sometimes relish sinking to that level of discourse. It's the diabolical twelve-year-old that resides in my psyche. Plus, as your mother always told you, *"It's better to give than to receive,"* and baby, I'm a giver.

Here's what happened. I try to never answer the phone at the restaurants for fear that I'll be asked a question that I know nothing about and, as the owner, that's a rather embarrassing position to be in. In my defense, I have a lot of stuff going on in the various restaurants with menus, special dinners, and promotions, so I don't always have the information at the ready. That's why God made receptionists. They are way better at it than I am, and I let them handle things. Besides, answering the phone is His way of telling me that I should have been in the kitchen doing something productive instead of hanging out in the office with my three-thousand-dollar Solitaire machine.

The phone rings.

I answered, "Hello, Coolfish."

A woman, sans greeting, said, "Where are you located?"

I said, "Where are you coming from? I'll tell you how to get here."

This is where I apparently pissed her off, because she seemed, at that moment, to go off the rails. She got very nasty and in a sarcastic tone said, "Why can't you just tell me where you're located?"

Okay, I'll admit she rubbed me the wrong way and that my patience level for rude people may have shrunk a bit but, like I've said numerous times, giving someone exactly what they ask for is the best revenge you can exact, if that's in fact what you're looking to do—which I was. I have heard about the high road but just like the woman on the phone, I was having trouble finding it. The only thing that makes me fighting-mad at a stage in my life where fighting is no longer a credible option is when someone mistakes kindness for weakness and starts bullying. I figure your right to be an asshole should be balanced by my right to be an asshole as well, so we can both act like assholes and see which asshole wins. I felt compelled to accommodate her: I never said I was grown-up.

I digested her, *"Why can't you just tell me where you're located?"* comment and the attitude that went along with it. Then I said, "Okay, we are *located* in Syosset."

She asked, "Where in Syosset?"

"6800 Jericho Turnpike."

She asked, "Where's that?"

"Next to the Chase Bank."

She said, "I'm not really sure where that is."

"It's just past the bowling alley."

She said, "I don't bowl."

I asked her, "Do you eat Chinese food?"

She asked me, "Why would you ask me that?"

I said, "Because the bowling alley is just down the block from the Szechuan restaurant."

She finally lost it and said, "You're being a jerk!"

I bowed to her laser-like sense of perception. I said, "Ma'am, I'm just giving you what you asked for and I could do this all night, by the way. I could take you right into Queens, building by building. Let me ask you a question, though: Do you really want to come here tonight?"

She said, "Yes."

I said, "Then why don't you just tell me where you are, and I'll be happy to tell you how to get here?"

She started screaming, "Fine! I'm on Jericho Turnpike, going west past Jackson Avenue! Are you happy?'

"Third light, make a left."

BURNING MAD

Now that you know my aversion to answering telephones, I must tell you that when I do, occasionally someone makes my day with a comment or request. I sometimes find myself being annoyed at the lengths people will go to eat in a restaurant. They lie about making reservations, they say they know you *("I'm a close personal friend of Tom Schmawdeley"),* and one lady even called claiming to be my mother. But when you give it some thought, it's kind of flattering that they will debase themselves to eat at your place. So, I'm trying to look at this from a healthier perspective since I've promised to be the new and improved version of myself. This was maybe the best phone call I've ever taken in my fifty years of doing this, but first a word about gift certificates. I love them. Love, love, love them. Why? Two reasons: Number one, they are paid for in advance by someone who is trying to be nice to someone else, thereby upping the ante and increasing the take. Some may think me greedy, but we do have bills to pay; this isn't the Peace Corps. The second reason I love them is that we only get about 50 percent of them back. That profit margin is either obscene or just right, depending on which side of the aisle your politics reside on. If all my sales were gift certificate sales, my salary would begin to approach that of a low-level federal bureaucrat. It's really the only profitable part that's left in our business. I'd love to talk to the fellow who dreamed up the gift certificate idea, to find out if he saw this coming or if it was just a happy accident. Either way, he has my gratitude. I'd also like to have a word with the person who decided that gift *cards* were to be the modern extension of the gift *certificate*. We were doing just fine without you. The problem with the gift *card* as opposed to the gift *certificate* is that it's made of plastic, and any environmentalist worth his windmill will tell you that plastic will not deteriorate for thousands of years, necessitating a slight change in setting the expiration dates. And being made of plastic and the size of a credit card, where do they end up? In your wallet, of course, sitting there as a reminder again and again that you haven't been to that particular restaurant in a while. Being made of paper, gift *certificates* find all kinds of ways to meet an untimely but welcomed end. They get mixed up in the wrapping paper around the holidays and get thrown out. They are left in the gift bags at the birthday party with those schmaltzy Hallmark cards and get thrown out. They find their way under the junk mail on the kitchen table and get thrown out. Some people even respect the expiration date, and they get thrown out. Where are the tree-huggers ranting about plastic when you need them? I can't believe they all got jobs. What's worse, losing a few trees or annexing North Dakota to use as a graveyard for all the discarded plastic?

And while we're on the subject of losing...

I was sitting in the office at Coolfish and working on menus when the phone rang ... and rang ... and rang.

I picked it up and said, "Coolfish, can I help you?"

A gentleman on the other end said, "I'd like to speak to whoever is in charge of gift certificates."

I said, "I can help you with that."

He asked, "What's your policy on them?"

"My policy?"

"Yes, your policy. What's your policy on gift certificates?"

I said, "I don't understand the question."

He said, "Don't you have a policy?"

I answered, "Well, yeah. My policy is I sell them to you and pray that you lose them."

He said, "Be serious. How strict are you on your expiration date policy?"

I was kidding him and asked, "Keep in mind we've only been here eleven years. How old is it?"

"My son bought it for my wife and me for Christmas last year, so it's probably close to two years old," he told me.

I said, "You know what? We're just looking to make friends. I'll be happy to honor it. Bring it on down. It's not a concern."

Then he paused a moment and said, "Thank you very much. I appreciate it, and we've been looking forward to coming there, but I have one other slight problem."

"What's that?" I asked.

He said, "I can't bring the gift certificate with me."

I asked, "Why not?"

He said, "About six months ago we had a fire in our house. It wasn't a huge fire, but we had some damage, and I think we lost the certificate in the fire."

"You lost the gift certificate in the fire?" I asked.

"Yes, and it was for two hundred dollars. My son is very generous."

"I'd say so. You must be big eaters."

He replied, "We like food and going to restaurants."

"That's nice."

He then said, "So it's not a problem with the expiration date? You'll still honor it?"

I said, "Honor what?"

He said, "Honor the gift certificate."

"Uh, sir, I'm not quite sure how to break this to you, but you don't have a gift certificate."

"But my son bought it. It was for two hundred dollars."

I sarcastically replied, "You sure it wasn't five?"

He said, "No, no. It was two hundred dollars."

"Okay, bring it in, and we'll be happy to honor it."

Frustrated, he shouted, "I can't bring it in! I told you I lost it in the house fire!"

I said, "Sir, I can't honor a gift certificate that you don't have."

Him, "But I had it before the fire. My son bought it."

"And I would have honored it before the fire, even though it was expired."

Not yet willing to let it go, he asked, "So you're really not going to honor my gift certificate?"

I repeated, "Sir, you don't have a gift certificate."

He screamed, "Are you dense or what? I lost it in the fire! I had it! It was in my house! I had a gift certificate!"

I said, "Okay, tell you what. Gather the ashes together and bring 'em to your local police station. With a bit of luck, they'll have a CSI unit. Have them piece it together, bring it in, and I'll honor it."

Bidding me a fond goodbye, he said, "You are such an asshole!"

"Maybe so, but you still don't have a gift certificate."

AND THE WINNERS ARE ...

There are some people who subscribe to the belief that there are such things as alien life forms and an alternate or a parallel universe. It has to do with a veritable pupu platter of space, time, matter, energy, cosmology, physics, religion, philosophy, fiction, and fantasy—a strange brew indeed. My head would explode trying to sort all of that out and, frankly, I have all I can do to get a meal to a table in the allotted time frame, hot and garnished, so I'll leave all the esoteric thinking to smarter people. Can I first take a second and dispense with the life on other planets stuff? The conclusive proof that aliens do not exist is that no one in government has found a way to funnel them foreign aid—period, end of story. And furthermore, not one enlightened official has come forth to offer the occasional extraterrestrial visitor, after a nocturnal tour of Tennessee, an amnesty with full citizenship and health care. Case closed; they don't exist. But I may be able to offer the hardcore proof that an alternate universe exists. All the evidence one needs is right here on Long Island: up is down, left is right, six reservations, six different times, six different names, six different restaurants, dressing on the side, chop my salad, steam my salmon, slice my steak, paint my house, mow my lawn, wipe my chin, and hold the chickpeas, capers, onions, wine, garlic, cream, herbs, and flavor—all of which sums up the typical Saturday night shenanigans. But do you know what the kicker was for me, the absolute indisputable proof? Only in an alternate universe could no fewer than three people tell me they were insulted, *insulted*, that they've weren't included in my first book or haven't been in one of my customer articles. Yes, there are those among us who consider my writings to be an awards ceremony, sort of like the Oscars without the egos. There are people longing to be recognized for their contributions to the annihilation of the restaurant experience as we know it.

A quick story: I was once in a restaurant in another state having dinner with a friend. I was looking around the dining room as I always do when I'm out for dinner, watching and observing, trying to pick up on what they were doing, when something suddenly struck me.

Bemused, I said to her, "Look around the dining room and tell me what you see."

She looked around and said, "I see people eating and drinking."

"That's it?" I asked.

She answered, "Yeah, Tom, that's it. Why, what do you see?"

I started to laugh and said, "I see people enjoying themselves. They seem to be having a good time. No one's giving the servers cooking instructions, nothing's getting sent back, no allergy trauma, people are ordering what's on the menu, and nobody's fighting, yelling, screaming, threatening, or dying. I've found Valhalla."

She said, "Sounds pretty normal to me."

I said, "You don't live in New York, where going out to dinner is a blood sport."

And just like any other sport, each contestant wants to be ultimately crowned the Champ. That's the purpose of competition, no? Well, then, what I seem to have on my hands are some folks who would like their efforts to be rewarded with the recognition that they feel they deserve for torturing their fellow man. They want to be considered the best pain in the ass they can possibly be. If that ain't an alternate universe, there isn't one. I've often said that if you lived west of New York City and east of LA and you read my writings, you would think I'm making this up because, after all, who really behaves like this anywhere else? The fact that the people I'm about to introduce you to asked to get into the book should tell you all you need to know about the state of dining out in New York. Well, here you go. You've made it; with all the pomp and circumstance that accompanies such an honor. So, puff out that chest, straighten that spine, stick out that chin and be proud; you've earned this. Congratulations, I guess?

For Best Supporting Actor, the Nominee Is:

When someone says to me, *"What do I have to do to get in your next article or book?"* I immediately think, by the very nature of the question, *"You probably just have to be yourself."* Because by asking that question, one must not only subscribe to a somewhat deviant view of restaurant etiquette, but you must also be confident that you can contend in that arena. And that alone, in my eyes, qualifies one as potential material. Was I surprised when this gentleman asked me, *"What do I have to do to get in your next book?"* No, I was not. What was rather amusing, though, was the lengths he was willing to go to in order to achieve that sort of infamy. Here's how it went.

He asked, "Hey, Tom, if I send my next ten dinners back, can I get in the book?"

I said, "That's nothing I haven't seen a hundred times."

He then asked, "What if I order a bottle of expensive wine and then refuse it because I didn't like it? Would that do it?"

I told him, "That would more than likely just get you tossed off the mailing list and buy you persona non grata status around here. You're going to have to work a lot harder than that. There's stiff competition out there."

Getting increasingly frustrated, he said, "Shit, man. I want to be in the next book. How do I get in?"

This is usually where I tend to reassure the readers that this conversation really did take place. I'm not paraphrasing or garnishing and that it's word for bloody word. I swear.

Thinking for a moment, he said, "What if I start a fight in the dining room?"

I responded, "As resourceful as that idea is—and it's a beauty—I'm way too old to be physical with the clientele, so it would only serve to get you banned and probably prosecuted. I'd say you should pass on that one."

He said, "Yeah, I guess you're right."

Ten minutes later, he said, "Hey, T, I've got it! What if I got naked and danced on the bar? You'd have to put that in the book."

I asked, "Dude, why would someone your age want to strip naked, dance on a bar, swinging the fellas around, just to get a few sentences in a book? It seems rather desperate, although I am going to weigh the comedic factor against the gag reflex before giving you an answer."

He said, "I just want to be in …"

The epilogue to this is that we did eventually have go our separate ways. I won't embarrass him by giving you the details of our parting, but I will tell you that the ironic part of this is just as I'd always suspected and with all his contrived scenarios notwithstanding, it was the direct result of him being himself. But he did get his wish ultimately, so how about a round of applause?

The Nominee for Best Actor in an Action Film:

Remember the movie *Like Water for Chocolate*? Let's call this one *Like Clipboards for Grown-Ups*. What is it about a brushed-metal menu clipboard with a fish on it that brings out the Clyde Barrow in otherwise law-abiding citizens? I just can't keep them in the house. I bring 'em in, and they take 'em out. It's come to the point where I'm considering a full range of options, because since the government has endorsed the adolescent technique of, *feeling up,* in airports as our best defense in the *War on Terror,* I'm assuming I can use enhanced pat-downs to keep my continued purchasing of menu clipboards from landing me in the proverbial poor house.

A table of four sixty-somethings were finishing their meals, and I'm assuming there was some alcohol involved. Scratch that—I'm praying there was some alcohol involved, because it would go a long way in explaining things. They paid their dinner check and were heading out.

As they approached the hostess stand, one of the gentlemen (*I did mention that he was in his sixties, didn't I?*) stopped and yelled, "Five … four … three … two … one!"

He then scooped up ten menu clipboards in his arms and ran out the front door.

Diane screamed, "Hey! Bring those back here!" and ran out after him. As she caught up to him near the parking lot, she said, "What are you doing?"

He said, "I'm just trying to get in the book. I'm just trying to get in the book! I wasn't really taking them."

Sir, you are one funny fellow. There's nothing I find funnier than a sixty-year-old man channeling a five-year-old child. It doesn't quite rise to the level of those knee-slapping classics like the water-squirting lapel flower, the electric hand buzzer, or that crowd favorite, the whoopee cushion, but I will give you points for style.

The Nominee for Best Actress in a Documentary or Drama, or Both at the Same Time:

This woman is the wife of a friend, golf partner, and customer; the mother of three beautiful and successful daughters; a person involved in various civic and fundraising organizations; a great friend to everyone she knows; and an all-around wonderful woman. Even with that resume, she's wondered aloud to me why she's never been included in my book. We've discussed it and I've told her that she's too nice to be in. Although she can be a little picky about her food choices, she's always polite and never a problem, so why would I include her in what is essentially a lampoon? She didn't quite see it that way and wanted to be in the book regardless. I steadfastly refused—that is, until now. I've recently discovered that my sweet little friend has been blessed with a culinary superpower, previously unbeknownst to me, that now qualifies her for inclusion. I'll refer to her as M. M can *hear* fennel. In my fifty plus years in the business, I must confess that she's the only person I've ever known to possess such ability. Yeah, that's right; I said it. She can *hear* fennel. I can't begin to know when or how she first became aware of her gift, but she sure as hell has it, and here's how I came to find out.

M hates fennel; hates it. I can't stress that fact enough. Think of the things you hate the most—taxes, okra, flight delays, budget cuts, colonoscopies, and Barry Manilow songs—factor that by ten, and you start to get a feel for the hatred this otherwise stable, lovely woman has for fennel. Fennel happens to be in the anise family and has that slight licorice flavor that anise has, as does its distant cousins basil, chervil, and tarragon. The thing is, M likes basil, chervil, and tarragon, and she has no problem or aversion to any of them, but she hates fennel. Go figure. I'm through trying to explain all the faux allergies, neuroses, and psychoses out there when it comes to the simple act of eating because it's well beyond my pay grade, and ultimately, who really cares? I just shake my head and try to accommodate them as best I can, which was what I was trying to do when I discovered that M had the gift.

She and her husband were eating at the bar, and she asked, "Does the halibut have any fennel in it?"

I said, "Nope."

She said, "If it has fennel in it, I'm sending it back."

I said, "I know I've seen this movie before. Would you like the halibut?"

She answered, "Yes, but only if it doesn't have fennel in it."

"I swear, M. What could possibly bring me to lie about fennel?"

As I was walking back to the kitchen, she said, "I'll know if it's in there."

I made her halibut without fennel, which was not part of the preparation in the first place and sent it out.

She sent it right back and said, "There's fennel in it. I'm not eating it."

Carefully positioning an index finger in each of my eyes, I told the server, "Tell her that I made it myself, and I swear there is no fennel in the dish, there was no fennel anywhere near the dish, and we took what fennel we did have in the walk-in box and put it out on the loading dock while cooking her meal so as not to defile it with even the slightest suggestion of the vegetable."

Upon getting the memo, she said, "There's fennel in it. I *know* there's fennel in it, and I'm not eating it."

As humans, we have five senses, and I guess maybe a sixth if you're John Edwards. Let's, for the moment, deal with five, assuming M doesn't chat with dead people. She couldn't see it because I never put any in, so in that sense, I'm sure. She couldn't smell it because it simply wasn't in the dish, and the only fennel I had was in the walk-in box. She couldn't taste it because she wouldn't eat it; that one was easy. She couldn't touch it because she's too old to be playing with her food. So, by the simple process of elimination, I'm forced to believe that M can *hear* fennel. It's not such a stretch. If we, as Americans, can believe that we can be taxed into prosperity and spent into solvency, why can't I believe that M can *hear* fennel? I'm happy to be a part of proving the hypothesis that there exists an alternate universe, and it's a lot closer to home than anyone originally thought.

RESERVATION JIHAD

When you can't sleep, the most entertaining thing you can do at four in the morning is turn on the television. That's primetime for infomercials. At four in the morning, if you are watching TV, you are either drunk or exhausted and neither condition makes for sound financial decisions. I once dislocated an index finger fumbling for my wallet while a considerably older Davy Jones, of the Monkees, was telling me that I couldn't live without the three-CD compilation of the British Invasion, while playing an Ed Sullivan clip of Herman' Hermits singing *Mrs. Brown, You've Got a Lovely Daughter.* Who could resist that? I'll leave it to you to decide whether I was drunk or exhausted. But why else would you shop for necessities like the Slap Chopper, the Potty Putter *(yes, my friends, it is just what it sounds like: a miniature putting green that you can spread out on the bathroom floor and practice your stroke, while straddling the hopper)*, a video where you exercise until you puke, or my favorite, the Music Vest? I believe that to this day, the Music Vest is the only article of clothing ever that had its inspiration from those two, joined-at-the-hip institutions, *NASA* and *Soul Train*. It was a silver vest that was a radio, or a radio that was a silver vest, but the brilliance of it was that because of the big hair trend that defined the times, it could be worn, heard, and danced to without the headphones that were the scourge of the spandex-loving eighties kids. No one wanted to spend all that time, effort, and gel to get vertical hair only to have a pair of headphones cut a trench through the middle of what some considered to be the height of fashion.

There are also any number of ways to become a millionaire by watching early morning television, sometimes in less than thirty minutes, and the people who've made these millions have taken the time that they would ordinarily use for counting, investing, or spending their fortunes to instead make an infomercial so they can share their knowledge with us. We should be grateful. At the risk of being called a champion of the obvious, why would someone who could work their own *get rich quick scheme,* spend all that money to film an infomercial, buy the airtime, create a website, establish an 800 number, and hire a conga line of telephone operators in order to let the secret out? And who's more clueless than the operators? They had to have seen the infomercial, no? You know the one with the guy on the one-hundred-foot yacht, sipping champagne, with a bevy of gorgeous women slobbering all over him. Then there's always a shot in front of the fountain, which is in front of the mansion, which is in front of the golf course, just to make sure you get the riches part of the rags-to-riches story. Those poor operators make $7.50 an hour, or whatever, taking the names of people subscribing to make millions in the time it takes them to take the call. It's hysterical. You would think that in the course of the hour, one of those operators would throw down the headset, stand up, and say, *"That's it! This is bullshit, pal. I need a raise."* But they don't. I only got into this to tell you that I have an idea that will make someone a fortune if they can just develop it. And I'm not going to film an infomercial with twenty beautiful women. I'm simply going to let this out because in an ironic twist, just as in those infomercials, I stand to gain as much as you.

Here it is: If someone could design a restaurant reservation system that would guarantee that everyone who made a reservation intended to show up for that reservation, that the number of people on the reservation would be at least partially accurate in relation to the number of people using the reservation, that the folks who made the reservation were compelled to show up on time and at the same time for the reservation, and that the name on the reservation matched the name on the driver's license of at least one of the diners who made the reservation, that person would not only become as wealthy as Ron Popeil but would also be the beloved hero of every restaurateur on Long Island. There you have it. Go ahead and give it a shot. If you believe you can learn how to buy twenty-five luxury properties with no money down and flip 'em in thirty days for five times what you bought them for, then for God's sake create a reservation system that works for three hours on a busy Saturday night.

"Simple," say you.

"My ass," say I.

It's never been done, I don't believe it ever will be done, and I blame it on the process of evolution. We are constantly tinkering with the reservation system, trying to get it right, but to be honest, we don't get a boatload of cooperation. Everyone wants to eat at the precise moment that they want to eat, and I understand that. But when you combine that desire with the need to invite guests, employ various means of transportation, enlist the services of MapQuest, numerous family issues, responsibility challenged babysitters, the art of makeup application, memory loss, poor cell phone reception, and the occasional marital dispute, it can throw shit off. We have tried all sorts of potential solutions to the myriad problems of getting someone's ass in the seat at their designated time, and we have been somewhat successful. But just as in nature, the strong must constantly adapt to survive, which is what the reservation jihadists have done. They are constantly evolving and developing better and more creative techniques to beat the system with the intent of turning Saturday Night into the St. Valentine's Day Massacre.

This was a new one that I must admit was brilliant in its simplicity. On a typical Saturday night, we have hundreds of reservations, and it really is a high-wire act dealing with them. Between misunderstood times, no shows, *A.K.A.* names that no one can remember, and a deteriorating patience level on the part of the public, it can get a little sketchy at the podium.

Diane is working the door, and a man walks up to her and says, "Hello."

She says, "Hi, do you have a reservation?"

The man says, "I do."

Diane asks, "What's the name?"

He says, "Jackson."

"Okay, I have you right here. A party of four," she says.

He tells her, "No, that's not me."

But before he can finish, Diane spots a second reservation under the name Jackson and says, "Oh, I see. We have two Jacksons. You're the six-top."

He then tells her, "No it's just the two of us."

Still looking at the reservation sheet and now a little bewildered, she sees a Jackson, party of two. Diane says, "Oh, here you are, I see a Jackson, party of two. It must be hard sometimes to have such a common name. I'm sure you get confused with people all the time. We have three different Jacksons coming here tonight."

He says, "Really?"

Diane tells him, "Yeah, we have a Jackson four-top and a Jackson six-top coming in besides you and your wife."

He says, "Well, to tell you the truth, I made those other two reservations because I wasn't sure who in our original party was or wasn't coming, so I was just covering myself. You can cancel those other two; my guests couldn't make it."

I'd like to ask why this is not considered theft of services. I'm sure if you reserved six airline seats and showed up at the gate and said, *"The other five couldn't get the time off and decided not to come,"* the price of six seats would show up on your Amex statement. What's the difference?

SPARE THE ROD

The most effective method and strongest case for birth control is a children's birthday party. From a restaurant perspective, the potential for trouble is limitless. Admittedly we don't do many of them and, for good reason, turn most of them down. There are three types of parties that I will never, under any circumstances, do: a bachelor party, a sweet sixteen party, and a children's party where the children total more than 30 percent of the guest count. The first two have to do with the wonton consumption of alcohol and out-of-control hormones.

The third one is trickier. We all love kids, but when they form a mob, they're scary. Throw in some sugar in the form of cake and soda and watch what happens. They turn a party into a ball busting contest. There's the *fork-bending competition*, the *stick the wet toilet paper to the ceiling in the bathroom* championship, and my favorite, the *hide the cake in the seams of the banquette* finale. There's no end to the trouble that can ensue from an imagination fueled by Coca-Cola. This is where the two-thirds parents, one-third children ratio becomes so important. It's why they put two policemen in a patrol car. There's safety in numbers. Besides, it takes a village to discipline a child because we have basically started treating them like Iran, hoping that being nice to them will make them like us. Being the wild animals that they are, the little darlings can smell the fear in adults and react accordingly by doing whatever they damned well please without any worry of reprisal, much like your run-of-the-mill mullah. This breakdown of discipline, aided and abetted by the psycho-sexual ramblings of one Sigmund Freud and the wisdom of Dr. Spock, who taught generations of young parents to understand their children instead of disciplining them, has turned the average children's party into an Alfred Hitchcock movie. A trip to your local Chuck E. Cheese will tell you all you need to know about how all the psychobabble worked out. Why are we afraid to discipline our kids? They crave it, yet we refuse to do it. Treating them as equals and frustrating both them and us when they're not up for the challenge is a pointless exercise in parental vanity. Kicking his or her little ass—figuratively speaking, of course—will go a long way in giving them the tools they need to become an accepted member of society who's respectful of others and doesn't believe that it's everyone's obligation to kowtow to his or her every whim. I'm always stunned when I see some poor, harried mother trying to reason with an out-of-control, tantrum-throwing five-year-old. *"Now, honey, try to calm down. You're letting your emotions get the best of you. Mommy only wants what's good for you, darling. Eating too much chocolate can cause your blood sugar to spike, increasing the chances of the onset of type one diabetes, sweetie. Mommy's only trying to keep you from having to take insulin for the rest of your life. And besides, honey, you don't like needles, and you don't want Mommy to have to give you a time-out, do you?"*

WTF is a time-out? I'm trying to imagine my father offering me a time-out. The only time out I got was time out for the healing process. *"If I catch you sneaking out your bedroom window to go joyriding in the family car at three in the morning one more time, you are getting a time-out!"* Yeah, okay.

The differences in disciplinary techniques today as opposed to my father's generation are night and day, and it's most evident in the schools. I got what eventually amounted to twenty-two years of detention (*they doubled it if you didn't show up*) for chewing gum, skipping class, and other various crimes against the state. I even got suspended in the sixth grade for pants that were a bit too tight. Today, unless you come to school wearing an AK-47, you can pretty much do whatever you want. We went from the Pol Pot school of child rearing to Dr. Spock without any transition whatsoever, which left some people confused, and no one was more confused than my high school gym teacher, Mr. Redden. That man was discipline personified. That guy was single-handedly responsible for putting the corporal in the punishment. He was a Marine Colonel—a drill instructor, I believe—and ran the gym like it was Paris Island. Have you ever been screamed at, nose to nose, by someone whose eyebrows are longer than his hair? That is some kind of cold fear right there. Man, he was a hard-ass. We'd heard that he was in the Korean War and that he was so tough, he didn't even carry a gun. They used to just fly him in behind enemy lines, and then he would get out of the plane, beat the living shit out of a whole platoon of Koreans, and fly back out. No one was scarier than Mr. Redden. But no one was more respected either. I once made the monumental booboo of making a wise-ass remark to Mr. Redden in the hallway outside the door of my history class. It was a lapse in judgment I would never repeat. He cracked me in the back of the head so hard that I walked around for three periods thinking I was Martha Washington. But you know what? I got the message. Mr. Redden has since retired because he couldn't make the transition from the Marine Corps to Sesame Street, and I hope he's enjoying the freedom that retirement brings because if he employed his brand of discipline in the school today, he'd be doing twenty to life. He made quite an impression, and I know of no one who had him as a teacher who doesn't speak fondly and respectfully of him to this day. He made me painfully aware that actions have consequences, and I'd like to belatedly thank him for that lesson.

And that brings us to Chucky. He was only about nine years old, and although he's not the first preteen I've written about, he's one of the more memorable. I'll give you the highlight reel. *Precocious* is society's way of calling a kid a pain in the ass without offending his parents. This *precocious* little boy came in with his mom, sister, and grandmother to book a birthday party for the sister. Apparently, he didn't want to be there, and he made us aware of that right from the start.

To the server, he said, "Get me a soda!"

The server replied, "I'll bring it with the rest of the order."

"Hurry up! Mom, when are we leaving?"

Mom, in that voice, said, "Honey, just be a little patient. We have to see about your sister's party."

"I hate it here. Can I wait outside?"

"No, darling. It's getting dark out, and we can't have you out there by yourself."

"Where's my soda?"

Mom explained, "The waitress went to get it, sweetie. Sometimes they get busy with other customers, and I'm sure that when she's done, she will bring it right over."

"I want it now!"

At this point, I was told that Grandma was starting to lose her patience with all the explanations and the coddling and said something to her daughter.

The *precocious* little fellow said to Grandma, "It's none of your business."

Mom, in as soothing a voice as she can muster, told him, "Honey, we don't talk to Grandma like that. It's not nice. You have to be nice to Grandma. Remember all the presents she got you for your birthday? She won't buy you those things if you're not nice to her."

"I don't care. When are we leaving? I don't want to stay here! Can I go over there?"

Mom replied, "No, honey. You have to stay at the table with Grandma while your sister and I talk to the man about her birthday party. You want her to have a nice birthday too, don't you? You had a nice birthday, didn't you? Well, she wants to have a nice birthday just like you did, so we need to talk to the man about it."

"I don't care. I don't want to stay here! Can I come with you?"

Mom said, "No, sweetie. We'll only be a couple of minutes. You have to stay at the table with Grandma."

He asked, "Why can't I go outside? I want to play outside!"

Mom replied, "It's getting dark, and you can't be outside in the dark by yourself, honey."

Frankly, the child was kidnap-proof. I can't imagine any kidnapper, after spending three minutes with him, not hooking a U-turn and paying the parents to take him back.

As Mom and Sis leave the table, he yelled at them, "I don't want to stay here with Grandma. I want to come with you!"

Grandma, tapping her pre-Spock sensibility, said, "Okay, buster. It's time for you to knock it off. Sit there and behave."

Employing an age-old cliché, the boy told Grandma, "You're not the boss of me. I have to go to the bathroom."

Grandma said, "No. Sit here and wait for your mother to get back."

The boy got off his chair. "I have to go, Grandma; I'm going to the bathroom."

Grandma said, "No, sit down. Your mother will be right back, and then you can go. What am I supposed to tell her when she comes back, and you're not here?"

This was what the little gangster told his eighty-something grandma. "Tell her I had to take a shit!"

Where's Mr. Redden when you need him?

LEVITTOWN, NY 11756

This little soap opera took place in a strip center parking lot in front of a television repair shop, but it qualifies as a customer story because in the middle of her seriously unscrewed tirade, this deranged soul stopped mid-rant, recognized me, told me that she had eaten in several of my restaurants, assured me that she would never again return, and then continued her yelling and screaming, ultimately forbidding me to ever return to Levittown. I have been officially banned from the municipality and I'm under the assumption that I stand alone in that regard. I've made some discreet inquiries since the incident but have yet to find anyone who shares the distinction that I could consult on with matters such as, has a ban ever been formally lifted, is there strict enforcement, and how the hell am I supposed to get from Bethpage to Seaford in under an hour? A ban should at least come with a set of instructions.

Anyway, here's how it went down. I used to be the proud owner of roughly twenty flat-screen televisions and have had to repair each one at least once. Flat screens are like women's fashion models in that they are all wispy thin and they're great to look at when you're bored but are prone to sudden breakdowns. And if you didn't know it, all flat screens have the exact same shelf life so if you plan on purchasing more than one buy them at least one week apart to ensure that you won't miss *Dancing with the Stars* on the second one when the first one goes into the repair shop. You'll also save a little gas by dropping the second one off to be fixed while picking up the first. An expert in the repairing of those suckers told me that it's quite normal for the screens to malfunction and that, for whatever reasons, they don't hold up as well as the plus-size televisions that used to last forever. I can't grasp it all and my brain, like my computer, has only so much memory, and I simply refuse to clear out some gigabytes to make room for new information regarding flat-screen repair. I consider it to be extraneous and I'm content to leave that to those who do such things and focus on food.

Upon my walking into Coolfish one evening, the bartender told me that both flat screens in the bar were down. I asked him if he knew anyone who fixed them, and he said that he didn't. I told him that I would take care of it.

The next day, I googled television repair and it gave me several choices, the closest being in Levittown. I called up and the nice gentleman on the phone told me he'd be happy to fix my flat screens, what the price would be, and even how much it would cost if he couldn't fix them. Much like the fashion models, they charge you for looking at them. The gentleman gave me directions and said that I could drop them off, and that he would probably have them back to me in a few days. I thanked him and hung up. We yanked down the flat screens, tossed them in my truck, and off to Levittown I went. The repair shop was in a small strip center on Jerusalem Avenue, and all the lined parking spaces in front of the stores were on a slight angle to accommodate the cars pulling in and out of the center because there wasn't much depth from the stores to the sidewalk. This created a flow problem that the owners of the center solved by designating an *In* entrance and an *Out* exit that I will readily attest were clearly marked as such. As I was barreling down Jerusalem Avenue the strip center came up fast and by the time I realized that it was the one I was looking for, I had just passed the *In* entrance. In a split second, while uttering an *Oh, shit,* and thinking I'd have to abort the landing, turn around, and try again, I spotted the *Out* exit. Seeing that there was only one car in the lot and having an opportunity to do something I wasn't supposed to do was too much for me to resist, so I turned the wheel and went in the *Out* exit. This presented a second problem. All the angled parking spaces were angled away from me, and it would have taken some extreme maneuvering to get into one, so I went past the parking spaces along the side of the building and turned around. My thought was to go back out the *Out* exit, make a left, and return via the *In* entrance, park the car and drop off the flat screens but it just wasn't in the cards. As I passed the end of the building, I looked left and saw that there was still only one car in the parking lot, presenting me with a second opportunity to do something I wasn't supposed to do. This was too good to be true, so naturally I seized the moment. I turned left against the grain of the one-way parking spots, and after turning a three-point turn into a nine-point turn, I nestled my truck into one of the spaces just as Pink Floyd's song, *Comfortably Numb,* came on the radio. I had no idea at the time that I was being watched. *Comfortably Numb* must be one of my favorite guitar solos ever. David Gilmore's soulful, wailing masterpiece never fails to stop me from whatever I'm doing, devoting all my attention to every note as I dab my eyes with a Kleenex and wish I could play like him. So, there I was with the radio volume on eleven, a tissue hanging from my face, air-guitaring the hell out of the solo, when this woman killed my buzz with a knock on the window.

She said, "Could you please get out of the car?"

Because I work with so many women, I'm accustomed to them telling me what to do. I shut the car off and did exactly like I was told. Given my proclivity for always doing what I'm not allowed to do, I will sometimes do what I'm told to do, but it does make me a bit cranky.

I got out and asked, "What can I do for you?"

She said, "Did you just turn in the *Out* exit, and then go against the one-way traffic when you parked your truck?"

I said, "Traffic? I didn't see any traffic. There was no one in the lot."

She asked, "Are you getting smart with me? Did you just come in that *Out* exit?"

Starting to see where this was headed, I couldn't help myself and said, "All right, you got me dead to rights, ma'am. It was I who made that *In* turn into the *Out* exit. I admit it, you caught me."

She then told me, "That sign says one way! Didn't you see the sign?"

I said, "I did, and if you noticed, I was only *going* one way." That nailed it.

"You think you're funny?"

"Yeah, kind of."

"You're not fucking funny. You're an asshole!"

Forgive me, but I had to play along.

Smirking, I said, "Okay, I promise, cross my heart, that I will never, ever again come *In* the *Out* exit, if you let me off just this once. You need a pinky on that, or is my word good enough?"

That was all it took. Seriously, that was all it took.

Her face scrunched all up and she yelled, "Wait a minute—you're that chef! I've been to a couple of your restaurants, and frankly they're not that good. I wouldn't think of going back!"

I said, "Oh, thank you," and I meant it.

She continued, "What, you think you can do anything you damned well please because you've been on TV? You think this is some sort of a joke? You think I'm kidding?"

It was all too much to think about, so I just said, "Well, if it's a joke, I wouldn't take it on the road—you'll bomb."

Her response was, "Oh yeah, you asshole? You'd better never—and I mean never—do that again!"

There was that word again. I was starting to get tired of being screamed at in a parking lot by a shrew of a woman who had obviously deputized herself after a couple of Red Bulls, making this huge scene and calling me an asshole.

I asked her, "Do you plan on letting me in on the, *or else?*"

She asked, "What?"

I said, "An, *or else. Do you have an, *or else? It's a simple question. You're issuing an ultimatum, and frankly without an *or else,* you look ridiculous. There's nothing behind the threat."

Looking like she was going to explode, she replied, "Yeah, well, fuck you, you asshole!"

I said, "Slow down. You're going too fast for me."

She took the bait, "Slow down? Fine! Fu … uh … uh … ck … youuuu, assssshoooole!"

I said, "Okay there, Wonder Woman. Why don't you grab a quaalude and go home and yell at that lucky husband of yours?"

This was when I realized that she was picking up her children from karate class because the karate instructor, who had heard the commotion, came running out of the dojo. He needed all his training to restrain this woman, who was now foaming at the mouth and screaming, "I'd better never see you in Levittown again! You hear me, asshole? You'd better never come to Levittown again, you fucking asshole!"

I believe that six *assholes* in the course of an exchange that probably didn't last more than three minutes is a record, even for me. Having now set that record, there's no reason to go back to Levittown because I'm pretty sure that it's unbreakable. I know a good number of people from Levittown and know of no one there who could produce a seven-asshole tirade in less than three minutes. Just my luck, I ran into Wonder Woman in my first ever tussle over there. I hope that rather excitable lady is okay, and she should be comforted by the fact that I don't get by her way very often. Flat screens have come down so low in price that it's cheaper to buy them than to repair them, so there's no need to drop in on her. Besides, I shudder to think what would happen if I blew a stop sign.

COMB-OVER HERE

Announcements are sometimes required in restaurants that take reservations. They are usually born at the hostess desk and shouted through the waiting area when one's interminable wait for a table has come to a merciful end. Some restaurants have tried getting around this by several different methods. Some give you a device that's a cross between a cattle prod and a vibrator and is designed to go off when your table is ready. To say they lost a few is an understatement. Then came cell phones and hostesses would take your number, and either call you or text you when your table was ready. It seemed like a good idea, and I tried it … briefly. The problem was the patience level of the customers. Fifty people trying to check if their table was ready, every three minutes, cramped up the hostess desk and the telephone beyond belief. It was chaos. We scrapped that idea and went back to the announcement technique. Saying, in soothing tones, *"Jones, table of four … Jones … Jones party … Jones, table of four,"* while walking through the waiting area seemed to be the safest and most economical bet, which was the preferred method one busy Saturday night when *Patty* was working the desk. Patty was a wonderful person in many ways. She was kind, good-natured, cheerful, and diligent. If she had one flaw, and it really wasn't a flaw as such, she was a bit sheltered, resulting in a certain level of naiveté. Now, that can be cute, frustrating, or unnerving at any given time, but it is always, in the end, funny. We did occasionally take full advantage of her condition when things got slow, or we got bored. Diane was usually the ringleader and would set Patty up. One afternoon, Patty was at the front desk between lunch and dinner.

Diane said to her, "Patty, are you very busy at the moment?"

Patty answered, "No, what do you need?"

Diane's ability to keep a straight face during her gags is the glorious result of miles of experience in the pursuit of a prank.

Diane tells her, "I need you to go downstairs and bring me up a board stretcher."

Patty says, "Okay, where do I get it?"

Diane says, "I'm not sure where they're keeping them. Ask the Spanish guys. They'll help you out."

One could only imagine Patty trying to explain to my dishwashers, in mangled Spanglish, that she needed a board stretcher. Off she went. I was totally unaware that this whole shenanigan was taking place at the time.

A winded Patty came up and said, "I can't find it. I asked the Spanish guys, but I don't think they understood me."

The *board stretcher* thing is the oldest gag in the restaurant book, along with the *bucket of steam* and the *cheese straightener.*

"I asked, "How long have you been looking?"

She said, "About fifteen minutes."

I said, "Let me guess. Diane sent you for the steam expander?"

She said, "No, the board stretcher."

I told her, "There is no board stretcher."

She said, "No? Oh, that stinker! She was pulling a practical joke?"

She started to laugh. No malice, no revenge, just pure nice.

Patty did finally get her revenge on Diane on the Saturday night in question, although unknowingly. We were packed to the rafters that evening. The hostess desk looked like the DMV on the last day of the month. People were everywhere and getting irritated about the wait. Patty was keeping her cool and it's not easy with impatient people constantly in your face. Diane saw that Patty was starting to drown and went over to help her out. As she was helping her get the guests seated, she saw a four-top leave and the table being bussed. Diane handed Patty four menus and told her that table thirty-one had just opened up and to get a four-top down as fast as she could.

Patty asked her, "Who's up?"

Diane pointed to the jam-packed bar and said, "Comb-over, over there," referring to the man's hair, and goes back to the

Open Table computer. Patty never quite got it. Not really seeing the man, she started walking slowly around the bar saying, "Mr. Comb-Over … Comb-Over, party of four …" Then she said it louder. "Comb-Over … Comb-Over party … Mr. Comb-Over … Comb-Over!"

One lap down, one to go.

Patty got louder still, "Comb-Over! Comb-Over, party of four! Mr. Comb-Over! Comb-Over party!"

She took two laps around the bar yelling for Mr. Comb-Over. And as if that wasn't bad enough, when Patty got back to the desk after giving up on Mr. Comb-Over, who showed up to check on his table? Yup, you guessed it.

He addressed Patty and Diane and said, "Excuse me, is my table ready yet?"

Patty looked him right in the eye and asks, "Are you Mr. Comb-Over?"

His hair was parted below his left ear

BASIC TRUTHS

There are a few basic truths that are hard to argue with.

1) It takes ten thousand hours of practice to become an expert at something.
2) Premarital sex leads to dancing.
3) Men look ridiculous in sandals.
4) If someone orders their salmon rare, they will send it back as many times as necessary in order to get it cooked all the way through.

Will someone please explain to me why people who like their salmon cooked to death order it rare? In all the years I've been doing this, I've never once had a rare salmon go out to the dining room and stay there. I know it's fashionable to eat your salmon rare, but no one does. Order it rare? Yup. Eat it rare? Never. I believe that salmon is best served medium rare to medium, and we suggest that when asked. But every week we play ping-pong with rare salmons to the point where now, if we get a rare salmon order, we will cook it medium to cut down the number of times it comes back to the kitchen for more fire. Taking into consideration the amount of mileage added to the waitstaff, the wear and tear on the kitchen, and the inconvenience to the rest of the dining companions at the table while the guest lays on the sophistication, we feel it's the best course of action. I guess medium well is the new rare. My theory is that there are some folks who go out to eat who aren't hungry but crave the attention, so they cause all kinds of mischief, drive everyone around them crazy, and leave as satiated as the folks who have eaten.

Here are a couple more truths.

5) Just when you think you've seen it all, some alien life form will come in and raise the bar another few feet.

Here was the phone request for the reservation. If you don't believe me, ask the hostess.

"This is a very special dinner for Jenny and me. We had nearly broken up last month, and now we are stronger than ever. Do you have the most romantic table anywhere? I would like a quiet, secluded table, fabulous attention when we look up, but nonintrusive in all other aspects."

How can you not know that this table will be a nightmare? When I saw this request and the directions on Open Table, I wanted to cane the hostess. Are you kidding, *"Jenny and me?"* I don't want to sound harsh but the only ones who give a hoot about you and Jenny are you and Jenny, and frankly I'm skeptical about Jenny.

Here's what the hostess wrote in the reservation notes: *When confirming this reservation, please let them know you will sincerely try your hardest to accommodate their request. Assure them you will be aware but ask them to be understanding that it is a Friday night with a live band. If slow, offer them a table in Beju?*

There were too many moving parts for this to go smoothly and, of course, it didn't.

Color me clairvoyant. The newly reunited duo arrived at about 7:00 on a Friday night in the summer. We have a healthy happy hour and bar scene, and on Fridays in the summer, we do a lobster special. This keeps things hopping, as they say, and that Friday was no different. They walked into a madhouse at the hostess desk. The gentleman spoke first.

He asked the hostess, "We called for a reservation and asked for your most romantic table. Do you have it ready for us?"

The hostess told him, "We're pretty busy tonight, so the only real quiet table will be in Beju." Beju is a little piece of sushi serenity in an otherwise busy restaurant.

He told her, "We didn't want to sit in Beju. We wanted to be in Jewel."

The hostess then said, "Okay, follow me."

She took him to the first table, and he said, "We can't sit here. It's too noisy."

She took him to the second table, and he said "No, this won't do. It's in the middle of the room, there's no privacy, and it's awfully loud."

Third table, same response. Fourth and fifth tables, same deal.

The hostess finally told him, "Well, that's it. I'm out of tables, but I assure you you'll be happy in Beju."

He asked her, "Do we have to order off the Beju menu?"

"No, you can have anything you'd like," she assured him.

He said, "Okay, because we came for the lobster special."

The hostess said, "That will be no problem, sir. You're welcome to order that in there." And that would have been that provided he wasn't insane. He was.

His table had a wobbling situation. It didn't wobble—it had a wobbling situation.

He called the server over and said, "My table has a wobbling situation. It doesn't wobble all the time, but I find that if I accidentally move it a certain way, it wobbles."

The server, channeling Elmer Fudd, asked, "Well, which way does it wobble? Maybe I can put something under one of the legs to stabilize it."

He told her, "I don't know what leg to tell you to put it under because it only wobbles occasionally when it's moved a certain way. I haven't figured out which way yet; that's why I told you we have a situation. I'll have to keep an eye on it and let you know."

The server said, "Okay, let me know if I can do anything," took the drink order, and headed for the bar.

The server returned with two glasses of Sparkling Pointe Topaz and set them down. Hers was perfect, his lacked a bit of effervescence.

He said, "Mine's a little flat. Could you take this back and get me another?"

The server replied, "Sure."

She came back to the bar and told the bartender what he said. The bartender informed her that both glasses came from the same bottle and that it had just been opened.

They told me what was going on, and I asked, "Romantic table for two, in Beju?"

The server said, "Yes, how did you know?"

"Good guess," I told her. I then said, "Wait two minutes and bring the same glass. I promise you he'll never know. He's trying to impress Jenny. I'm telling you; it'll be fine."

The server asked me, "Do you know them?"

I said, "No, but I've seen these two a hundred times. Just take the wine out before the bubbles really do dissipate."

She got to the table and set down the wine. He took a sip while looking suspiciously at the glass.

The server asked him, "Is that all right?"

He put his glass down and said, "Yes, much better. Did the bartender open a new bottle?"

The server said, "As a matter of fact, he did." And she wasn't lying, really.

He said, "Yeah, I thought so. That other one was kind of flat."

She took their order, and it was two lobster specials, but he wanted the octopus appetizer instead of the salad that came with it because salad, *wasn't his thing.* Then he threw a minor hissy-fit when informed there would be an upcharge. We explained that octopus costs more than lettuce, something that I think would be obvious to most, and he reluctantly agreed to part with the cash. The real trouble came when the lobster was served. Lobster can be a pain in the ass for several reasons. One, no one believes the lobsters weigh what they weigh. If I'm going to try to screw a customer, it's not going to be for four ounces of lobster. I'm going big. I once offered to bet a customer ten thousand dollars that the two-pound lobster weighed two pounds. He refused, of course. Number two, when you remove a two-pound lobster from the shell, it doesn't weigh two pounds anymore. I don't see what's so hard to comprehend. If you'd like to chew on the shells, we're happy to provide them, but I know of no dentist who recommends it. Number three, people who order a steamed lobster and then send it back to have the meat taken out of the shell are a *royal* pain in the ass, and anyone who tells you differently is lying to you. Restaurant kitchens are busy very places, so you have to pay attention to what you're doing. We develop routines and moves, a ballet of sorts, where people are moving in and around each other quickly and deftly, handling hot and sharp items, trying their best to allot the same care and time to each dish and each customer. Sending a dish back means we have to handle it twice, and if it's a legitimate complaint, we're happy to fix it, but it does take valuable time away from someone else's meal preparation.

If you're over the age of twelve, you should be able to negotiate a lobster with a lobster cracker. If you can't, order something else. Sending a lobster back to be deshelled on a busy night is the equivalent of driving a Harley through a performance of Swan Lake. But of all the lobster shenanigans that I've been through, this one was unique.

The two, two-pound lobsters go to the table, and the server asked, "Is there anything else I can get for you at the moment?"

They both shook their heads no. The server saw him studying his lobster intently, had a feeling, and hung back by the station waiting. The man turned around, made eye contact with the waitress, and called her over.

He said, "I can't eat this lobster. Take it back. I want another one."

The server asked, "What's the problem?"

He said, "This lobster is pregnant!"

Just my luck. We were dealing with a practicing lobster-trician. It was my first to date, and my only.

He asked her, "Didn't the chef see that this lobster was pregnant?"

She responded, "I don't know. Let me go ask him."

She brought the lobster back to the pass where I was standing and said, "He can't eat the lobster because it's pregnant."

I looked at her and burst out laughing. "What did you say?"

The server asked, "How can you tell if a lobster is pregnant?"

We said, "Well, you look for the one with swollen chest and butter pecan ice cream and pickle juice dripping off its chin."

After five minutes of this we realized that we'd better get another lobster to the table.

I said to one of the cooks, "Go get a male lobster and get it out as fast as you can."

There's an easy way to tell the difference but the cook didn't know it, so he asked, "How do I know which ones are male?"

We told him, "Well, this one's a female, so take her down to the walk-in box where the others are. Pose all her sexy in your hand over the crate, and at the first sign of interest, grab his ass and get him into the steamer. We need to have this out quickly."

And we did.

Dessert was a tragedy, with gelato flavors being returned and changed, various garnishes having to be served on the side, and sauces from other desserts thrown into the mix. What a night. It was our own fault. If I'd have gotten that initial phone call, I would have told him we were booked solid. People always tip their hand if you pay attention. It's called profiling, and it works. That's why the bad guys don't like it—which brings me to basic truth number six.

6) If it looks like a duck, quacks like a duck, and waddles like a duck, there's a very good chance it's a duck.

THE WHOLE WORLD IS GOING TO POT

Valet parking is to restaurants what laws are to politicians: a necessary evil that gets in the way of your everyday business and applies to everyone else but you. I know that valet companies try their damnedest to find good, responsible people to park cars, but it's harder than it sounds. These are jobs filled by people who are usually waiting for something else to come through or by folks who smoke copious amounts of weed. Either way, there's a measurable degree of apathy, which regularly results in a problem or two. My experience has been that these problems range from small dents, missing keys, a joyride, cars smelling like smoke, and allegations of petty theft, to a stolen hundred-thousand-dollar Mercedes that one of our less-than-astute valets handed over to a guy who looked like he lived under a bridge. It's a long story. Suffice it to say, valet parking is a major pain in the ass, but you must have it in certain places and in certain situations. And just like the politicians do with our laws, I try to skirt around the valet parking as best as I can. What most customers don't fully understand is that valet parkers are not my employees. They don't work for me per se;

they provide a service and have their own contract, insurance, and procedures. That said, because they are on-site and working at the restaurant, I feel responsible for their actions … to a point. Here's what happened.

A woman came to dinner one recent Saturday, pulled up, saw there was a valet, and explained to him that she wanted to park her own car. She said, "I never use valet parking. I don't want anyone else in my car."

Whether it was that or the expected tip that bothered her, we'll never know, so I'm taking her at her word.

The valet told her, "Okay, if you want to park your own car, you can go right around that side of the building. There are spaces over there."

She answered, "What about those spaces here by the door?"

He told her, "Those are reserved for valet."

She said, "That's ridiculous! It's raining. I don't want to park over there and walk in the rain. I want to park here."

He said, "I'm sorry but these are reserved. I'll be happy to park your car for you, so you don't get wet."

She responded, "I'm going to see the manager. This is bullshit."

The valet said, "Okay, but leave your keys in the car in case I have to move it while you're talking to him."

She reluctantly left her car with the keys in it right there in the middle of all the activity, went inside, and started in on the manager. "I want to park my own car! I don't want anyone else in it! This is bullshit! Why do I have to park around the side like some second-class citizen?"

He explained—patiently, I might add—that the spaces were reserved for the valet for ease of retrieval, expediency, and lack of wear and tear on their feet. Exasperated, she went back outside. She told the valet, who now had seven other cars to deal with, that she would allow him to park her car, but she was not happy about it and would probably write something on Yelp. I always chuckle at that threat. Who cares? There's a small amount of people who value their own opinions to the extent that they feel everyone needs to hear them, agree, and riot against the offender. Get a life, for God's sake. The rest of us see some pathetic soul whining after three martinis.

Anyway, the woman finished her dinner, paid her check and went to the valet stand. The valet got her keys and delivered her car to the front door. She got in and was about to drive off when she slammed on the brakes. She got out, accosted the valet, and asked, "Where's the bag?"

The valet said, "What bag?"

The lady yelled, "The bag that was in the car. Where is it?"

The valet replied, "Ma'am, I have no idea what you're talking about. I didn't see any bag."

The woman said, "Don't give me that! There was a bag in the car and now it's gone. You were the only other person who was in the car. This is why I don't use valet. Where's the bag?"

The valet told her, "Ma'am, I swear I didn't see a bag, touch a bag, or look at a bag. I have no idea what you're talking about." The cars were piling up, and the valet told her, "I have to get back to work. I suggest you talk to the manager inside. I can't help you."

She came back into the restaurant and repeated the whole story to the manager.

The manager asked her, "You mean a pocketbook type of bag?"

She answered, "No, just a bag."

The manager then asked, "Was there anything in it?"

She said, "Yes."

He asked, "What was in it?"

She told him, "It doesn't matter but it was valuable, and I think the valet took it. I told him that I wanted to park my own car and I think he took it to get even with me."

The drama of it all was something to behold. The manager talked to the valet who, again, swore that he knew nothing of any bag. At this point, we had to make a call on this. It wouldn't be the first time a valet poached something out of a car but it's very unusual. We told her again that the valet denied having taken the bag and we suggested that we would call the police to come and get to the bottom of the caper.

She said, "No, no, no. I don't want you to call the police. I don't want them involved." That was the light bulb moment where we felt we knew what was in the bag.

We said, "Okay, you obviously don't want the cops involved for a reason, so what would you like us to do?"

She said, "I'd like you to call his boss."

We did, and it went about how you would imagine it would. His boss told us that he called the valet and asked him about it and that he told his boss the same thing he told us. He didn't know anything about it.

The lady decided to play the fear card. She said, "The person I'm delivering that for is going to be very upset if I show up without the bag."

I told the manager, "Unless that person is Pablo Escobar, I'm not worried. This is *Housewives of the North Shore* not the *Sinaloa Cartel*, for heaven's sake. And by the way, if you're dumb enough to leave a bag of pot in a car that you're having parked for you, I'm rooting for the valet."

Five minutes later, she came back in and asked to see the manager again. He walked over to her, and she said to him, "I don't know how to tell you this, but I'm very sorry. I found the bag."

The manager said, "That's great. Where was it?"

She told him, "It was home."

The manager asked, "It was never in the car?"

She told him, "No, it was home the whole time. My husband called to tell me that I forgot it. I never put it in the car. I'm going to call his boss and apologize—and apologize to the valet, of course. And I'm sorry for causing such a ruckus, but I was flipping out thinking he stole it. Again, I apologize."

To her credit, she wrote the valet a formal letter of apology. That was a very nice gesture, and we don't see that very often, so I thank her for that. I've always heard that chronic pot smoking can wreak havoc with your memory, so I'm sure there's a connection. I wish I could remember who told me that.

A LEARNING EXPERIENCE

There have been some doozies when it comes to people who want to get out of paying the bill, but this one is up there. A couple came in one night on a blind date. She was a very pretty thirty-five- to forty-year-old woman and you could tell she had style. Her hair, clothes, and makeup were all well thought out and appointed, and she carried herself with a certain air about her that spoke of sophistication. He was none of the above. A nice enough guy, I guess, but very blue collar and rough around the edges. Why people put themselves in these situations is beyond me, but I'm thrilled that they do, because otherwise you'd be reading Nelson DeMille. This was an oil and water thing that even the most casual of observers could see didn't have a prayer of a successful outcome. One of them had to know and I'm guessing it was her. My experience has been that most men who are very clumsy at dating believe themselves to be Rico Suave. Where this confidence comes from is mystifying due to their strikeout records, but I imagine there's a false sense of experience after so many dates, the failure rate notwithstanding, and an evolutionary defense mechanism in one's psyche that prevents you from believing that you're an asshole. They sat down at the bar, where she ordered a soda, and he ordered a dry vodka martini straight up. This is your classic first date mistake. A martini is a drone strike on your brain and that's the last thing you need when you're trying to make an impression. Vodka is the second problem here. With beer or wine. and even with some liquor, you get a feeling of where you're going relating to your degree of inebriation. It allows you the time and awareness to either pull the stick back or push it forward. Vodka isn't like that. With vodka, you're sober, sober, sober, and then whacked. There's no transitional period that would allow you to make any adjustments. He orders a second martini. By this time, he's starting to talk a little louder, being very animated and telling farmer's daughter jokes to the bartender. You could see that the woman was hanging on by her fingernails. One of them decided it was time to sit and have some dinner. I'm sure it was her.

They sat in one of the booths, he scooted over a little too close, and told her, "I'll be right back. I'm dying for a cigarette." He left her sitting there.

The server told me she was on the phone the whole time he was gone, so we figured she was making contingency plans with a girlfriend. The server asked her if she would like to order anything while she was waiting, and she politely declined.

Romeo came back in, slid into the booth smelling like a Camel, and said, "So, what are you in the mood for?"

Before she could answer him, he spotted a couple of his buddies walking in the door and shouted, "Hey! Johnny, Jimmy, over here." They walked over to the table, and he said, "Hey, I want you two to meet Sharon. Sharon, meet Johnny and Jimmy."

They all exchanged pleasantries and the two men headed for the bar. As they were walking away, Romeo said, "Hey! Why don't you join us?"

One of the men said, "No, man. You guys have a nice dinner. We're going to the bar."

Romeo said, "Come on, sit down. She won't mind, will you, sweetheart? Come on, it'll be fun. Sit down, sit down."

Reluctantly they sat. Romeo grabbed the server by the arm as she was going by and told her, "Listen, darling. I'll have another vodka martini, she'll have one too, and get these two idiots whatever they want." He proceeded to laugh at his own joke while trying to high-five the other two guys simultaneously.

The woman wore a look of disbelief and oddly enough a bit of a smirk.

Romeo announced that he was going out for another cigarette and wanted to know if anyone would like to join him. All three declined. When he left, the other two men, who were completely sober, started talking to her, and it looked like the three of them were having some fun at Romeo's expense. He came back in with a woman he had apparently met over a cigarette and introduced her to the group. I'm assuming it was for the benefit of either Johnny or Jimmy, but he was pretty far gone at that point, so it was impossible to tell. As all this commotion was swirling around the table his date excused herself to go to the bathroom. The other woman retreated to the bar, leaving the three men on their own. Guys are how guys are, so they started talking about the woman.

Johnny said, "Hey, Romeo, wow, man. She's beautiful."

Jimmy added, "Yeah, don't screw it up like you usually do."

Romeo said, "I don't know if I like this chick. She doesn't talk too much." He ordered another round. Five minutes went by, then ten, then twenty, and there was no sign of the woman.

Romeo was the first to notice and said, "What, is she taking a shit? Where the hell is she?"

Johnny chimed in with, "Was she drinking? She could be getting sick."

Romeo answered, "No she had a soda."

Jimmy stated the obvious. "Maybe she left."

Clueless, Romeo said, "Why would she leave? We haven't had dinner yet."

They're always the last to know. Thirty minutes more went by and Romeo asked a server to check the ladies' room for his date. She came back and told him she wasn't in there. After an hour and fifteen minutes, it was apparent that she'd left, and Romeo wasn't happy about it. He went back to the bar and tried to order another round, but the bartender wouldn't serve him. That was the match on the gasoline.

He said, "You're cutting me off?"

The bartender replied, "Yes, sir. It's the law. I'm sorry."

To make a long story short, Romeo made an ass—or should I say more of an ass—of himself for the next half hour. Yelling, threatening, and using my favorite line of all: *"You know who I am?"*

How can you not know who you are? I don't know about you, but I'd be too embarrassed to ask if I'd forgotten. Yeah, yeah, we know who you are. You're an over-served failure of a serial dater whose chances of scoring are lower than a fourth-string soccer hopeful. Pardon the sixth-grade humor. We finally called him a cab. The next day, we got a call.

The hostess answered, "Hello, can I help you?"

The man said, "Yes, I'd like to come down and speak to a manager."

The hostess responded, "Is there something I can help you with?"

The man said, "Yes, you can tell me what time a manager will be there."

A bit taken back, the hostess replied, "Well, they're here now, sir."

He answered, "Fine, I'll be there in twenty minutes," and slammed down the phone.

He arrived brimming with attitude and rudely announced that he was there to talk to a manager. The hostess fetched one.

He said to the manager, "I was here last night for dinner."

The manager told him, "Yes, I remember."

Romeo then said, "I made an ass of myself."

The manager repeated, "Yes, I remember."

He continued. "My date left without saying a word, I never got dinner, and my car keys were taken from me."

The manager said, "We were worried about you getting home. Your friend has your keys and we called you a cab."

Romeo explained, "Yeah, yeah, I know. I want that check taken off my Amex card—last night's check. I'm not paying it."

The manager said, "What do you mean, you're not paying it?"

The man said, "I'm not paying it."

"Why not?"

Romeo said, "Because someone in this bar slipped a roofie into my drink."

The manager said, "What?"

Romeo replied, "Yeah, that's right. And I want the cameras checked to see who did it! Why do you think I made such an ass of myself last night?"

There's a question for the ages. Why do drunken men make asses of themselves? I'll have to get back to you on that.

The manager told him, "I have to check that with my boss." He came and told me, "I have a guy out there who was in for dinner last night. He got hammered and now he's saying he doesn't want to pay his bill because he thinks someone slipped a date-rape drug in his drink, and he wants us to check the cameras to see if we can find out who did it."

My response was, "He what?"

The manager said, "Yeah, he's serious. He's telling me that someone slipped him a roofie and that's why he was acting like an ass. He said that he lost his date and had his car keys taken away, so he's not paying his bill."

"Are you shitting me?"

The manager said, "Nope, that's his position. What do you want to me to tell him?"

I said, "I'd like you to ask him a question for me."

The manager replied, "Okay."

I continued. "I'd like you to ask him who he thinks was trying to boink him."

The manager burst out laughing and said, "You're not serious."

I said, "No, I'm curious. I've heard an awful lot of excuses from conniving people over the years about why they shouldn't have to pay their bill but, *Someone slipped me a roofie?* It's brilliant."

The manager then asked, "Do you want me to check the cameras?"

I said, "You're kidding right? No. He's nuts, and he's also paying the bill. Ask him who would want to boink him and why the rapist would want him passed out during the violation. It's not supposed to work that way, if I'm not mistaken."

The manager informed him that we weren't taking anything off the bill. The guy went off with all the usual threats: *"I'm never coming back, I'm telling all my friends not to come here, I'm going to close you."* Yeah, whatever, dude.

He then told the manager, "I'm going to the police station to file a report."

The manager came back to the office and said, "He told me he's going to file a police report."

I responded, "I would love to have an eight by ten glossy of the look on the face of the officer taking his statement."

Can you picture it?

Romeo: *"Okay, Officer, here's what happened. I had three martinis and twelve cigarettes in the first fifteen minutes of a blind date. I then invited two friends and a strange woman to join us in the booth for dinner, had another drink, and ordered a round for the group. Then my date went to the lady's room. When she didn't come back, I went to the bar, made an ass of myself, had my keys stolen from me, and was given a cab ride home. I believe someone slipped me a roofie—you know, Officer, the date-rape drug—and I want to hold the restaurant responsible. I also would like them to check the cameras to see who did it, and I don't think I should have to pay the bill."*

The Policeman: *"Okay, sir. Let's get to the bottom of this. I'm putting out an all-points bulletin for a sneaky as shit female rapist. Her modus operandi is using a date-rape drug, also known as a roofie, to render her victim's 220-pound body helpless so she can toss him over her shoulder while walking out of the restaurant to her car and then take him home to her lair, where she could have her way with his passed-out, impotent ass until the medication wears off. Does that about nail it, sir?"*

What can I say? All you can hope for in a situation like this is that someone learned something from it. I'm thinking it was her.

DO ME A FAVOR ... RIGHT NOW

I was involved in a restaurant in Montauk in the nineties. It was maybe my favorite out of all the ones I've had for several reasons. First, I love Montauk. There's nowhere else I'd rather be for six months of the year and it's where I met Mike Buffa, who made me a partner in his business, allowing me to dig myself out of a financial hole caused by my inability to see that I made a series of monumentally bad business decisions, impaling myself on my own ego, and was therefore unable to admit that I was incapable of rescuing the white elephant of a restaurant that I had opened in East Hampton. After four years of trying and turning small losses into gigantic ones I walked— or rather ran—away.

Three months later I met Mike and we opened the restaurant in Montauk. Mike had a friend who was in the music business, and he used to come to the restaurant quite often. He had two things in common with every other human being I have ever met. Number one, he had always thought it would be fun to own a restaurant and, number two, he knew exactly what to do to make it a smashing success. This business must be an awful lot easier than I realize because it seems that I'm the only one who struggles to figure it out. You can't imagine the advice I've gotten over the years from well-meaning customers, friends, and strangers alike. Try these.

This one was from an extremely overweight customer: *"Did you ever think of giving out free desserts? People would really go for free desserts."*

And then from a friend: *"How come no one's ever opened a Chinese-Italian fusion place? Those are my two favorite cuisines. Let's you and I do it."*

Here's one from a well-meaning stranger: *"You know what would be a great idea for a restaurant? A place where you could bring in a fish that you just caught, then the waiter could ask you how you wanted it cooked, and the chef would just make it for you. Think of all the money you would save not having to buy fish."* I'm guessing he frequently dines alone.

Here's one from a friend of a friend that I was forced to endure: *"Let's open a place that serves an inexpensive lunch, no tablecloths. We could do sandwiches and salads and soups and pasta, and even sushi if you want to give it a little Asian flair. Then we could do a happy hour with dollar drinks, but then after happy hour, we throw on the tablecloths, lower the lights, and do a very upscale dinner with tableside cooking and live music. And get this: we dress up the wait staff to resemble famous people. Famous people, Tom. Can you picture it? Can you imagine being waited on by President Kennedy, or Elizabeth Taylor, or even Phyllis Diller? And we could do a comedy night or a reggae night to build up the weekdays."*

It's amazing that the mortality rate of restaurants is only around 90 percent. I once had a concerned family member tell me, "You'd better not spread yourself too thin." Sound advice for sure but I was surprised to hear that he thought I'd never considered it. Everyone I've ever met knows exactly how to run a successful restaurant and has no problem sharing the information. I can't tell you how many times I've been involved in a conversation that started with, *"You know what you should do here?"*

Now, as soon as I hear those words, I say, "Yeah, I do," and walk away.

You can't imagine the frustration that those concerned folks feel from me not taking such sage advice.

Anyway, Mike's music friend became interested in getting involved with us in the restaurant, which we welcomed for a couple of reasons. I thought his connections to the industry would be good for business from the standpoint of attracting a high-profile crowd and other successful people who would maybe like to invest in the projects that we were thinking about doing. The PR certainly doesn't hurt. Mike liked the camaraderie of having his friend involved and the safety of having another financially strong partner to rely on considering my net worth at the time was slightly north of eighty-six dollars. But the best part of having him involved was that for all his big shot-ness, he was a down-to-earth, nice guy.

One day he came to me and asked if I would like to do the catering for a rock concert that his company was sponsoring in Montauk. Wanting to make sure to start the relationship on the right foot, I said, "Of course, whatever you need."

He said, "You'll have to feed about one hundred people three meals a day for seven days. There will be a lot of workers there building the stage and setting up the sound systems and all the other stuff that we need. Are you up for that?"

To do anything extra in Montauk in August, the highest of high season, is a very large order. At that time of year, business is nuts and it's all you can do to keep up. To throw another two thousand meals on top of that, and off premise no less, is nothing short of insanity. I certainly fit the profile and at that time in my life, the combination of being crazy and broke led me to make one of the worst decisions of my life.

I said, "No problem. Who's playing?"

I had visions of being debt free in one week's time and figured that if I could survive the thing, I would make a substantial amount of money and make some creditors very happy. My crack staff and I set about planning the feeding of this sea of folks that were due to arrive in two weeks. We set breakfast, lunch, and dinner menus, did scheduling for the employees, dealt with the rental equipment, prepared paper and plastic goods, arranged trash removal, got tables and chairs, and organized every last detail of the operation. We had decided to do three buffets per day, and we would issue voucher tickets for the people who were to be fed at each meal to make sure it didn't turn into a free-for-all. We prepped ourselves as best we could while doing two to three hundred covers a night at the restaurant and we waited for the day to arrive.

The first day was a gorgeous August morning. I began prepping at 4:00 a.m. trying to get a head start on the breakfast and lunch buffets. Breakfast was to be served at 7:30, lunch at 1:00, and dinner at 6:00. Being that it was first day, and not knowing what to expect when we arrived at the site, I called for an all-hands-on deck situation. My entire kitchen staff was helping me get ready for this assault on the restaurant and I must tell you we ultimately pulled off a culinary miracle that week. We were doing basically the same menus for the concert as we were in the restaurant, which made the prepping somewhat easier, but we couldn't serve them the same thing every day, so we had to bring in some new product each morning, taxing the walk-in refrigerators to the limit. We spent half of our time loading, unloading, and rearranging the box. Off we went with the first breakfast. We got there and set up the buffet, and to my surprise, it went rather well—except for my first encounter with "Jason." Jason was the underweight, overwrought, key employee to one of the two headlining rock stars. I believe his official title was Road Manager and he appeared to be unduly impressed by it.

He started our relationship with a question. "Are you the cook?"

"That would be yes," I responded.

He said, "Good, then make me an egg sandwich. Three scrambled eggs but not snotty, with very crisp bacon, and it *better* be crisp, on a roll with the bready part of the inside pulled out, salt and a little pepper, and ketchup, but don't drown it— and make it quick, I have a lot going on."

This was quite the opening line. I was having a bit of trouble formulating a response because it was 7:00 in the morning, I hadn't had anyone order me around like that since my divorce, and I was trying to think of a way to dispose of the body.

To say that Jason and I got off to a rough start would be the understatement of the year. He was maybe the most arrogant little twit I'd ever met. *(You're a road manager. You've created nothing, you haven't written the tunes, you don't play an instrument, and I haven't noticed any groupies hanging off your pant legs.)* My inability to keep my mouth shut has on occasion gotten in the way of more than one diplomatic solution. Knowing that you have a problem is the first step in fixing it, providing you're of the mind to. At that time, I was not, nor was I about to reward Jason for being so boorish, but we had a lot at stake, and I wasn't prepared to blow it all up six minutes into the gig.

I took a very deep breath and said, "Sorry, dude, we're not cooking eggs to order or making sandwiches. There's a frittata on the buffet if you want, and eggs, bacon, and rolls. You can make your own sandwich, if you'd like.

Jason said, "Did you say dude?"

"Excuse me?"

Jason repeated, "Did you call me dude?"

I said, "I might have, yes."

Jason said, "Let's get something straight. Unfortunately, we're going to be stuck with each other this week. For the remainder of the week, you will address me as sir, Jason, or Mr. 'So and So.' Got it?"

As I considered the lost revenue and the lack of proper bathroom facilities in a prison cell, I got hold of myself and said, "Yeah, I think I've got it, Jase."

I'm sure he was unaware, but Jason was perilously close to getting it himself. I've spent a good part of my life around people who are used to getting what they want, and sometimes through the process of association, their underlings feel entitled to the same treatment. It's just a little harder to take coming from the flunkies. I avoided Jason like the plague for the rest of the week because I didn't trust myself to not blow the whole party in a fit of anger. Although it would feel good to go a couple of rounds with Jason, I'd ultimately regret it, not to mention the lost revenue.

The week was a beast. We we're getting it done but it was taking its toll. Everyone was on the edge, exhausted and cranky. The stress on me was so severe that five days into the week, I lost my voice. I've been in highly stressful situations before—I'm in the restaurant business, for God's sake—but I'd never had it affect me that way. I was working from 4:00 a.m. to 12:00 a.m. five days in a row, and with two more to go, I was hanging on by my fingernails.

As I was getting ready for the lunch buffet on day six, my music man partner arrived from Manhattan and stopped in to see how it was going. He said, "Hey Tom, how are things at the ranch?"

Sounding like an articulate frog, I said, "Good. Five down, two to go."

He said, "What the hell's with your voice?"

"Lost it somewhere at the ranch. It's actually better than yesterday."

He said, "Sounds like it hurts."

I replied, "Only when I sing."

He laughed and said, "Okay, carry on."

I said, "Before you go, I'm making up the bill today and I need to know who to give it to."

He said, "What bill?"

I said, "The bill for the catering."

He said, "Oh, there's no bill. We're donating it for the Nature Conservancy."

I said, "What?"

"Yeah, the concert proceeds go to benefit the Nature Conservancy, so I wanted to donate the food too. It's a great cause. They preserve land on the East End. I have a brochure on it upstairs if you'd like to read it."

I had just gone from pauper to philanthropist. I can be as generous as the next guy but when you're destitute, it's a little harder to muster the charity. It felt like someone told me my dog had died. There I was, still broke, with five more buffets to go. I arrived on day six in an admittedly more irritable mood than the previous five. The buffet went smoothly and as we were cleaning things up and getting ready to break down, a bus full of backup musicians pulled into our area. We were contracted to serve 120 people for lunch that day. I had 120 vouchers in my pocket that had been redeemed at the buffet attesting to the fact that we had served 120 people. We even fed some of the fishermen I knew who were working security that day.

As the bus pulled in, I saw Jason running toward me and yelling, "Hey, Tom, get over here."

I now had no reason to hide my disdain for this horrible little guy and said, "What is it there, my man?"

He said, "We have a problem here. We need to feed these guys and you don't have any food left."

With my hand over my mouth, I said, "Oh, my. That would seem to be your problem now, wouldn't it?"

He then said, "You call this a buffet for 120 people?"

I said, "Actually, I call it a buffet for 130, but who's counting? Oh, and here are the 120 vouchers, if you care to count."

Straddling the line between courage and stupidity, Jason got right in my face and, while poking me very hard in the chest, said, "Well, then, you'd better get back to your fucking restaurant and get some fucking food back here, or your fucking ass is finished."

Forgetting for a second that I couldn't wait for my ass to be finished, as he so eloquently put it, I had a fantasy about finishing his as well. I believe that anything that begins in anger ends in shame and I probably have about two minutes of tough-guy stuff left in me before I have to go to the couch to rest, so with that in mind, I decided not to kill Jason. He was making this scene in front of about fifty people and although I'm sure he was doing so to demonstrate his authority while adding a little street cred to his resume, he was simply being a jerk, and an aggressive one at that. I resisted the urge to snap his finger in half, removed it from my chest, and dug in my pocket for a quarter.

I asked him, "Are you armed?"

He said, "What?"

I repeated, "Are you armed? Are you carrying a weapon, a gun?"

With a quizzical look on his face, he replied, "No, of course not."

I handed him the quarter and said, "Good. Here you go. Call an ambulance."

He went white on me and asked, "What?"

I said with a Zen calm, "Call an ambulance. I'm just giving you a heads-up. Make the call. You're going to need a ride to the hospital and being from Manhattan I'm sure you don't have a car."

I enjoyed watching Jason's whole deal change right before my eyes. Consequences are pesky little things, especially when you're not used to experiencing them. Needless to say, it went no further, but Jason and I had quite a different relationship for the remainder of the week. We both grew from our brief time together. Jason had grown a newfound humility, at least around me, and I learned a great lesson about giving. I realized that it's much more fun to give people shit than it is to receive it.

∾❦∾

LAWYERS

D on't you just love lawyers? My affection for William
Shakespeare grows with each personal injury attorney
commercial that I've been subjected to in the last
twenty-five years, flooding the airwaves and billboards from
sea to shining sea. I recently saw a huge sign in Las Vegas
for a barrister whose specialty was suing hotels in Las Vegas
and whose lawyerly puss was emblazoned across half of the
billboard. His countenance oozed integrity, compassion, and
concern, but I found myself wondering how someone who
is intelligent enough to graduate law school and pass the bar
exam wasn't smart enough to be embarrassed by his area of
expertise. It's hard to imagine a top of his class Harvard Law
School graduate suing the Bellagio over the resultant chaffed
ass caused by a fifteen-hour blackjack marathon. How the man
hasn't found his way to Washington is mystifying. A career in
government would seem to be a good place to lend those talents
if the hotel business dries up because there's not a place on the

planet that sells more integrity, compassion, and concern, to more desperate folks than DC. A natural fit, I'd say, and what town couldn't use another lawyer?

WHAT GOES AROUND COMES AROUND

I'm not prepared to write a sweeping indictment of lawyers, but they are an interesting breed. If you need some convincing, just look at Washington. There are more lawyers per square inch in our nation's capital than anywhere else on the planet and it speaks volumes as to why, as a nation, we stumble around bumping into walls. Lawyers, by the very nature of their profession, find it impossible to agree with one another. They are literally paid to argue. It's all about manufacturing billable hours. A lawyer makes his or her living by talking, and if he's talking, he's billing. Now, that's totally cool until it reaches a point where they're just talking for talking's sake as the bill keeps going up. There isn't lot of money changing hands in an uncontested divorce but one of those, *War of the Roses,* deals can be very lucrative. I lived with a lawyer for a while, and do you know when I knew it was time to go?

I looked out the window one day and said, "It started out as such a nice day, and now it's raining."

In a knee-jerk reaction, she said, "No, it's not."

Last time I checked, rain was not an opinion and if you're willing to argue about rain, you'll just have to do it with someone else. I guess that's what's called practicing law. Call it what you may, I call it exhausting. My only point here is that the profession thrives on talking and disagreement and the more disagreement, the more money comes rolling in, so I think it becomes an ingrained instinct. Assuming you can't get two lawyers to agree on anything, can you imagine the folly of assigning five hundred of them the task of fixing the nation's problems that were, in more cases than not, a direct result of their talents in the first place? I've met very few lawyers who didn't automatically believe they were the smartest person in the room. Knowing a lot about your chosen profession doesn't make you smart—it makes you trained. I know a lot about preparing fish that have met an untimely end, but that certainly doesn't make me a genius. I love when I hear a politician, whose primary talent is the ability to disagree, pontificating on the application of nuclear power, or how to build better automobiles, or the economics of baggage charges by certain airline companies, or the salt content of our diets, or the Middle East, or oil spills and the subsequent cleanup, or the price of gas, or mortgage schemes, or how to jump-start the mating habits of the spotted owl. If these people are so well versed in all these myriad subjects, why are we so short on answers? In a nutshell, it's the arguing. As soon as someone comes up with a solution, there are 499 other people telling them why it's a bad idea. Then they argue over who's right and wrong for eight or ten years and solve nothing while attending fundraisers aimed at reelecting themselves to keep the argument going indefinitely. It's quite a gig. I love it when they trot out answers for the troubled economy. If they knew what to do, how did we get into the mess? These are people who can't make a profit running a gambling (OTB) operation with a built-in *"vig"* that insures it against losses. They still managed to bankrupt the thing and then they explain to the rest of us morons the concept of spending our way out of debt. I'm waiting for just one reporter with a mischievous sense of humor to stand up at a press conference and ask one of these guys, *"Sir, before you take over the entire private sector of our economy, could we just try balancing a checkbook as a good-faith demonstration to the American people that you have any idea what you're doing?"* How much fun would that be to hear the response?

("Well, let's define the meaning of checkbook, blah, blah, blah ...")

Sorry about the rant and I do know that it's only 98% of lawyers give the rest of them a bad name. I'm not sure which side of that the following gentleman falls on, so I'll just tell you what happened, and you can decide for yourself. We had a regular bar customer some years back who worked in a law office near the restaurant. He was a highly educated, affable fellow who had recently graduated from law school, a loyal customer, and an all-around good guy. I wouldn't have called us friends because we never socialized out of the restaurant, but we had grown friendly due to his good nature and constant patronage. A friend of mine had gotten himself into some legal trouble at the time and was at a loss to know how to handle it. He was explaining his problem to me one night over a glass of grenache, and it occurred to me that maybe my lawyer/customer, whom I'll refer to as *John,* would be able to give me some insight that could help my friend. We're not talking felonies here, but he was trying to figure out whether he should fight the thing or pay the fines. I told him that I had a buddy who was a lawyer, and I would call him to see what he thought about my friend's predicament. The next day when I got to work, I called my lawyer buddy.

"Hey, John, how are you doing?" I asked.

He said, "Hey there, Cheffy. What's up?"

I said, "I need some quick legal advice on something for a friend of mine."

He said, "Sure, no problem."

I went on to explain my friend's dilemma, he told me what he thought the best course of action would be, and we were probably on the phone for fifteen or twenty minutes. I thanked him, hung up, and said, "I'll see you at the restaurant."

"See you there," he said.

All was normal for about a week and then I got a letter from him sent from his office. I opened it to find a bill for eighty-five dollars for legal services rendered and applied to what I thought was our casual conversation. Let me say something here. I don't expect anyone to work for free, but this wasn't like that. This, I thought, was two buddies talking. Apparently, I was mistaken. I called him that day.

I said, "Hey, John, how are you?"

"Good, Tom, and you?"

I said, "Good, I think. I just got your bill in the mail, and I'm not sure what to make of it."

He asked, "What do you mean?"

"I mean, what's with the bill? I thought we were just yapping about my friend. I didn't hire you to defend him."

He then said, "Listen, Tom. This is how I earn my living. Its billable hours, man. I can't give out free advice to anyone who calls. And I don't really know your friend."

I said, "Wow, I just wasn't expecting that. Eighty-five, huh? That's pretty good for fifteen minutes."

John said, "It's a living."

We hung up but I must tell you, I was annoyed. It wasn't the money; I've spent more on M&M's. It was the principle. I paid the bill and in a rare display of self-control, I didn't say anything further about it to John in order to not rock the boat. We need all the customers we can get but it felt like a low-grade fever whenever he was in the restaurant. Well, despite what any of my atheist friends may believe, there is a God, and She has a whopper of a sense of humor. One day about eight months after I received the bill for legal services rendered, I got a call from John.

I picked up the phone and he said, "Hey, Cheffy, what's going on?"

"Nothing, dude, just working. My life is like the movie *Groundhog Day*, same thing over and over."

John said, "I wonder if you could do me a favor?"

I said, "Of course."

"My wife and I are having a family party at the house, and I think she's a little insecure about her cooking. She's better than she thinks she is, but she asked me to ask you if you could suggest some appetizer items that aren't that hard or time-consuming to make. She also wanted me to ask you how to improve the flavor of her meatballs and if you knew of an easy dessert that would impress the guests. Do you have any ideas?"

My day had just brightened considerably, and I had about fifteen minutes of good ideas about to sell him. I spent that time patiently attending to his wife's culinary shortcomings as he was writing down recipes and suggestions. As we were about to hang up, he said, "Thank you, I really appreciate it. She was flipping out."

I said, "John, it was my pleasure." And I really, really meant it.

You can probably guess what happened next but let me explain it. Before the phone hit the receiver, I was typing the bill. Giggling, I ran it to the post office and mailed it four minutes and thirty-seven seconds after the phone call. Then I returned to the restaurant to wait with breathless anticipation for the follow-up call I knew I'd be shortly receiving. A few days went by and then it happened.

The hostess rang me in the kitchen and said, "There's a call for you on line one."

I picked up line one and said, "Hello."

John said, "Hi, Tom, it's John."

"Hey, John, how are you?"

John said, "Well, that's why I'm calling you. I'm sitting here with a bill in my hand for eighty-five dollars for culinary services rendered. You're joking, right?"

I said, "What would make you think I was joking?"

"Let me get this straight. You sent me a bill for *talking* about food?"

I said, "You sent me a bill for *talking* about law, right? What's so hard to understand?"

John said, "I was in my law office, where I make my living, when we talked about your friend's legal problems. Get it, Tom? *Law* office … *legal* problem?"

Admittedly, I was being an asshole, "I do get it. That's why I sent you the bill. I was in my *kitchen* discussing a *culinary* problem. *Kitchen* … *culinary* problem. It's as clear as a bell to me."

John said, "This is ridiculous. I can't even believe I'm arguing about this."

I replied, "I can, but I'll spare you the reasons why. John, I'm going to tell you something. I was shocked when I got your bill. I thought we were kind of off the clock. But you pointed out something valuable to me, and that's time. Time is valuable, and I'm a little late to that party, which is probably why I'll die broke, but I thank you for that lesson. Surely someone of your intelligence can see the value of other people's time through the same pair of glasses that you use on your own. With that said, I would hope that you pay your bill in the timely manner that I paid mine."

I'm not sure if this is proper, courtroom tested legalese, but he told me, "Go fuck yourself."

To his credit he did mail the check, but he never came back to the restaurant, and he hasn't spoken to me since. After a little self-reflection, it dawns on me that I cost myself a customer who probably spent a thousand dollars a month with us for the grand total of eighty-five bucks. I showed him a thing or two, didn't I? You know what, though? I'd do it all over again.

THE BALL'S IN YOUR COURT

Question: How many ambulances do you have to chase to earn seventy-five million dollars?

Answer: The right one.

When did we lose our minds over medical awards? All ribbing aside, let me first preface my comments by saying that I believe that the legal profession is largely populated by moral, hardworking, upstanding individuals. There, the disclaimer is out of the way. If you are a successful lawyer making a living, you practice law. If you're a failed lawyer who can't argue his way out of a marital spat, you chase ambulances on TV, advertise inflated labor claim victories in Spanish-speaking newspapers, or *(the worst-case scenario)* run for elective office. Let's deal with the first group for now. I'll get to the other two later. Have you seen the ads?

"Hello, I'm John So-and-So. Have you been in an accident? Have you witnessed an accident? Have you dreamt you were in an accident? Chances are we can get you the settlement you deserve. We'll sue the shit out of 'em, and if we don't win, you don't pay. Call for a free, no-obligation consultation."

Hadn't Shakespeare warned us all those years ago? There were abundant good reasons that these people weren't allowed to advertise on television for all those years. An accident, whether in a car, cutting oneself, or even falling down, often requires a fair amount of stupidity. When was the last time you heard someone say, *"That was the fourth car that John's totaled in the last three years? He should start his own limo service."* This is the only place in the world a scenario as ridiculous as that can play out. Why, you ask? Because we are hell-bent on rewarding stupidity. We will search out stupidity for the expressed *intention* of rewarding it. Ambulance-chasing lawyers will spend tens of thousands of dollars in television and radio ads to find someone who did something stupid enough to make them a millionaire. Yeah, yeah, I'm sure there's an occasional victim out there who's duly rewarded for their suffering, but from what I can see, most are in the business of creating victims. Why else would you add the, *if we don't win, you don't pay,* caveat? Sounds like trolling to me. Think I'm exaggerating? How about the elderly woman who spilled a cup of McDonald's coffee in her lap and for that she was rewarded with a few million dollars? Nice work if you can get it. Picture the initial consultation.

The lawyer said, "Hello, Mrs. Smith, how can we help you?"

The victim replied, "Well, sir, I was driving to work, and I stopped at McDonald's for a hot cup of coffee."

"Yes, go on."

The victim said, "I feel a little silly telling you this, but I had it between my legs, and I took one hand off the wheel to open the top so I could drink it, and I wound up spilling the hot coffee in my lap."

The lawyer replied, "Hmm, okay. I have a couple of questions. Did anyone at McDonald's inform you that the hot coffee was going to be served hot or were there any signs posted warning of the perils of hot coffee?"

"No."

"Really? Did anyone advise you of the danger in opening your coffee after placing it in your lap while driving?"

"No."

The lawyer said, "Okay, now I want you to think carefully about this. Did anyone at McDonald's, at any time, instruct you in the proper opening procedures of the container, or make available a manual with diagrams, printed in seven languages, showing how to safely remove the cover of the container when placed between your knees and traveling at sixty-five miles per hour?"

The victim said, "No, sir, they did not."

"And because of that negligence, you burned yourself opening the coffee, correct?"

The victim replied, "Yes, sir, that's correct."

The lawyer said, "And you were treated for the burn?"

"Yes, I went to the emergency room."

"Did they take any pictures of the injury for insurance purposes?"

The victim said, "Yes, I brought them with me."

The lawyer asked, "May I see them?"

The victim replied, "It's a little embarrassing."

The lawyer said, "I assure you, I'm a professional and very discreet. Wow, what a nasty burn that is, and it's in such a sensitive spot."

"Yes, it was very painful."

"Well then, Mrs. Smith, I'd say we have a very strong case. In my experience, looking at those photos, my gut feeling says that you have yourself a three- or four-million dollar-burn there. I'd put pain and suffering at another million. Let me ask you this: Do you now *have fears of opening coffee containers or dread having something hot between your legs?"*

The victim replied, "I do."

The lawyer said, "Well, I'd say that's worth another million or so. The fact that not only is your sex life in jeopardy, at your advanced age, but also your fear of opening coffee containers won't allow you the caffeine you need to throw the hubby a proper tumble, puts us at about six million. My fee will be a third, and don't worry; if we don't win, you don't pay. Let's start by asking for ten million, and maybe we can settle for six. I'll call you when I need you."

"Thank you."

"No, thank you, Mrs. Smith."

Apparently, McDonald's has a big pool of insurance money just waiting to be drained. Rewarding stupidity is very profitable, but so is punishing good intentions.

This brings us to group two. I've been working with Hispanic people, who start in entry-level positions in restaurants, my whole life. I've always told them that if they want to be career dishwashers, they should be lazy and not bother to learn English. I've always insisted that my guys learn the language. I speak fluent Spanish, so it's not a hassle for me; I just thought I could help them more by forcing them to do so. It's worked out well. For the most part, these are very hardworking people with dreams and ambitions, and I'm proud to say that we've sent many on the American dream path to successful careers. The other thing I always tell my dishwashers is to watch the pantry people and the cooks. Ask them questions, learn what they're doing, and help them out in your downtime because that's the next step in your restaurant career. I might have been wrong about that.

I had a friend in the restaurant business who was so disillusioned, he had to get out. Here's the straw that broke his back. He had a great kid from El Salvador working for him as a dishwasher. The kid was a beast, a hard worker, polite, friendly, and motivated. He was also a sponge, absorbing all he could take in, and he was a real bright kid. He wanted to get out of the dish station badly. Who could blame him? He asked if he could come in on his own time to work in the salad station to begin to learn the pantry. My friend was happy to let him. He probably figured the kid would do it once or twice and lose interest. He seriously underestimated the seriousness of the motivation. The kid stayed after his day shifts, came in on his nights off, and worked his ass off learning the salads and desserts. My friend, being a sweetheart, told him that he would give him the same hourly rate for his *learning* time as he got for working the dish station; even though the kid was willing to do it just for the experience, hoping to one day move up, my friend's conscience wouldn't allow him to not compensate the young man. This went on for a couple of months and then the kid got his promotion and was working in the pantry; a year later, he moved to line cook. Then one of the guys in the kitchen read an ad in a Spanish-speaking newspaper advertising big cash settlements for hourly employees who were not properly paid. I'm sure that it goes on, and you know what? I'm on their side—the side of the employees, that is—but this kid was talked into suing a guy who paid him out of kindness when the kid was willing and offered to learn on his own time. My friend was eventually forced to compensate him at time and a half for hours that the kid had volunteered to try to better himself, after he'd already paid him for something that he didn't have to let him do. So, the next time you hear someone crowing about helping the downtrodden, try to get the facts before high fiving anyone for their sensitivity or judging someone for the stupidity of trying to do the right thing.

Doing the right thing and having it turn out to be the stupidest thing you've ever done happens all the time, which gets me to the third group of lawyers that chafe my ass: elected officials. The all-time greatest example of rewarding stupidity, in the history of humankind—and I say this at the risk of a sudden IRS audit—is *(cue the trumpets)* Joseph Biden. And that's saying a mouthful considering his predecessor. Never has there been a dumber soul entrusted with so much power and responsibility and I'm sure the electorate thought they were doing the right thing. The only intelligent words he's ever uttered were ultimately plagiarized and I'm shocked that he thought he could get away with it considering that Joe, whipping out a cogent sentence, would raise a suspicious eyebrow on anyone with an IQ greater than twenty-six. The good news is that he's absolutely hilarious, and I'm hoping the terrorists get it because it's difficult to plot any mischief while pissing your robes. He may accidentally turn out to be our single greatest deterrent in the War on Terror. One can hope.

Okay, back to the private sector. I opened Panama Hattie's in 1983. We had a smokin' bar crowd on most nights, but Fridays were crazy. One Friday night, two gentlemen came in and ordered some drinks at the bar, hoping to chat up the ladies. As hard as they tried, they were striking out more than Alex Rodriguez. After a while, one of the fellows went to the men's room. His buddy, I found out later, was a cousin of mine—fourth or fifth, once removed, and eventually, as it turned out, completely removed. As related to me later and verified by the bartender, my cousin followed his buddy into the john. His friend was in the booth when my cousin walked in. My cousin—and I'm afraid to think what side of the family he belongs to—placed his hands on the top of the wall of the booth, pulled himself up, hung his head over the wall, and said whatever it is you say to someone who is in the process of cranking one out.

I'm assuming it was, *"Feeling better?"*

It turns out that when you exert the effort to pull yourself up, gravity is working just as hard to pull you down. Apparently, my cousin didn't have the strength to keep himself up on the wall hovering over the bowl, and he came sliding down at about four times the rate that he ascended. About halfway through his descent—and I'm going to try to be sensitive here—his scrotum met the latch. Bent over and barely able to breathe, he exited the bathroom with both hands on his crotch, a position he seemed to be all too familiar with. You have to cradle that kind of pain. He told the bartender in a voice like that of the, *ah, ah, ah,* part of the Bee Gee's song, *Staying Alive,* that he had to leave but would be back, and to hold his tab open. The friend came out of the men's room and off to the hospital they went, one with a spring in his step and one not so much. After what I assume was a thorough examination of the affected area, the diagnosis was that he'd scratched the scrotum and bruised a ball. Judging by his prowess with the ladies, he wasn't using them all that much anyway, but it's better to be safe and sore than sorry and celibate. He was patched up and sent on his way … right back to the bar. They returned to the bar, hung until closing time, paid the tab, and left.

About a week later, I received a letter informing me I was being sued for seventy-five million dollars. It's quite a sum. It had the usual litany of boilerplate bullshit like because of the force of the ball bouncing off the latch, his girlfriend was breaking up with him for lack of service, his chances of contracting testicular cancer had quadrupled, and it blew his masturbation schedule to smithereens. Plus, the blow had knocked one of those babies out of round, and the sight of the newly deformed testicle would scare away any chance at all he had of being able to mate in captivity. We gave it to the insurance company. Several months later we were summoned to an examination before trial *(EBT).* I guess this is supposed to filter fantasy from reality before getting to court. Marty, my partner, was to be our spokesperson. Thank God, because he's more levelheaded, disciplined, and articulate than I am. They even got to him. Each side had a lawyer—theirs, familiar with ambulances; ours, familiar with fickle jurors—and a referee was there to complete the farce. Their side was contending that because there had been water on the floor, my cousin slipped and hurt himself, and if it wasn't for the fact that we kept the men's room in a, *perpetual state of disrepair,* their client would have two perfectly round balls.

Our common-sense defense was, *"What the fuck are you talking about?"* It wasn't exactly grounds on which to compromise. They got my cousin on the stand and asked him about his girlfriend, any recent biopsies, candlelight dinners for one, and the oblong ball. He told them that she'd left him, so far, he was cancer free, his time alone wasn't quite what it used to be, and besides being unsightly, the ball in question doesn't sit quite right in his preferred tighty-whities, so he was forced to purchase a new stash of looser-fitting boxer shorts. There wasn't a dry eye in the room. It was time for them to call a witness. They called Marty.

Their lawyer said, "Marty, could there have been water on the floor of your men's room on the night my client injured himself?"

Marty replied, "Sure, there could have been."

Their lawyer said, "So you're admitting that there could have been water on the floor creating the danger of slipping and falling."

Marty answered, "It's a bathroom. It's why they tile the floors. There's water in bathrooms."

Their lawyer said, "Well, it's obvious to me that through your negligence, my client sustained his injury."

I said Marty was level-headed, disciplined, and articulate I didn't say he was Gandhi.

Marty raised his hand four feet from the floor and said, "Counselor, here's the latch." Then he lowered his hand to two and a half feet and said, "Here's his balls! Why are we here?"

The referee, not accustomed to outbursts of common sense, woke up and started banging his mallet. He said, "This is a court of law. I'll not have that language in here. One more outburst, and I'll hold you in contempt."

I'm not totally sure that contempt of common sense is a judicable offense, but Marty obliged the referee just to be safe. The insurance company's lawyer, in an attempt to earn his keep and calm Marty down, asked for and got a timeout. He took Marty out in the hallway and, after a brief phone conversation with his office, told Marty, "This is just like a court of law. You can't act like that!"

Marty said, "A court of law? I've been listening to this shit for an hour, and I can't take it anymore. He's saying his client levitated himself into cutting a nut, that other idiot is smacking a mallet down and telling me to shut up when I'm the only one saying anything that makes any sense, and you're telling me I need to have some respect? Are you shitting me? This is *The Three Stooges*.

After another quick consultation with his office our lawyer told Marty, "Okay look. Due to the nature of the injury, we're prepared to offer him seventy-five thousand dollars to settle the case. It's one percent of what he's asking for."

Marty looked at him a moment and said, "Don't tell me you're going to give this moron seventy-five thousand dollars. Don't tell me that!"

The lawyer said, "Well, you never know what's going to happen if it goes before a jury."

Marty said, "If you give him seventy-five thousand, I want ten grand for showing up and putting myself through this."

They were called back in. Our lawyer said, "In the light of the injury and to avoid a court case, we're prepared to offer the plaintiff seventy-five thousand dollars."

This was 1983. That's seventy-five grand in 1983 money.

My cousin said, "No. I'll go to court."

And that's precisely the moment when I knew what side of the family he was on. He was working for Home Depot at the time, making whatever they make an hour. He turned down seventy-five grand and never even hit his head on the way down the wall. How do you explain it? He did go to court and I'm happy to say he was awarded nothing by a jury of his peers— maybe the last jury of peers to ever reach such a common-sense decision. On the way out of the courtroom, Marty flashed him a big right-handed okay sign that doubled as a zero, smiled at him, and left. In conclusion I bear him no ill will and wish him a decent life, a new girlfriend, and full use of both boys regardless of their shape.

SUCCESS IS 10 PERCENT INSPIRATION AND 90 PERCENT PERSPIRATION

We've defined lying to the point where we've immunized ourselves to it. Not only have we accepted it as standard operating procedure, but we lionize the more accomplished practitioners of the art. Why we don't demand more honesty is a question for the ages. The fact that lawyers and politicians can be so blatant sends the message that lying is merely conversation and the preferred method of removing one's ass from a sling. It's hysterical to watch these folks who know everything about everything, the self-anointed masters of the universe, go all Sergeant Schultz at the sudden appearance of an inconvenient truth. But really, where's the outrage? Have we suspended all common sense and twisted the language and the courts into knots, giving free passes to all the Pinocchio's in power just to avoid hearing the truth? What's the lesson, and more important, what's the price? Forgetting the moral cost—and that would seem to be heavy from what I'm seeing—what about the actual monetary cost of all this lying? How many lawsuits would see a courtroom if both parties told the truth? After all, the main purpose of a judge or jury is to determine who's full of shit and who isn't. I suspect I'd have no trouble finding waiters with the spike in unemployed lawyers if that were the case. I think we should just go all in and make O. J. Simpson the truth czar. What the hell? He's a poster boy for the legal system's cartoon antics and we'd have the added benefit of maybe having him scouring every golf course in Florida, searching for Nicole and Ron's real killer. You may suspect from my rant that I'm about to tell you about another lawsuit, and I am, but I gotta tell ya, this one actually made me laugh.

We opened Jewel some years back. A month or so before we opened, we hired a dining room staff and started training. When hiring a floor staff, if you need twenty, you'd better hire sixty because the attrition rate is extremely high. We seem to be experiencing the glorious results of participation trophies. Everyone is told they are great at everything they do, mediocrity is celebrated, and failure is rewarded. Now I have to deal with them. The problem with all the feel-good psychology is that it evaporates in the heat of reality. Marking one plus one equals five, correct, on little Johnny's test because he tried hard is a wonderful self-esteem confection—until Johnny tries computing a bar check on a busy Saturday night. Also, a little criticism is healthy once in a while. It rights the ship and allows you to get used to the application of the art. Most of my employees have no stomach for it and I think it's because it's a relatively new experience for them. Waiting tables at Jewel, or any restaurant for that matter, is not an inherent skill. Policy and procedure are different everywhere you go and those must be learned and respected, a room full of participation trophies notwithstanding. And, you know what? I took the risk, I pay the bills, and I'm the one owing the purveyors and everyone else if it doesn't work out, so I'm making the rules, and that, my friends, is trophy worthy.

We had a nice young guy who was hired to be a server. Every time I saw him at one of the orientation or training meetings, he was wearing a hat. Full disclosure, I'm a hat bigot. I think they look ridiculous, have never worn them, and every enthusiastic hat wearer I've ever known was a psychopath: The bigger the hat, the bigger the crazy. Okay, so being a hat bigot requires me to monitor the cyclical and stylistic offerings of the market in order to decide to what degree I hate which hat, and to form the appropriate responses to each. We are in the fedora phase of the hat-wearing cycle, and other than the derby, which hasn't reared its ugly hat in years, the fedora is my least favorite. Nothing looks goofier to me than some hipster kid in tight pants, white socks, a short-sleeved pastel madras shirt, and a fedora. I can't help but hate him. I could almost get by it all without the hat, but the fedora seals it. I didn't hate this kid, try as I might have for his chapeau preference, but I made a mental note that he always wore the same hat, he never once took it off, and it was a bit too small. If you're a serial hat-wearer, change it up occasionally, take it off once in a while, and buy one that fits. Is that too much to ask? The rest of us have to look at you. Truth be told, I thought his hat fetish was because he was prematurely bald, and I know a lot of bald or balding guys who wear hats. I was about to find out differently. The first day we were to open, he was scheduled to work. He showed up on time, uniform pressed, new shoes, with his own pens and what could only be described as a bright red do-rag wrapped around his head. I assumed it was some hip-hop culture fashion statement that he wore into work and was going to go to the locker room and remove it and store it with his coat. Again, I was to find out differently. He went down to the locker room, removed and stored his coat, and came back up rockin' the rag. I stared in disbelief. He was walking around the dining room like nothing was amiss.

I asked, "Okay, I'll bite. What's with the do-rag?"

He said, "Oh, I wear it because my head sweats."

I stated the obvious. "You can't wear that in the dining room. You look ridiculous."

He persisted. "I have to wear it. I have a condition that makes my head sweat and I need it to keep me from perspiring in the food."

Do I need this? Opening a restaurant is a monumental task for those of you who have never had the pleasure and the last thing you need to deal with is this brand of absurdity.

I told him, "You're not wearing that in the dining room. You look like a bad, white imitation of a Bloods member. Get rid of it."

He asked, "What if I bring a doctor's note explaining my condition?"

I said, "Son, you can bring a doctor's note, an attending psychiatrist, a hat maker, and the scientist who developed Arid Extra Dry, but you ain't getting on the floor with that thing on your head."

He said, "That's discrimination! I have a disease."

The disease is called entitlement and it may well be an epidemic. If sweat was a race, I'd be in deep trouble, but thankfully, *sweaty-head-itis,* has not reached its full potential as a protected disease … yet.

I said, "That's right, I'm discriminating against do-rags. I confess I'm a *do-ragist.* Take it off, or you can't work here."

And home he went. The next day, he came in for his shift with his uniform pressed, new shoes, his own pens, and a slightly more subtle black do-rag wrapped around his head, with a note from his doctor stating that his head does, in fact, sweat.

I said, "You're not serious."

He said, "Look, I have a doctor's note."

"I don't care about the note. You can come in here with a court order; you're not walking around the floor with that thing on your head."

Suddenly, he turned into Johnny Cochran. "You can't legally keep me from working here. I have a medical condition!"

I said, "Fine, I have a dishwasher opening. You can wrap a whole roll of Bounty around your head, walk around with your unit hanging out, and take off one shoe, if you'd like. The point is no one has to look at you. If you're out there, you need to be presentable, and I've earned the right to determine what that is. Why don't you just buy a toupee?"

He said, "Because it would look ridiculous."

Oh, the irony.

He took off the do-rag, donned his fedora, and stormed out. Several months later, I got a call from someone in some bureaucracy in Albany. He said that he needed me to answer a few questions about so-and-so, who had filed a claim against me. I didn't remember at first. He asked me to give my side of the story.

I said, "I really don't have a side. Here's what happened." I told him.

Being the sensitive soul that I am, I looked up excessive head sweating on the internet. There are a few reasons that it can happen, but do you know what the number one condition that causes excessive head sweating? I'll tell you. The number one cause for excessive head sweating, right there on the excessive head sweating website, at the top of the page, is the main cause: an elevated atmospheric condition. Yup, it seems the hotter it gets, the more the head will sweat. I'm confident that there is no end to the governmental studies initiated to support the conclusion. Just when I was about to dismiss it as a myth, it turns out that global warming continues to wreak havoc on the heads of people prone to perspiring. Not only does global warming cause global warming, global cooling, static temperatures, the ice floes to shrink, the ice flows to swell, the oceans to rise, the oceans to fall, car accidents, tripping and falling, gastrointestinal mayhem, carpal tunnel, incontinence, migraines, tooth decay, good weather, bad weather, diminished mathematical skills, impotence, polar bears to eat each other, Alzheimer's, and colicky babies, it also causes excessively sweaty heads. The judge said his suffering was worth eight thousand dollars. Can you believe that? Lol. I'm under no illusion about what goes on in the minds of those who make those decisions. They will give away any amount of money to buy a single constituent. But I will tell you that if I were his lawyer arguing for a settlement, and although I might bring up the global warming argument as a sidebar for a sure and lucrative pay off, I would lay the blame exactly where it belongs: at the feet of Donald Trump. I'm guessing eight thousand is reasonable compensation for a sweaty head. I'm surprised, though, that the judge didn't throw in another five grand, considering I'm a hat bigot, and call it a hate crime. I can't wait until my first hemorrhoid sufferer applies for a bartending position.

LEGALLY INSANE

All I ever wanted to do was cook. Who knew that in the end, I would wind up being an electrician, a plumber, a sensitivity counselor, an insurance adjustor, an immigration agent, a plaintiff, a defendant, a logistics expert, an advertising executive, a nose wiper, a marriage mediator, a psychologist, a loan shark, a labor lawyer, a pot washer, and a golden tax goose? It can get to you after a while. What irks me the most are the insurance issues. I pay ridiculous insurance rates and I'm sure that I'm not alone. What used to be referred to as an accident is now referred to as a lawsuit. Ever watch TV at night? I know the injury attorney's jingle and phone number by heart. At the restaurants, we have any number of attempted suicides every month with people trying to get to and from their car to the building and back. It's a journey fraught with danger. I eat out every night that I'm not working, and not once, since 1968, have I fallen down on the ice, tripped getting out of my car, slipped off a curb, somersaulted into the ladies room, somersaulted out of the ladies room, swan-dived down a flight of stairs, tripped over a carpet, slid across a tile floor, banged my head on a urinal, chipped a tooth while attempting to dismount from my chair, danced on broken glass, fell into a DJ booth, knocked over a Christmas tree, cracked an antique mirror with a tooth, walked straight into a glass wall, went ass over head at a wedding table, or shing-a-linged off a balcony … and I drink more wine than the average customer. And the Academy Award–worthy performances of pain and suffering are worth the price of admission. You would think that someone who did something so stupid would just get up from sheer embarrassment and leave, but no, they start hearing that jingle in their heads. *"Cellino and*

Barnes, injury attorneys, 1-800-888-8888." It would take ten of these books to detail the insurance hijinks over the years but suffice it to say there were enough to hire a gentleman to show us how to minimize the accidents. For those of you who don't deal with this on an ongoing basis, it will seem like a rather strange calling but there are folks out there who do this for a living. So, this gentleman comes to see me and explains that he does this for several big companies because the business climate has dictated that necessity. It seems like the politicians, in their never-ending quest to entitle, have convinced the public that they're entitled to be compensated for just about anything, the side benefit being a bonanza for the trial lawyers.

He sat me down and said, "Okay, we're going to examine some ways to prevent accidents to minimize your exposure."

I said, "Great."

He asked me, "What do you think causes most accidents and their resulting lawsuits?"

I said, "Abject stupidity."

He said, "No, Tom. Slipping and falling."

I said, "Oh."

He told me, "We have to find ways to minimize slipping and falling."

I said to him, "You mean real slipping and falling as opposed to taking a dive? Because I believe we've had a few of those and they wind up giving these folks ten grand and two months off for a skinned knee. It's a cottage industry."

"What do you do when one of your employees slips and falls in the kitchen?" he asked me.

I said, "I tell them to get up."

He said, "You can't do that, Tom."

"Too much common sense?" I asked.

He said, "We'll get back to that in a bit. What's your plan in case of a fire in the building?"

I said, "Huh?"

He said, "A fire. What is your plan in case of a massive fire in the building?"

I said, "My plan is to get the hell out." Are you serious?

He said, "You need a plan, Tom—a written, well-thought-out plan and it needs to be where people can find it."

I then said, "Let me understand this. You want me to write up a plan for what to do in case of a fire and laminate and secure it, so when a fire breaks out, instead of using my, *"get the hell out,"* option—which is brilliant in its simplicity if I do say so myself—my employees can run around the restaurant, in the fire, looking for a manual that will essentially tell them to get the hell out. Do I have this right?"

"Um, well, yes, but only to cover yourself later if there is a lawsuit," he told me.

One would have to have at least seven years of college to come up with something this idiotic.

I asked him, "How many lives do you think have been saved by the, *run around the restaurant in the fire looking for the manual,* plan?"

"It's not about saving lives. It's about avoiding lawsuits," he said.

I said, "Oh."

He then asked me, "What do you do if an angry spouse comes to confront their partner at the restaurant?"

I told him, "I take the spouse aside and tell *them* to get the hell out."

My plan is flexible and has multiple applications, as you may have noticed.

He then asked, "But Tom, what if the spouse is having an affair with another employee and the husband shows up with a gun and starts threatening people? What do you do?"

"I get the hell *down*," I told him.

Let's call that a variation on a theme.

"I'm assuming you don't have a written plan for that situation either," he noted.

I said, "No, that one slipped my mind when we were getting ready to open."

He said, "Well you need one of those too."

I'm trying to imagine a scenario where a husband, whose wife has been out drinking five nights a week, neglecting her children, and *boinking* a coworker, comes to the restaurant armed to the teeth to kill them both, and I go up to him and say, *"Could you just calm down and wait here in the lobby while I go get the Homicidal Husband Manual? I just want to make sure I don't do or say anything that's going to piss you off."*

How did we get here as a nation, and how do these people take themselves seriously? I'm not talking about the gentleman who was trying to help me; he's serving an important function, keeping my ass out of court. But the authors of all this legislation? It's a sitcom, and here's the evidence.

We now have dating guidelines. That's right, dating guidelines within the company to quell any potential sexual harassment claims. Have you ever tried to keep restaurant employees from *boinking* each other? It's like herding cats. You have young, hormone-riddled, alcohol-fueled, twenty-somethings stuck in a building with each other for eight to ten hours a day. What do you think is going to happen? And the government, whose regulatory nose is already in marriage, bathrooms, healthcare, twenty-ounce sodas, trans fat calories, and name-calling, has decided to regulate dating … because they're so good at all the other stuff. I'm the father of a daughter, so I'm very sensitive to this, but there is some real gray area here and all kinds of opportunity for problems. A friend of mine had a sexual harassment situation in one of his restaurants and decided to vigorously defend against the charges. It turned out that the woman had filed similar charges in her five previous places of employment. It was, essentially, a part-time job. Thankfully, nothing came of it, but it could have been a huge problem for those involved, all because of something that had never happened. I also think that sometimes the difference between sexual harassment and dating gets down to how much you are attracted to your harasser. I don't recall Brad Pitt ever being accused of sexual harassment, do you? Woody Allen would be a different story. So aside from my other responsibilities as described before, I am now the sex sheriff, dutifully sworn to make sure there is no funny business going down—unless of course the two parties have a mutually agreed-upon contract specifying foreplay technique, a full description of the act in advance, duration of the blessed event, the brand of cigarette to be used in the cooldown period and is signed by no less than two witnesses. Believe me, they are serious about this, as funny as it sounds. That said, here's a quick little tale about a situation I ran into before I earned my badge.

A bartender who worked for me some years back was quite the player. In a very quiet way, that bartender bedded just about anyone with a pulse. We all have standards. I was basically unaware of the goings-on because I try to avoid all the employee stuff and I don't hang out with them. But I do hear snippets from time to time and I did hear some things that I didn't really want to believe for reasons I won't go into here. I wasn't sure if it was gossip or gospel, so I shrugged it off and never really gave it any further thought … until that night. I had noticed that the bartender was very flirtatious with one of the servers and had been for some time. The feelings seemed to be mutual and it's always problematic when two employees get together, but like I said before, it's hard to avoid. It was a busy Saturday night and as it wound down, I headed out to meet a friend who was playing in a club several miles away. I got there around eleven and I was going to play a set with him from about eleven thirty until about twelve thirty, which we did. After the set, we were sitting there having a glass of wine, and I said, "How do you like this gig?"

He said, "It's cool. The people are nice."

I asked him, "How long have you been playing here?"

He answered, "A few weeks. It doesn't pay very well. I took it because I needed the cash but I'm going to have to ask him for a raise."

And that was when it all blew up. As soon as he said the word, *"raise,"* my heart stopped and my brain screamed, *"Braise,"* as in, *"I left the short ribs in the oven."* I frantically tried calling the restaurant but got no answer. By that time, it was one o'clock in the morning and everyone had gone … or so I'd thought. I raced back to the restaurant, jumped out of the car, was relieved to see there was no smoke pouring out of the building, and ran to the door. I wasn't paying too much attention to my surroundings as I unlocked the door and went inside. I was more concerned for my pounding chest and the short ribs that were an hour overdue. As I approached the kitchen, I thought I heard something but assumed they were kitchen noises—ice machines, compressors, and such. I was also in a hurry, as you might imagine, because of the short ribs and the thought that I'd destroyed them. It turned out that the ribs were the least of my troubles. I rushed into the kitchen and snapped on the light.

Have you ever walked in on anyone? It's an emotional nightmare. At first, I was horrified. The two of them were stark naked on the chest freezer, inserting the hopeless into the romantic. As the magnitude of what I was seeing settled in, I began to chuckle. Trying to cover a naked body in a commercial kitchen is a challenge. That's why I don't recommend you have sex there. The man definitely has the advantage. Unless he's Godzilla, he can cover up with both hands, a Vita-mix blender, a spatula, a salad bowl, a dinner plate, a water pitcher, or any number of other utensils because there's only one area of concern. The woman, in contrast, has three, which causes a number of problems for someone with two hands. After watching two naked people trying to pretend they were in a prayer meeting, one covering up with both hands between his legs and the other desperately trying to get to three places with two hands and failing, I lost it.

I said, "Excuse me. I need to get the ribs out of the oven," and did just that.

The two of them stood there looking at me in disbelief as I took the ribs out and put them in the walk-in. Neither moved a muscle nor said a word. What can you really say? I shut the walk-in and walked past the two of them a second time and when I got to the kitchen door, I turned around and said, "Well, at least I know who to call when I need a shift covered." Then I turned out the light and left.

None of us ever said another word about it and no one filed a lawsuit. Ah, the good old days.

꙰

RESTAURANT WEek

Restaurant Week is the one week that comes around about five times a year. Just when you think you've survived the onslaught another one rolls around. It started years ago with Hamptons Restaurant Week, and everyone except those of us who had to work it, thought it was such a good idea it expanded to now include Long Island Restaurant Week, Huntington Restaurant Week, Melville Restaurant Week, March Restaurant Week, Main Street Restaurant Week … you get the idea. It's become Restaurant Year. And after having had multiple restaurants in multiple towns, I feel like I've participated in more than my share. The good news is that Restaurant Week, by its very nature, supplies fabulous material. Some of these folks are customers that we only get the pleasure of serving once or twice a year and although their restaurant tabs are minimal, their contributions are many.

SALMON GRILLING

Ah, Restaurant Week. When Restaurant Week rolls around the percentages of screwy people swell considerably. Here's my breakdown, pun intended.

- I believe that sixty percent of Restaurant Week customers love the fact that they can get to try restaurants that they may ordinarily shy away from because of price and if they like your place, they may consider you for holidays or special occasions in the future. We love those folks and they're the main reason we participate.
- About twenty percent are customers who ordinarily eat at your restaurant, and they may or may not be aware that it's Restaurant Week, show up for dinner, are pleasantly surprised by the bargain, buy a nice bottle of wine or an extra appetizer, and consider it a reward for being a regular. We obviously love those folks as well.
- Then twelve percent of Restaurant Week customers are just there for the $24.95 price, drink water with their meal and will not set foot in your restaurant—or anyone else's for that matter—until it rolls around again next year. We like those folks and understand the motivation.
- Finally, eight percent of Restaurant Week aficionados are certifiably nuts. These people are the reason I harbor homicidal fantasies toward a friend of mine, the creator of Long Island Restaurant Week.

I'm convinced that if you had a copy of the Creedmoor social calendar, you would see Restaurant Week highlighted in yellow.

"All right, listen up. There will be a seven-day drying out period for Restaurant Week. We want you to represent well, so your meds will not resume until a week from Monday. Okay, pay attention. Monday night, the bed wetter's are going to Coolfish. Paranoids, you folks head over to A Mano; just don't let anyone see you.

Schizophrenics will be dining at A Lure, no, A Mano, no, A Lure. And the Multiple Personalities can hang at Jewel because it has the most seats."

As entertaining as these folks can be and they are, occasionally I'm stunned into silence by a thought process that's as brilliant as it needs to be monitored. I'm convinced that saving money—real money—is something that if you want to be successful at you must practice daily in every aspect of your life. I know some incredibly thrifty people *(thrifty when you love them, cheap when you don't)*, and they've all managed to do very well financially regardless of their income levels. I have an old buddy who was the poster boy for not spending a dime. He had moves that would make me stare in awe at his flagrant disregard for anyone's feelings and he possessed an unrivaled ability to feel no shame, all in the pursuit of saving money. I once went to Florida with him and our wives some years back. *Ken* told me that he would get the limo because I was buying dinner that night in Miami. I should have known. At precisely 6:30 the next morning the limo showed up at my house. It was a rather boxy number in gunmetal gray, and true to its color, it looked like it had survived a drive-by shooting. On the side door, emblazoned in the hand-painted, cursive penmanship of a nine-year-old, was the name and telephone number of the company: *"The Always Ready Limousine Service."* I kid you not, that's what it said. Ken and his wife were in the back-most seat of this twelve-seat monstrosity along with two Protestant ministers, a mother, her two extremely uncomfortable children, and a dog in a carrier.

I stood there in the street with my mouth open and finally managed to say, "Are you shitting me?"

Ken said, "What?"

I really don't believe it occurred to him how ridiculous this was.

I asked, "This is your idea of a limo to the airport?"

Ken replied, "What's your problem? It's just a ride to Kennedy. What's the difference?"

I said, "This is a vacation. The purpose of a vacation is to elevate your standard of living for a week, not lower it."

Ken aid, "Oh, sorry, Mister High End. Why didn't you order a helicopter to take us in?"

I said, "I don't need a helicopter, shithead, but a little upholstery would have been nice. How many more people are we picking up?"

While this exchange was taking place and the driver was tying our luggage to the top of the car, my ex-wife said, "Will you just shut up and get in?"

I shut up and got in. When we got to the airport, as luck would have it, we were the last stop. The driver, who couldn't have been nicer or more talkative at that hour, began to untie my suitcase.

I said, "I've got these. Why don't you give Rockefeller a hand over there? He looks like he's struggling."

I travel light—very light. Ken and his wife do not. They each had two bags bursting at the seams, probably with coupons, and he was having a rough time getting it together.

As the driver went to help Ken, whose bags were bigger than he was, I said, "I'll go inside and save a place on line."

Ken said, "Okay, we'll be right in," and my ex and I headed for the door.

As we were about to enter the terminal, I hear the driver yell, "Hey, Meester, hey, punta, I hope chu fucking plane craches, chu peets o chit!"

Horrified, my ex turned her head to see what was going on and said, "What the hell?"

Without a glance back or breaking stride and before she could finish her sentence, I said, "Ken tipped the driver."

Saving money is an art form and, for most of us, a learned behavior. As good as Ken was at avoiding payment at all costs, I may have met a woman who is his equal. I've recently experienced the Suze Orman of Restaurant Week and if you were insecure about your ability to save money, this lesson may be just what the accountant ordered.

One night at A Mano, a woman came in with a four-top. As she was looking over the menu she was hemming and hawing about the selections. "I can't have this, or that, or any of the other things. This makes me fat, that makes me fart …" On and on.

She finally asked the waitress, "So this is Restaurant Week?"

The waitress said, "Yes."

The woman, like she didn't know, asked, "What's the deal again?"

The waitress replied, "Its three courses for $24.95. The only catch is that you must order off the Restaurant Week menu."

For general information's sake, we do a very ambitious Restaurant Week menu. Some places do the minimum required number of selections: three apps, three entrees, and three desserts. Long ago, I decided that if I was going to do this thing, I would make the most of it and do the best that we could, so we list about ten apps, ten entrees, and four desserts. Although it was a diverse selection, Suze couldn't find anything she liked.

She called the waitress over and said, "I really don't like anything on the menu and I'm really not that hungry, so what can you do for me?"

The waitress told her, "Well, you can order off the à la carte menu. You don't have to participate in Restaurant Week."

The woman said, "Oh, I could just have the salmon off the regular menu and nothing else?"

The waitress told her, "Absolutely," and took the order.

The woman then said to the waitress, "That's so nice of you to let me know that. I preferred the à la carte salmon preparation to the Restaurant Week menu."

The waitress said, "Great, we'll have that out for you in no time."

Suze sat there through cocktails drinking water. Suze sat there through the appetizers eating bread. When her fish arrived, Suze tore into the salmon like a grizzly bear breaking fast in the spring. Suze sat through dessert picking at everyone else's. When the bill came, Suze reached for it, opened it up, and went nuts.

Suze said, "Excuse me, Miss!"

The waitress hurried over. "What's the matter?"

Suze said, "You overcharged me!"

The waitress replied, "I'm sorry. Calm down and let me see."

Suze got louder. "You overcharged me!"

The waitress said, "Ma'am, please don't scream at me. I don't see where you were overcharged."

"Right there. Right there! You charged me twenty-five dollars for my salmon!"

The waitress told her, "That's the à la carte price of the salmon on the regular menu, which you specifically ordered."

Suze said at the top of her lungs, "You never told me it was going to be twenty-five dollars!"

The waitress replied, "The price is on the menu right next to the salmon. I'll get a manager."

You couldn't help but hear what was going on and the manager was already on her way. She got to the table and said, "Ma'am, please calm down. What's the problem?"

Suze turned her fury to the manager. "Don't you tell me to calm down. You people are trying to screw me!"

The manager said, "What are you talking about? You ordered the menu salmon à la carte. You were told that you'd be charged à la carte for your menu salmon, with the menu preparation that you specifically asked for. No one is trying to screw you."

Suze said, "There's no way I'm paying that! This is Restaurant Week, $24.95 for three courses, no? I had one course, salmon, which just happens to be on your Restaurant Week menu! I'm only paying for one course, not three!"

The manager was exasperated. "What are you telling me? You're going to walk out of here without paying? Do you want me to call the police? I'll be happy to do it."

Suze said, "No. I'll pay you when you give me the correct bill! You're serving three courses for $24.95! I had one! Do the math, sister! Twenty-four divided by three is eight. That's what I ate, that's what it's worth, and that's what you'll get!"

You know, all in all, as screwy as the logic is, you've got to admire the passion. I've never been that gung-ho about anything. It's the inability to feel shame when there's money involved that allows some folks to fatten their wallets at the expense of others, much like when Ken flipped the cabbie, what I suspect was, a quarter. I can't compete with these people, so I don't try. She left after paying eight dollars for her twenty-five-dollar salmon because the manager just wanted to shut her up and get her out of there. That's seventeen dollars in profit. I can honestly say, as God is my witness, I've been in the restaurant business fifty-two years, and I have yet to make seventeen dollars on an order of salmon and most likely never will. I'm sure she does it routinely. There's no other week but Restaurant Week where the person selling the salmon could make less on the deal than the person buying the salmon. I believe I'm unique in that regard.

YOU CAN'T ALWAYS GET WHAT YOU WANT

I've spent a good part of my life in the town of East Hampton. It's my adopted hometown at this point, and I've enjoyed almost every moment I've spent there. I started going out there in 1970, and it was a very different place back then, as you can probably imagine. When I first started spending time there, usually to see my college roommate who was a local, it was a sleepy little hamlet that reminded me of Mayberry RFD of Andy Griffith fame. It was still farm-y and everyone knew everyone else. It almost had a Midwestern kind of feel to it with people wishing you good morning and always stopping for a chat on the street. It was stone dead in the winter with absolutely nothing to do, except of course for the occasional alcoholic beverage, consumed in one of the very few establishments that chose to endure the off-season. It was even hard to stay home and watch TV because they only had two stations out of Connecticut, channels three and eight, so your choices were extremely limited. Some folks think that a lot of the East Enders are Boston Red Sox fans because of Carl Yastrzemski growing up in Bridgehampton but it really had more to do with the fact that before cable TV they couldn't get the signal out of New York, so they had to watch the Red Sox on channel eight. I don't care all that much about baseball, but I do know there's a hell of a rivalry between the Yankees and the Red Sox and I just want the Yankee fans to not judge the East End Red Sox fans too harshly because it wasn't their fault. Anyway, back on topic.

My college roommate and I would hit the two or three bars that were open, sit there drinking beer after beer, and bitch that there was nothing to do. As the eighties rolled around, the music industry discovered East Hampton, and the place has never been the same. There was always the occasional movie star or famous author or artist who would hang out there in the summer, but no one really seemed to notice. You'd be in line in the supermarket standing between Kevin Bacon and Christie Brinkley, and it was business as usual. But for whatever reason, that changed in the eighties with the influx of the music industry people. The town became more crowded, the summer crowd became more aggressive and impatient, and all the little mom-and-pop stores started to disappear, to be replaced by the usual high-end stores that appeal to the super wealthy. That was when I realized that the way of life I'd experienced in East Hampton when I'd first arrived there was gone. Those stores— Ralph Lauren, Elie Tahari, Coach, and the like—were constant reminders that the torch had been passed.

And it was in one of those stores, London Jewelers, where I had an epiphany. I'd been sort of trying to live up to the rising standard of what was going on, from a demographic standpoint, as it was happening. You can get caught up in it all, and it certainly can be fun, but I never had the financial firepower to hang with even the poorest of the wealthy for very long. That fact became painfully clear, and the resulting weight-off-the-shoulders moment happened right there in London Jewelers, in the earring section, on Main Street in beautiful downtown East Hampton. It was the day I learned how to say, "*no*." Well, kind of. Some years ago, I was dating a very nice, kind, wonderful woman who was just a tad … spoiled. High maintenance wouldn't really describe her because in essence, she wasn't. She was just a tad spoiled—a clothes, jewelry, and vacation kind of spoiled.

We were walking through East Hampton on a beautiful fall afternoon and as we got to the corner of Newtown Lane and Main Street, she said, "Let's stop in London Jewelers."

Let me first say that there is absolutely nothing in London Jewelers that even mildly interests me. I don't wear jewelry and rarely buy it as a gift. Until recently receiving one for my birthday, the only watch I owned was bought in a panic in an airport gift shop because I hate being on an overseas flight not knowing how much longer I'll have to suffer.

I told her, "I'm not going into London Jewelers."

She asked, "Please, can we just go in and look?"

"At what?"

"Jewelry, Thomas."

I said, "I have absolutely zero interest in London Jewelers or anything in it. I have a huge interest in being outside on a gorgeous fall day. There's no way I'm going inside on a day like today."

Five minutes later, I was standing in the earring section of London Jewelers. Call me a coward or, more accurately, a pragmatist. She was chatting away with an earring specialist. How a guy earns a living talking about earrings is beyond me, but he was keeping her occupied and for that I was grateful. I was wandering through the watch section, which I find to be fascinating, looking at the different designs and, solely out of curiosity, inquiring about the prices. From the corner of my eye, I saw the salesman bring out one of those felt trays that they keep the goods on, which is the first step in a series that leads to crushing your credit.

The two of them were chatting and laughing, I'm assuming at me, and having a merry time of it when I said, "Can we get going? I don't want to miss the day."

She answered, "Wait. I just want to try a few on."

I said, "There's a dressing room?"

It seems that trying on earrings means holding them by your ears and looking in the mirror. So, he was holding the mirror, expressing way too much interest in the selection, and she was holding up pair after pair of earrings.

She said, "Come here and tell me which ones you like."

I said, "I'm out of here. Let's go."

She said, "Come on, five minutes. Help me out."

I walked over just as she was dangling a dropped diamond, deadly fabulous, killer earring that went from her ear to her shoulder, next to her blonde highlighted, long wavy hair, and a fresh-from-Florida tan.

This was a beautiful woman and a beautiful piece of jewelry that even a Neanderthal like me could appreciate.

As she asked me, "What do you think?" the little, teensy-weensy, white tag turned just enough to reveal its somewhat north of six-thousand-dollar price.

It hit me like a gift from the cosmos and without missing a beat, I said, "I think they make your ass look big."

She had a great sense of humor, thank God—the only reason I got away with a comment like that—and cracked up. The earring specialist failed to see the funny, as expected, but given that he plies his trade in East Hampton, I'm sure he'll recover the sale. I'm still friends with her to this day and I'm happy to report she's with a very nice guy who can afford any earring London Jewelers has to offer. What a relief it was to just say, "*no*," and

I'm starting to do it more and more. It's quite therapeutic, as you'll soon see. Speaking of big …

Restaurant Week had recently passed, and I'd just gotten my bi-yearly dose of the word *big*. Not big as in, *I'll make a big profit this week*, or *I've got a big deposit to make*. No, it's more like, *"His linguini is bigger than mine,"* or, *"Which is bigger, the apple cobbler or the strawberry-rhubarb shortcake?"* It's the only week where you'll hear a grown man admit to having a smaller linguini. Big is what it's all about and given the fact that the price went up three whole bucks, to $27.95, big is bigger than ever. This past Restaurant Week, we decided to put a skirt steak on the menu. I will never do it again. The problem is that skirt steaks can differ in size and shape and just like the Restaurant Week folks who order them, some are shorter and fatter, and some longer and leaner. That being the case and being the seasoned pros that we are, we cut them to weight. The other way we get around the shape thing is that we always try to send the same shaped steaks out to the same table if there are multiple steaks ordered, to avoid the whole, *"His is bigger than mine,"* melodrama. Nothing turns a grown-up into a tantrum-throwing three-year-old faster than the impression that one's skirt steak is smaller than his dining companion's, which is exactly what happened after I bone headedly sent out two different shaped steaks to the same table. Hey, it was busy.

The server came back to the pass with the two steaks in hand and said, "The man at table twenty-three sent these back and said that he can't believe you had the audacity to send these two steaks out to the same table. He wants you to fix it."

Because he brought up the subject of audacity, let's define it. If I understand my dictionary correctly, *audacity* is defined as *shameless boldness, with an arrogant disregard for personal safety.* I believe that pretty much nails it. He was shameless by telling me that for the kingly sum of $27.95—for three courses, mind you—he felt that *he* was getting screwed. Bold in telling me that, *I* was the audacious party even after serving him what amounts to a nondeductible, charitable donation on my part. The, *fix it* comment reeked of arrogance, and the combination of the three put his personal safety in jeopardy. If the Mets could cover four bases as thoroughly as that they'd finish the season undefeated. You know, emotion is a funny thing. It's a lot like fire: useful if you can control it, and destructive if you can't. The best deals I have ever made were the ones that I didn't care if they happened or not. When you're not wrapped up emotionally you can say no and wait until it gets good enough to say yes. I feel the same way about Restaurant Week. I used to get all emotional about it, running around like headless chickens, hoping against all odds to break even. But now I simply go with it and, frankly, laugh about what goes on and the antics that some people are willing to pull. Maybe I'm just mellowing with age.

I said, "He wants me to fix what?"

She told me, "He said that these two steaks aren't the same size and he wants you to fix it. He wants two of the same size steaks."

I've made it a priority to enjoy every single day of my life and I've been very successful at it. Some would say even a bit too successful, but personally, I think its jealousy. We're so busy during Restaurant Week that it's hard to jam some enjoyment in there, but this presented a golden opportunity to do just that, and I suspect you know what's coming.

I asked her, "That's it? He just wants two of the same size steaks?"

She answers, "Yes."

I said, "No problem." To the cook, I said, "Jose, take this longer one back and give me one of the shorter ones."

I proceeded to send out two perfectly matched steaks back to table twenty-three. The man lost his mind, and I mean lost it. He was f-bombing the server, me, the hostess, and my grandmother, and then he demanded to see the manager, the owner, my parents, everyone. It was hilarious. You had to see this guy. He went completely nuts, but funny nuts. All I really did was give him exactly what he asked for, and honestly, I knew what would happen. There's a limited amount of shit that I'm willing to listen to for $27.95. Now, $2,795.00 will get you a more sympathetic ear, and for $27,095.00 I will listen to you wax poetically for days while I fan you and feed you grapes. But $27.95? Nope, can't do it.

He started with the finger pointing. "Let me tell you ..."

I put up my hand and said, "Sir, before you say anything, I must tell you, most people who ordered two Restaurant Week steaks and got one Restaurant Week steak and one à la carte steak would have just kept quiet and eaten the bigger one. But not you, sir. No, you had the integrity to see the mistake, and even though it was in your favor, send it back to be corrected. Not many people would have done that, and we want you to know that we admire your honesty."

He said, "Blu ... gack ... cuh ... di ... wew ... chit ... ow."

I guess he got all choked up.

When he could finally spit it out, he said, "This is why I usually eat at the Four Seasons!"

Excuse me. Do they have a $27.95, three-course, price-fixed menu that I'm unaware of? Because I've eaten there, and I've spent considerably more money than that. The Four Seasons. Isn't that rich? There's an equitable choice. "Hmm, should we go to the Four Seasons or Jewel for Restaurant Week?"

It's befuddling. Don't pretend you're a big spender—prove it. Order one of the five-dollar supplemental entrees; it's still a good deal.

He then said, "That's it. I'm calling the owner tomorrow and having you fired!"

I said, "Okay, sir. I guess we'll chat in the morning."

As I said before, I've come to embrace Restaurant Week. It's crazy busy but the fact is that it is good exposure. I've met a lot of lovely people over the years who might not have had the opportunity to dine with us otherwise, and for that alone, it's been well worth the effort. For the few folks who need to twist this thing into a knot, well, your personal safety could be in jeopardy, figuratively speaking of course, but be aware that you just may find yourself on the dark side of that enjoyment jamming thing I mentioned earlier.

GIVE THE BABY A BOTTLE

Here's another out of that goldmine known as Restaurant Week. Large tables are a phenomenon not unique to Restaurant Week, but it seems to be the popular way to gather for the bargain. I think people feel that there's safety in numbers and if you can convince twelve of your friends not to request twelve separate checks, there's a good chance that rusty mathematical skills will reward you for ordering that second Singapore Sling. This is my first ever story that's featured bottled water at the heart of the problem. You ask, *"What can possibly go wrong with a bottle of water?"* If I hadn't experienced it for myself I wouldn't have believed it. It started innocently enough. A rather loud and large party of six Restaurant Week aficionados sat down and breathlessly awaited the arrival of their, soon to be sainted, server.

"Can I get anyone anything from the bar?" Pam, the server, asked.

"We'll take a bottle of sparkling water."

"Will that be all?"

"Yes," they said in unison.

Pam delivered the bottle of water, opened it up, poured out six glasses of crystal pure, glacial water imported straight out of some warehouse in Denmark, and left the rest of the bottle in the middle of the table. The table gave her their orders and proceeded with the task at hand, devouring $140 worth of food priced at $21.95 each. The problem started with the second bottle of water. Pam was busy, so she sent the bus girl to deliver the second bottle of water, which she did. Where things seemed to have gone wrong was that the bus girl, having a heavier pour than Pam, poured out the entire second bottle of glacial water, imported from a warehouse in Denmark, among the six glasses and removed the empty water bottles from the table, disposing of them properly in a recycle bin so as not to send any of our greener friends into apoplexy. Nevertheless, this caused one of the less stable women at the table to lose her shit. I'm not quite sure to this day what it was about the removal of an empty water bottle that caused the infantile tantrum of a grown woman, but whatever it was, it worked.

The woman called the bus girl over and asked in a not-so-pleasant tone, "What did you do with the water bottle?"

The bus girl said, "I threw it out."

"Why would you do that?"

"It was empty."

The woman got madder. "The first one wasn't empty when the waitress poured our water."

The bus girl, all of seventeen and displaying wisdom beyond her years, said, "I probably filled the glasses a little higher than she did."

Undeterred, the woman continued. "This is ridiculous! You call this service? Where's our waitress?"

The bus girl, who couldn't be happier to go find her if it meant getting away from the table, took off with the woman yelling after her as only the disturbed can do, "Get her over here!"

The bus girl told the waitress, "You'd better get to table eighty-two. The woman's upset with me for removing the water bottle."

"Why is she upset about you removing an empty water bottle?"

"I don't know."

Me neither, and if any of my readers can somehow explain it to me, I'd be grateful. This was where I unknowingly stepped into the fracas. I was talking with Eileen, the manager, and as

I looked out the window and onto the patio, I see this woman giving away what appeared to be her few remaining marbles over the premature removal of an empty water bottle. At that point, I had no idea what all the commotion was about, just that there was a commotion. I sent Eileen out to find out what was going on, and after a valiantly futile attempt to placate the woman, she reported back to me on the missing water bottle. We had to go over it twice because I just couldn't get it. The woman was so out of her mind over the bottle that I was becoming concerned … for her. I told Eileen to give her another bottle of water to pacify her, and let's see if we can get through dessert without anyone getting hurt. Dessert was included, after all. Eileen went out and gave the table a fresh bottle of crystal-pure, glacier water, imported from a warehouse in Denmark, only to be told that although they were fully prepared to accept the freebie, a new bottle of water was not the point and in no way assuaged the grievance that the removal of the empty bottle had caused. I know what you're thinking: *he's exaggerating.* There's no need to and it gets better. They finished dinner and paid their check. Somehow, the free bottle of crystal-pure, glacier water, imported from the warehouse in Denmark, found its way onto the bill. I don't know how it happened. It was either an innocent waitress mistake or karmic retribution for some forgotten offense. The woman lost her mind again, and this time she invited her husband into the fray. We made the correction, and they paid the bill. As they were walking out, they passed Eileen and me as we were talking in the service station. For some strange reason the woman thought we were laughing at her. I've heard that psychosis can be often accompanied by visions.

She said, "You know, we appreciated the free water, but I do not appreciate you laughing at me."

I've got to tell you, folks, the fastest way to get me to laugh at you is to tell me that I'm not allowed to—especially if you're being ridiculous. I started to giggle, which of course started

Eileen giggling, which made the woman even more furious, which pissed off her husband.

The husband, who was a big guy, got in my face and said, "Why was the water bottle removed from the table?"

I would kill to be able to focus this narrowly.

My response was, "Because it was empty?"

He said, "And you call that good service?"

"Yeah."

He then said, "So let me ask you something. If I had a bottle of wine with dinner and I finished it, you would take it off the table?"

"Yeah."

"And you call that good service?"

"Yup."

"You should be ashamed to call yourself a restaurateur."

The only shame involved would be leaving an empty wine bottle on the table for the whole world to see that you sprang for $21.95 on a *whole* bottle of *wine (specially priced for Restaurant Week).*

He then announced, "This is the last time I'll ever set foot in this place. This is disgraceful."

I never really got what fired up this whole fountain of angst. Could it have been something in that Danish warehouse–imported, crystal-pure, glacier water? I don't know, but if it was, and those glaciers are melting at the rate that Al Gore was making all that money telling us they were, we could be in much deeper shit than he initially anticipated. Their reaction was a bit severe even by Restaurant Week standards, so I'm guessing that it had to be the water. Sometimes there's just no explaining it.

BALLS, COURAGE, OR AUDACITY?

I find television to be extremely entertaining these days. I'm not talking about the sitcoms with their predictable plot lines, overacting, and laugh tracks. After all, if you need a laugh track as a cue for your audience, you should be looking for new writers. I'm talking about the news. That, my friends, is where the comedy resides. There was a time when there was great news reporting, and people tuned in to be informed about world events, politics, and the like, but it's turned into the modern-day version of *Rowan and Martin's Laugh-In.* Our news outlets have become sketch comedies with formulaic talking heads desperately trying to make agendas fit events. They don't even have to start reporting to start the chuckling; just look at the cast. In their zeal not to offend anyone, every station has one African American, one Asian, one woman, one white guy, one Latino, and one gay movie critic. Okay, we get it: you're inclusive. I'd rather have five Black, gay Latino women, married to white guys and living in Asia, telling me the truth than a politically correct version of, *The Brady Bunch,* bullshitting their way through a twenty-four-hour news cycle, wouldn't you? Regardless of where you stand on issues a good dose of truth serves you well. One station has a motto: *We report. You decide.* If that was only the case. We're not told the news; we're told what to think. The news motto should be, s*hut up and vote the way we tell you.*

Remember Caitlin Jenner? She's that woman who won a slew of Olympic medals as a guy and transitioned from a Wheaties box to a Vanity Fair cover. What a long, strange trip that had to be. Anyway, Ms. Jenner was given the Arthur Ashe Award for courage, which I guess was nice, but I couldn't help thinking that there might have been one or two other people who were, just a bit, more courageous than Caitlin. The people in the newsrooms were all fawning over her and talking about her bravery for that spectacle of a transition. I would think tens of millions of dollars would take the edge off your anxiety, and after all, this isn't exactly Christine Jorgensen in the early sixties. Caitlin had a cheering section for heaven's sake. Had she gone all the way and removed the junk swinging freely under that tennis dress, I would have to have given her the nod because that would've taken a set of balls. But then it was said that she was having second thoughts. What then? If she went back to being Bruce, would they have taken back the award or given her another for being brave enough to admit that the whole thing just might have been a colossal booboo? It would certainly have given new meaning to the phrase, *woman's prerogative*. And while we're on the subject, did you hear about the couple that was fined $185,000 for refusing to make a gay couple's wedding cake? It seems a bit severe, no? What I don't understand is that if they didn't want to make the cake, why they didn't give the couple an estimate of $185,000 to make the cake and stop the whole mess before it got started? Then the couple could have simply gone to another baker, which would seem like a solution that would satisfy all parties. Who really cares if homosexual couples get married? I certainly wouldn't want them to miss out on all the fun the rest of us have been having. I guess it was a religious something or other, because they were warned that, religious beliefs notwithstanding, they were going to get it good if they didn't make the cake and the powers that be, in an act of what they deemed political courage, stuck it to them just like they said they would. I'd be curious to see if the powers that be and the talking heads who cheered them on would have had the same political courage if a Muslim baker refused to make a cake for a Jewish wedding. Now, that would be worthy of a Courage Award.

Another great news story that was covered awhile back was Harry Reid showing up to the Senate floor looking like he had had the shit beaten out of him. Not that that could ever happen to a corrupted politician in the city of Las Vegas. Whom did he piss off? But when asked why his eyes were hidden behind his Foster Grants and his nose was where his ear should be, Harry had the audacity to reply, "I had an accident working out at home."

Does Harry look like a gym rat to you? I swear this is true. Harry explained that he was working out in his bathroom—his *bathroom*; I have to say it twice—when the safety harness (*the safety harness?*) let loose, and he crashed into the shower door. I don't know about you but when I'm in my bathroom working out, strapped onto my treadmill, I'm very careful not to point it at the shower door for fear of killing myself. It's common sense. The news people who were interviewing him looked him in the eye and asked him the brand name of the faulty equipment he was using—as a public service, I suppose, to make sure the rest of us didn't install said brand next to our toilets. Not one person told him he was full of shit. Not one. How do you keep from laughing in the guy's face? Of all the stories to tell, you pick working out in the bathroom.

I would have asked him, *"Senator, sir, how many cans of Hormel Chili do you have to consume to propel yourself from the toilet bowl, face first, into the shower door?"* It's the only plausible bathroom explanation. This idiot was once the Senate majority leader, and he couldn't lie any better than that, with all the practice?

And try this for nerve. As I've said before, Restaurant Week is a challenge. My dear ex-friend came up with this idea some years back to boost business in the Hamptons during slower times of the year. Okay, fair enough. But now everyone's on the bandwagon and like I mentioned before we have, L. I. Restaurant Week, Hampton's Restaurant Week, Huntington Restaurant Week, Summer Restaurant Week, Winter Restaurant Week—the list goes on and on. It's a lot like when someone, years ago, realized that you could raise a significant amount of money with free food and wine. I get four or five phone calls a week asking us to participate in one charity function or another and they always tell you how much business you'll get by signing on. Well, then why do we have slow nights occasionally? I must have done a thousand of these in the last forty years or so. I don't mind doing the ones that we do, but trust me, it's not for the added business that's promised. Restaurant Week is sort of the same deal. Oh, yes, you do get busy. Nothing brings out folks like a bargain, but we make very little on it, and the extra stress that goes along with it can be taxing on those of us who are involved. Restaurant Week is like going to war. You must prepare. You need to physically prepare the restaurant, the food, the ordering, extra tables and chairs, and more. And you need to prepare mentally: the waitstaff for lowered tips, the kitchen for higher volume, and yourself for higher food costs. It's like an invasion, and my job as general is to prepare a response. So, there we were, cruising to the end of Restaurant Week 2016, when I got a curious phone call.

The hostess said, "Jewel, may I help you?"

The customer said, "Hello, Jewel, I need to cancel my reservation for tonight."

"Okay, what is your name?"

The customer said, "Jones. A party of six at 7:15."

The hostess said, "Okay, Mrs. Jones, I have you right here. I'll cancel the reservation for tonight. Can I reschedule you or help you with anything else?"

"You know, you could. Is Tom there?"

The hostess told her, "I believe he is. Hold on, and I'll find him for you."

"Thank you."

The hostess located me in the office and told me that a woman was on the phone and would like to speak to me. I picked up the phone. Mrs. Jones asked, "Is this Tom?"

I said, "Yes."

She said, "Tom, we come to your restaurant every year for Restaurant Week, and we love the fact that you do an expanded menu that week."

"Thank you."

She continued. "We were coming tonight with a party of six but two of the guests are sick and can't make it, so I had to cancel the reservation."

I said, "Well, that's a shame but I certainly do appreciate you taking the time to call and cancel."

"That's okay, I was happy to do it." Then she added, "Tom, could I ask you a favor?"

I replied, "Of course. What can I do for you?"

She said, "We would like to come a week from next Saturday with the same group."

I say, "Okay, I'll put you down for a six-top for one week from Saturday."

She then said, "Great, and you'll honor the Restaurant Week prices, right?"

I answered, "Excuse me?"

"You'll honor the Restaurant Week prices."

I asked, "Why would I do that? Restaurant Week is over."

She told me, "Because we had a reservation for Restaurant Week, but we couldn't make it, so you should give us the Restaurant Week prices when we can make it, and that's a week from next Saturday."

I told her, "The reason they call it Restaurant Week is because it lasts eight days, Sunday to Sunday and for you to enjoy the benefits, you have to bend to the criteria. Otherwise, they would have to name it Restaurant Month or Restaurant Year. But sadly, it's Restaurant Week and we only honor it for the eight designated days."

She said, "That's ridiculous. What's the big deal? We had a reservation for Restaurant Week, and that should count for something. We couldn't make it. We come to your restaurant every year for Restaurant Week. We're loyal customers and I can't see why you can't accommodate us."

Honestly, I was running out of steam. I said, "Look, we'll be happy to accommodate you, but it will be at the regular menu prices. Eight days of Restaurant Week is quite enough. Do you want me to keep the reservation?"

She said, "Absolutely not."

"So, you're not coming?"

"No, we're not coming. Take my name out of the book."

I then asked her, "So we'll see you next year for Restaurant Week?"

She said, "No, you won't see us again because you're a cheap bastard!"

How funny is that? Here's someone trolling for a discount and calling me cheap for not giving it to her. Is it balls, courage, or audacity? I'd say all the above.

THE POLITICALLY INCORRECT POLITICS OF FOOD

We live in interesting times. Free speech is under assault from all different angles and it's hard to know what can and cannot be said. Phrases and terms that were perfectly acceptable last week can get you canceled tomorrow. When I finished the manuscript of this book, I enlisted the help of several friends to pre-edit it to see what they thought. I got some honest assessments, sometimes to the point of pain, on my writings and storytelling that at first made me a bit defensive. I know full well that the biggest mistake a writer can make is to fall in love with his words and upon further reflection, I realized that they were right to point out those excesses and were able to save me from myself. I'll be forever grateful for their honesty and wisdom. A true friend tells you the truth; a smart friend hears it.

One of my pre-editors had a problem with my imagery of accents. Let me fully explain. I have been working, hanging, and eating with heavily accented people for over fifty years. Mostly Spanish, for certain, but there have also been French, Chinese, Japanese, Middle Eastern, Indian, Italian, Eastern European, Southern, Massachusetts, Jamaican, Antiguan, and one guy from northern Louisiana who required subtitles. When I hear these accents applied to English, I find them funny, and when they blow a word, a phrase, or a sentence, it cracks me up. I'm not laughing at *them*; I'm simply laughing at the blown call, what it *sounds* like, and the picture my twisted brain conjures up. It's an accent for heaven's sake; we all have one. There's no malice, no moral or intellectual superiority, and no condescension there. Have you ever seen Richard Pryor do the, *white people,* accent? It's hilarious. It simply sounds funny to me. That's the long and short of it. Oh, and by the way, I have sent some of these folks into convulsions explaining a recipe or kitchen situation with five mispronounced words in Spanish or Japanese when forty-five or fifty well-articulated ones were the minimum requirement for understanding. We poke fun at each other all day with this stuff and no one gets mad or offended. The only people who become incensed are the political types who manufacture outrage in order to use these people as chess pieces in their social engineering schemes. It's all about having a laugh, camaraderie, and passing time together, something I think the world at large could use a little more of. The kitchen is the true melting pot and those three things—laughter, camaraderie, and pleasantly passing the time—are the seasoning that makes the soup turn out so well. This may be news to the elites, but people have senses of humor, even foreigners. They're adults; they can poke fun at themselves. They don't require being told when to be offended or saved by some well-meaning or politically motivated soul. It's called having a laugh, so relax. If you're offended by pointing out that a person has an accent—which is fairly common in America, I'm told—I would suggest you move on past this chapter to the next unless you have a readily available supply of Pepto Bismol. If not, read on and giggle if you must. It's all in good fun. I promise.

DIAMONDS ARE A GIRL'S BEST FRAUD

You will need a little imagination, some patience, a sense of humor, and heightened literary skills to appreciate what I'm about to attempt to convey. I'm already on record saying that I'm amused by accents, mine included. *(I hear myself on my radio show and cringe.)* It's not to say I enjoy laughing at someone struggling with a language barrier; I don't. It just that it sounds funny to me, the same way someone blowing a word or phrase does, and like I've stated numerous times, if there's no malice behind the giggling, there's no harm. My Latin American employees have had some very hard laughs at my expense, listening to my version of their language. It's all in good fun. We seem to have lost the ability to laugh at ourselves, and at the expense of being accused of offering unlicensed, armchair psychiatry, along with it we've lost the pressure-release valve that keeps us from taking ourselves too seriously, emphasis on seriously. For the purpose of brevity, I would like to concentrate on three for illustrative purposes: Chinese, French, and Indian. For a variety of different reasons, I am unable to keep a straight face when I hear broken English garnished with either of the three. Call it immature, but those three accents have brought me and those around me countless laughs over the years. I'll start with the Chinese. I studied kung fu and as a result spent a whole lot of time trying to figure out just what the hell it was the Chinese were trying to say. Not only is it hard to understand, with no relationship to English like Italian or Spanish have through their Latin roots, but also there doesn't seem to be any *romance* to the language. The elevated decibel levels of casual conversational Chinese could cause one to believe that there's a mass murder about to occur. Regardless of the subject matter, they're always screaming at each other, and they have the vocal dexterity to stop on a dime and then resume screaming at the same level with no decibel transition whatsoever. Even when we were sparring, they would yell at you while beating the shit out of you.

And when they decide to whip a little English out, it becomes hysterical. *"Herrow, I rike a make a lesavation at a you lestalaunt dis a night fo a fo a peepo on a seven o'crock."*

I warned you.

I'm affected by French and Indian accents for different reasons, but it results in the same puerile behavior. The reason for this can be summed up in two words: Peter Sellers. His purposeful annihilation of those two accents in his movies has rendered me unable to get through a conversation with anyone employing them. A French case in point: I was visiting Opus One winery in Napa some years back. My appointment was 8:30 a.m. Unfortunately, the night before, I found a few things *(red, white, and pink)* to do that took a little longer than I anticipated, resulting in an acute lack of sleep and a head the size of a beach ball. This general feeling of disorientation combined with the fact that I was made to wait twenty or so minutes in front of a roaring, garage door–sized fireplace, its heat adding to my lethargy, sent me right to silly central. I found everything around me funny. Opus One is like the Vatican of wineries and an appointment there is like an audience with the pope. For some strange reason, I found that my being there in that less-than-perfect condition was a good enough reason to morph into a giggling idiot.

As I was being told by my companion, in not so uncertain terms, to behave, and as I was trying desperately to exercise a smidgen of control, our guide arrived and announced in a thick French accent, "Elluuh, I am Christine, end I wheel be for uuuhh, a giiiide."

As I ran for the men's room, I heard Christine ask my horrified companion, "What ees zee mattear wiz Tum? Ees ee, ow uuuhh say, zick?"

My companion said, "Yes, Christine, sicker than you can imagine."

Well…it was quite a tour. I lost it about halfway through and had to come clean about the Peter Sellers accent deal, and to Christine's credit she was a good sport, and we shared a laugh over it.

That brings me to the Indian accent and the reason for writing this. Forgetting Mr. Sellers for a moment, there is something about the clipped cadence, the fact that the tip of the tongue never leaves its position behind the front teeth on the roof of the mouth, all the *t*'s pronounced as *d*'s, the *p*'s being *b*'s, the *v*'s sounding like *wee*'s, the *w*'s changing into *v*'s, and the *h*'s being silent that brings out the shithead in me every time. One night, a party of ten came in for dinner last fall at Amano. One of the women was recently engaged and although it wasn't officially an engagement party or shower, they were celebrating her good fortune. Everyone was enjoying themselves except for the waitress, who was trying to take the dinner order in a language she was unfamiliar with.

"Vee vill start vit doo bizza for da dable."

"Den I will get da weal chope and eee vood like a steck."

"My vife an me vant to begin vit doo octobuses, and den bring a Duscan bot roast and a yellow vin duna."

"I am getting biece of vish, any kind, vit just biece of lemon and bodado. My vife would vould care to ave the sveet bee rawioli."

"Vee are gooing doo start vit doo meats and doo cheeses, and den I can ave ganocchi, and eee vill do soft shell crap."

"Okay, I go? Vell den, give to me vun broscuitto and cauiflower appetizer and duck breast, vell done, for my beauteeful fiancé, and I vould like werry much doo ave goat cheese bizza to begin, and I am wegatarian so permit me to ave vegetable blate."

I'm sorry, it cracks me up. As the server puts the order in, two of the ladies, one of them the recently betrothed, headed for the ladies' room. When they returned to the table all hell broke loose. It seemed that the woman lost her engagement ring and the whole table was desperate to find it. Realizing it was nowhere in sight the search party turned its focus to the ladies' room. The ladies' room at Amano is a, *one holer,* and therefore rather small. There are only four places in there that it could have possibly been: the floor, the waste basket, the sink, or the toilet.

They checked the floor, waste basket, and the sink and found nothing. This led them to surmise that it had to be in the toilet. They decided to enlist the help of a toilet specialist, Adam.

The woman said, "Bardon me, sir. It seems dat I may have dropped my engagement ring in da doilet."

Adam said, "How'd you do that?"

It's a fair question. I'm trying to imagine the technique, the hand speed, and the ferocity of purpose it would take to dislodge an engagement ring from a finger while wiping one's rear end.

"I'm not sure it's in da doilet, but I vas oping dat maybe you could reach down in dare and check for me. It's werry waluable, six karats."

This begs another question. I would want to know if it was dropped before or after she sat down. That's a crucial piece of information that would weigh heavily on deciding whether or not to call off the search. This was where we started to become suspicious. It would seem to me that if a six-karat diamond fell into a toilet you would be able to hear the splash and see the ripples all the way to the Taj Mahal. Someone at the table advanced the theory that maybe one of the staff grabbed the ring, hopefully sterilizing it before stashing it.

"Check bockets of vaitstaff! I vant bockets checked!"

It got crazy to the point where we had to bring in Mattituck's finest. The cavalry came in the person of a nice, young police officer who, although he looked like he was twelve, handled the situation with a practiced professionalism that belied his years.

Someone at the table said, "Officer, I vant bockets of vaitstaff checked!"

The officer said, "Hold on there a minute. Let's hear what's going on." As everyone was trying to explain what was happening, the fiancé had a brainstorm.

"Officer, this is six-karat diamond, custom made. It is werry, werry, werry waluable. I vant you doo arrest vaitstaff!"

The officer took the complaint information down and questioned the waitstaff about what had gone on. Satisfied that there was no foul play and thus sparing us both incarceration and the humiliation of a full cavity search he told the party that he would follow up with them upon the completion of his investigation. Everyone finally left. The epilogue is that about two weeks later, one of my staff heard through the friend of a friend that the woman said she hadn't lost the ring at the restaurant but that it had happened earlier in the day, that the whole deal was a ruse, and that she was hoping to claim damages on our insurance policy. Yep, we do it all there at Amano. It's a full-service restaurant: good food, great wines, warm and friendly service, and … insurance fraud.

SING SING

Now that I've documented my inability to act like an adult when I'm around heavily accented people trying to speak English, noting that French, Indian, and Chinese are the three I have the most trouble keeping a straight face while listening to, you can now add Japanese to the list. I love the Japanese culture for its history and customs that date back to who knows when, but what a chore the language and the accents are. I was once in the process of building a sushi bar and, as a result, I was eating a ton of the stuff trying to find inspiration, and I'd interviewed quite a few sushi chefs. It's not easy hanging on every word but, occasionally, they would say some very funny stuff. Trying to decipher broken English is exhausting after three minutes, so I think in order to keep you from checking out completely, they will massacre a word or sentence just to keep you listening. It's brilliant, really. Here's an example.

I was chatting with this guy, and I asked him, "Where's the best place to find a sushi chef?"

He looked at me straight-faced and said, "In sushi lestaulant."

Who knew?

After composing myself, I said, "No I mean to advertise for a position."

He thought a moment and said, "Oh, you mean for job."

"Yes."

He said, "Besta prace you find a sushi chef, Japanese newspapel. But mouth to mouth good too."

I said, "Yup, I've heard that mouth-to-mouth advertising can be very effective. It's also fairly direct."

He said, "Maybe you try dat."

I said, "I just may. I need some waitresses."

You're telling me that's not funny? You would need to have a Coexist bumper sticker on your Kia, a Free Mumia button on your lapel, a Che Guevara T-shirt, and tenure at Harvard to be politically correct enough not to laugh at that. The guy was a Japanese Joe Biden.

One day, after two hours of trying to translate what should have been a half-hour interview, I was at the end of my rope. I decided to go to a sushi bar and spend another couple of hours drinking sake and chatting with folks I don't understand. I got there around six o'clock and was the only one in the place.

I sat at the sushi bar and the chef came over and said, "Herro."

I gave him my order and as he was preparing it, I was looking around as I always do in restaurants. I saw one of the waitresses wheeling out a karaoke machine. She spent a good fifteen minutes turning knobs and flipping switches, and when she was satisfied that it was time for a test run, she came over to me and said, "Hi-eee. You wan' sing?"

I said, "Me? No, I'm good."

She then said, "Okay den, I sing."

She went back to the machine and after fiddling with some switches and making some adjustments, made her selection. Three seconds later, *"My Way"* came blaring out of the speakers like Deep Purple at the Garden.

She ran back to turn it off and sheepishly said, "A rittre rowd."

She started it up again and right there in the middle of the empty restaurant, all by her lonesome, she started singing, *"My Way,"* like there were two hundred people in the room.

"So, day a tine / I shoe you know / when I bite off, moe I chew / but from it orrrrrrr / when I have dowwww / I eat up / and spit on house / da lecod show / I took a bro / an do it rike-a my wayyyy."

If it was, *"Layla"* or *"My Boy Lollipop,"* I'd have been hospitalized.

As I was straining to regain some measure of composure the sushi chef walked over with his face in his hands and said, "Sometime she think she Cerene Dion." He turned away laughing.

Check, please.

I bet I laughed for an hour. My only regret is that no one other than the sushi chef and I were there. It might have been the single most entertaining performance I'd ever seen. I had spoken to six or seven Japanese people that day, in person or on the phone, and she was the only one I could understand.

And understanding, you see, is the key to a successful transaction. We recently had a miss—a misunderstanding, that is. We got a call from a woman who wanted to book a party for twenty.

She asked if we had a private room. We told her yes. We gave her a choice of menus and she chose the one for ninety dollars per person.

We asked her how she wanted to handle the drinks. She said, "Let them have whatever they want."

Okay, that was easy. A few days later, they had their party, and everything went off without a hitch. The final bill after drinks, tip, and tax were added came to about $140 per person. No problem. They paid the check and left.

The next day Diane pulled me aside and said, "The woman who had the party last night is on the phone and she's saying we overcharged her, and she wants you to adjust the bill."

I asked, "She says we overcharged her?"

Diane said, "That's what she's saying."

I then asked, "Could we have made a mistake?"

Diane said, "No, I checked it. The bill is correct."

"Then I don't understand what she wants me to do."

Diane said, "She's saying that she didn't understand that there was a room fee and no one told her about it, and her boss is going to kill her because she spent too much money. Could you please talk to her?"

I asked Diane, "Did we charge her a room fee?"

Diane said, "No."

"Then what's she talking about?"

"I don't know. Just go take the call."

I picked up the phone and said, "Hi, this is Tom. How can I help you?"

She told me. "I had a party in the restaurant last night and I was overcharged because no one told me there was a room fee. My boss is going to be furious when he sees the bill, so I want you to take one hundred dollars off."

I asked, "Why would I do that?"

She said, "Because no one told me. I didn't understand that there was a room fee."

I told her, "We didn't charge you a room fee. Look at the bill. We wouldn't just sneak a room fee on without telling you."

She then said, "I know it's not on the bill but when I looked at the regular menu, I figured out that if I'd ordered a lobster, a salad, and a dessert, it would have come out cheaper."

I said, "Yes, but you wouldn't have had a private room, which is what you asked for and got. You could have eaten in the dining room à la carte, if you wished."

She said, "I know, but I didn't understand about the room fee. No one told me."

Again, with the room fee.

I finally said, "Okay, we gave you a choice of three menus, right?"

She said, "Yes."

I said, "You chose the ninety-dollar menu, correct?"

She said, "Yes."

"We asked you how you wanted to handle the alcohol, and you said to let them have whatever they wanted, yes?"

She said, "Yes."

I said, "You were aware that there was a twenty percent gratuity and tax, right?"

Again, she said, "Yes."

I asked, "Then could you please explain to me where we went wrong? If we screwed up in any way, I'd be happy to help you out."

She said, "I didn't understand about the room fee and my boss is going to kill me."

Exasperated, I asked her, "Do you want me to explain it to him? I'll be happy to talk to him."

In a panic, she said, "No, no, no, don't talk to him." I knew right then and there that she'd effed up and wanted her boss to think it was us. She then asked, "Can't you just reduce the bill one hundred dollars? We're good customers and we come in all the time."

Feeling a bit sorry for her, I said, "Tell you what. The next time you come in, I'll take one hundred dollars off your check as a goodwill gesture."

Perking up, she said, "Well, I'm not sure when we're coming so I'll just take the discount this time."

"Well, you come in quite often, no?"

She said, "Yes."

"Then I'll take it off next time," I said.

She said, "Okay, how about you just take fifty dollars off the check this time?"

"I'm sorry, but we didn't do anything wrong, and I'm not in the practice of giving discounts for doing a good job."

She said, "My boss is going to kill me. Our budget was $120.00, and I spent $140.00. I didn't understand that there was a room fee."

I replied, "Ma'am, there was no room fee. You knew what it was going to cost going in. No one played a trick on you; no one padded your bill. That was a menu and a price you agreed to. I don't feel any responsibility to change anything. I'm willing to give you a one-hundred-dollar credit because you say you're a good customer but that's out of kindness, not guilt. Yours is a math problem and I'm sorry you're in trouble with your boss but you had the dinner and drank the drinks. What more can I say?"

She said, "You could say you will take twenty-five dollars off this bill."

I was at a loss for words. It rarely happens.

RARE FISH

This is more of a restaurant story than a customer story, but bear with me. Some years ago, I was coming back from my home out east and I was getting that little hunger pang. Not the *I'm starving* one, but the one where you think that if you don't eat something you'll be sorry a few hours later. It's probably worse for me because, being rarely home, I keep very little food in my house, so there's no room for error. We decided to hit this Italian restaurant, grab a salad each and maybe split some pasta, and get out quick.

As we walked in the door, we were greeted by a nice maître d', who informed us, "Tonight a Signor y Signora, we have a beau-ti-ful a six a course a wine a deener a from a Tuscano, for a one a hundred and forty dollars a person a. We hava Vernaccia from a San Gimignano, a nice a Trebbiano to a starta, a gorgeous a Malvasia, two a stunning a Sangiovese, and a one a Super a Tuscano that a willa make a you feel a like a you in a Montalcino. And Signor y Signora, we have a first a course a sautéed egg a plant a, with a touch of a garlic and a splash of a tomato ..."

I always get a kick out of talking to someone from Italy. Have you ever noticed that when an Italian speaks to you in English, they stick an "*a*" on the end of every word that doesn't come with one? Example: "Come-a here-a, I wann-a talk-a to you-a."

But when there's an "*a*" there, ready and waiting, they take the "*a*" off the back of the word and stick it in the front and then say it. Example: "Hey, Luigi, you wann-a slice a-pizz?"

I find it hilarious, but that's me.

Anyway, I interrupted him and said, "Um okay, listen, I'm sure it's all fabulous but we just stopped for something quick and light. We'll come back another time."

He said, "Oh, you no wann-a the wine a deener-a?"

I said, "No, we just wanted something light. We had a late lunch."

He then said, "Okay, I sit a-you in a the back a room-a, and you can a have-a what-ev you like-a."

I asked him, "Are you sure? I don't want to be any trouble."

He assured me, "No trouble a, Signor. I got-a other customers a back-a there-a too, no wann-a wine-a deener-a."

I said, "Okay, if you don't mind, we'll do that."

He said, "Come-a dis-a way."

We followed him to a private room off the main dining room where the wine dinner was taking place. There were two or three other couples eating there, so I didn't feel too bad about putting out the kitchen. I must tell you; I absolutely love the Italian people. I've visited Italy many times and have been through most of the country, and I find them to be among the warmest, most welcoming people I've ever met. They're either kissing you or feeding you. I also love Italian food and Italian restaurants, as well as the sense of hospitality they try to convey, but there are two things that a lot of them have in common that I find infinitely amusing. The first is the menu and specials relationship. A lot of Italian restaurants have these benign, formulaic menus that have a section for appetizers; one for pastas; and one each for chicken, veal, and seafood. Then there are a couple of steaks and most of the other selections are the usual suspects like, Francaise, Marsala, Valdostana, and Scampi. Most of these items are in the twenty-dollar range with the steaks costing a bit more. But when you get to the specials, things start to change. Here's where the chef gets a chance to shine and God knows it's reflected in the price, but they never tell you that during the recitation. The specials generally start in the forties and top out quite higher depending on the ingredient list. And that, my friends, is called commerce. The second is the recitation of the specials. They're almost always the same and can be funnier than an Eddie Murphy routine. The waiter brought us our menus and wine list, and we looked them over.

I said to my companion, "I always love to hear the specials in an Italian restaurant because nobody can inject more passion into a specials speech than a Salvadorian masquerading as an Italian."

She asked, "You don't think the waiters are Italian?"

I answered, "No, I'd bet they're from Central America and between the language barrier, the fact that almost all Italian restaurants have the same specials, and that there can be as many as two dozen, I always get a kick out of hearing them."

She said, "You know you're out of your mind, right?"

I said, "No, I'm telling you the truth. You watch. I swear, they'll be baby clams; some kind of artichoke; a portabella something or other; a branzino; two pastas, one with seafood and one gnocchi; one veal chop served two ways; and a splash, a touch, and a kiss of something."

She laughed and said, "You're absolutely nuts."

The waiter came over with the bottle of wine that I'd ordered and asked, "Are chu ready for order?"

I asked him, "Are there any specials tonight?" Then I leaned back and smiled.

He said, "Si, Signore. Tonighta, we hab a sauté baby clam. A sauté nice for chu in a touch a white wine, butter, and yust a leetle beet ob balsamic binegar. Also, for chu tonight, we hab a stuffa ar-tee-choke, a stuffa with a leetle bread crumb, a touch ob garlic, and a leetle olib oil, etra bergin. We hab for chu tonight also a greel portabella muchroom, ober arugula solid, wiif roast a pepper and balsamic binegar, wiif etra bergin olib oil. Branzino! Tonight, I make a for chu a nice a branzino, a sauté wiif a touch of white a wine, baby clam, mussel, garlic, and a splash of tomato. We serb it ho, but I fillet for chu at dee table. Tonight, also for chu, we hab a two pastas. Dee first one hab a angel hair wiif lowster, scallaks, shrink, clam and mussel, serb wiif light tomato sauce, garlic, honion, and a kiss o bodka. We hab tonight too, gnocchi Bolognese, nice tomato sauce, may wiif beef, pork and beal. And also, tonight if you wanna, I make for chu Beal Baldostana, a stuffa wiif a leetle prosciut and a mozzarella and a demi gloss, o if you like a we can a pound it down, bread a leetle beet, fry, and put a solid on top wiif a splash o binagrette. Whateva you like it. And for berry special tonight, we hab a beautiful pompano from a Florida. He jus swim up a today. I make a yolk, he no really swim up, he was deelibered. berry fresh, and I make it for chu wiif a leetle white wine, butter and a touch of basil, or if you lika, Livornese, wiif tomato, olibs, an a caper. Chu know what chu like?"

We were crying.

I said, "Could you repeat that?" and my companion bolted for the ladies' room. I told him that we needed a couple of minutes and truer words were never spoken.

When she got back, she said, "If I hadn't heard it …"

I said, "I told you. It's worth the price of the dinner. He hit on all the salient points."

As we were laughing, he came over and asked, "Chu ready for order now?"

I said, "Yes, she'll have the house salad, I'll have the portabella, we'll split the angel hair pasta, and we'll split an order of the pompano."

He wrote down our order and said, "I bring dee solid and muchroom rye now," and did so.

We had a leisurely meal talking and laughing about the language thing and I was explaining that if there's no malice, it's okay to laugh at things you find funny. If I was a waiter in Mexico, I'm sure I'd provide my share of chuckles. It went on for the whole meal. Well, it turns out God likes Central American waiters. When we finished, I asked for the bill.

The waiter responded, "I get for chu. Can I bring a chu leetle Sambucca o spresso?"

I said, "No, we have to get going."

He dropped the bill and when I opened it, I couldn't believe what I saw. The pasta was forty-two dollars, and the pompano was eighty-five. This was in 1996! I thought maybe he'd made a mistake and charged us for two orders of each because we'd split both dishes.

I called him over and said, "I think there's a mistake on the bill. The pasta's on here for forty-two dollars and the pompano is on for eighty-five. We only had one of each and split them, so I think you mistakenly charged us for two."

He looked the bill over carefully and said, "No, Signore, deese bill is a rye. I yust a check. Eats correc."

I asked, "That pasta was forty-two dollars?"

He said, "Si, Signore, forty-two."

I then asked, "And the pompano is eighty-five?"

He answered, "Si, eighty-five."

I said, "You're telling me you get eighty-five dollars for one pompano filet?"

He said, "Si, Signore, eats a berry rare feesh."

I started to laugh and said, "It must be on the endangered species list. I can get lion fillet for less than that."

He said, "But I no tink lion tase too good." Then he gave me a conspiratorial glance and said, "I neber hab lion, but I ting maybe eat tase like a chit."

That was it for me. We laughed all the way home. The bill was north of $225 with the wine. I'd have been better off with the wine dinner from a financial standpoint but I wouldn't have had nearly as much fun. And although we were laughing at my new friend's execution of the language, we weren't laughing *at* him, and in my book that makes it okay. It was all in fun, and it turned out he got the last laugh anyway, whether he knew it or not, and I had one of the most enjoyable meals that I've had to date. It was total serendipity, completely unexpected, and worth every penny. God, I love restaurants!

STICKING TO PLAN A

A young, local guy was working for us for a while, and we all came to like him very much. He was super macho in an inoffensive way and unwittingly provided us with some fabulous moments. He was a bit of a cowboy and liked to do things his own way, which can be okay provided you know what the hell you're doing. That wasn't the case. We finally told him to not try so hard and to listen a little more. He never really got it.

I said, "Please, just do what I tell you to do, nothing more, nothing less. And please don't improvise, okay?"

He replied, "Well, I just thought that if—"

I cut him off, "Don't think, John, please. I'll do that. Simply do what I ask. You'll be fine, and my life expectancy will have a much more optimistic outlook. Are we good here?"

He said, "We're good."

I love it when an employee screws up and says, "Well, I just thought …"

I never say it, but I always think, *"Please don't think. If I were paying you to think, you'd be making a lot less money."*

Just do what I ask. Is it that hard? We're certainly not perfect but we've been at this for a while. We were having a wine dinner with Domaine Wolffer the following Sunday. They sent a case of rosé to the restaurant in advance and were bringing the rest of the wines with them that day. Because our wine cellar has a lot of inventory, I asked John to put the case of rosé in the liquor room so I wouldn't be panicked trying to find it when I needed it that weekend. He dutifully took it downstairs. I forgot about it until Sunday. Sunday rolled around, and because Domaine Wolffer was going to use it as their reception wine, I wanted to get it up and get it chilled. I asked him to go down to the liquor room and bring it up. He did, and I went about getting ready for the wine dinner. About forty-five minutes later, I realized he hadn't come back.

I asked, "Where's John?"

The waiter said, "I thought I saw him downstairs."

I said, "Do me a favor. Tell him I want to see him."

The waiter said, "Okay."

Ten minutes later, John came into the kitchen and said, "Tony said you wanted to see me."

I said, "Yeah. Where have you been?"

He said, "Downstairs getting fruit for the bar setups."

I said, "I thought I asked you to go to the liquor room and get the rosé."

He then told me, "I did. I went down there and looked but it wasn't there, so I thought I'd get the bar set up in the meantime."

I stood there looking at him for a moment and then asked him, "Didn't I ask you to put it in the liquor room last Tuesday when it first came in?"

He said, "Yeah."

I asked, "And you checked the entire liquor room?"

He said, "Yup, just like you *"axed"* me to."

"And it's not there?"

He said, "No."

I said, "And you put it there Tuesday when I asked you to?"

He said, "No, I put it in the wine cage."

Incredulous, I asked him, "You put it in the wine cage ... on Tuesday ... when I asked you to put it in the liquor room?"

He said, "Yes. I thought you screwed up the difference between the liquor room and the wine cage when you told me to do that, and I didn't want to embarrass you by correcting you."

I replied, "Okay, but when I asked you *today* to go to the liquor room to get it, you actually went to the liquor room and looked for it, knowing all along it was in the wine cage?"

He said, "Yeah, 'cause that's what you told me to do."

I was staring at my shoes. I asked him, "I have to know. How long did you look for the rosé?"

He said, "I was in there for about three minutes. The room isn't that big."

I then asked him, "Three minutes? What were you thinking about when you were in there looking for wine that you knew was in the other wine cage?"

He said, "I thought it was kind of ridiculous."

I said, "Yeah, I guess it was. Why did you go down there in the first place when you knew it wasn't there?"

He said, "Because you told me not to think and just do what you *"axe"* me to do."

I said, "John, can I ask you another question?"

"Sure, chef."

"How do you spell ask?'"

He said, "A-S-K."

I said, "That's good, John. Now, pronounce it."

He looked at me quizzically and said, "Axe."

A PIP OFF THE OLD BLOCK

I'm aware that there are those of you who think I exaggerate when I tell these tales. Try this one. We did a rehearsal dinner for a prospective bride who, when she was finished setting up the date, time, and menu, informed us that she would be sending a list of her allergies. A list of

allergies. A list. And she did. The bride's allergies were as follows: soy, soy sauce, soybean oil, soy flour, edamame, tofu, miso, mayo *(unless made without soybean oil)*, stir-fry sauces made with soy sauce *(teriyaki, black bean sauce, ponzu, etc.)*, and a side note saying that if any oil says vegetable oil without specifying the type of vegetable it is, it is likely made with soybean oil. One can see a pattern here that the bride obviously has a problem with soy. I get it, no soy for you, and we're more than happy to accommodate. But there was a second page of allergies for her mother. I must tell you that, every once in a while, I'll get a doozy of an allergy, one I've never heard of before. Last year, I had my first bergamot sufferer, but lo and behold, there's another one out there. Mom's list of allergies—and I swear this is allergy for allergy, and I saved the list in case I'm questioned—is as follows: Moroccan herbs, Moroccan spices, Indian herbs, Indian spices, Turkish herbs, Turkish spices, mustard greens, mustard cress, kuzo, kai choi, Chinese mustard greens *(a variation on a theme)*, komatsuna, mustard seeds, musk plant, monkey flower, kohlrabi, bergamot *(it's an epidemic)*, Greek oregano, chili peppers, ajowan seeds, Aleppo pepper, charnushka, curry leaves, garam masala, orris root, galangal *(but curiously not ginger)*, cumin, fenugreek, za'atar, hot paprika, caraway seed, nigella seed, juniper berries, lemongrass, cardamom, cilantro, coriander, capers, caper flowers, turmeric, vermouth, gin, triple sec, absinthe, Campari, Lillet, Pernod, Bragg's amino acids, olives, Mrs. Dash *(not my first)*, Worcestershire sauce, Old Bay seasoning, pickling spices, kafte spice, jerk seasoning, adobo, mesquite, smoke flavor, chutney, and last but not least, poultry seasoning. Two questions come to mind. The first is, What the hell are ajowan seeds, orris root, and monkey flower? The second is, who would marry into this family?

GETTING WHAT ONE PAID FOR

This turned out to be the most entertaining dinner party in the history of dinner parties. The whole problem centered on inexplicable thrift and a flash drive. After booking a party costing thousands of dollars, the woman's fiancé asked if we had a screen on which he could show a montage. We told him we did. He asked my IT guy if he gave us a flash drive, would that be okay and be compatible with our system. We told him that would be fine.

He then asked, "If there are other pictures on the flash drive, will it affect my montage?"

My IT guy said, "It's always better to have a new flash drive with nothing on it. You can save your stuff to a file, but if it continues to play, it may wind up shuffling the files."

This is all Greek to me, by the way, but it's what I was told.

The man said, "Well, I'm not paying for another flash drive. I'll do it myself, so nothing gets screwed up. I'm pretty good with this type of thing."

I'll never understand cheap people. I do get that it is a pathology and one that I'm sure is beyond the control of the folks who are afflicted because I've seen these people do things to save a nickel that blow up all they negotiated for. How much can a flash drive cost? The party was set up where everyone in the party got one free drink. I don't know about you but the parties I'm invited to usually provide the guests with complimentary drinks. Not this one. The first one is free; the next one is on you. It was incredible but that was what the host wanted. And everyone got a ticket to redeem their drink ... but just one.

Most of the guests were a bit bewildered when a bartender would say, "That'll be thirty-two fifty, sir," after handing over the drinks but what could anyone do? We were as bewildered as the guests—except for one resourceful fellow sitting on Pat's table. He got his free drink and then enlisted an army of accomplices to fill out the rest of his requests.

Apparently, the DJs were going to the bar and ordering sodas and such, so he said to one of them as one was passing his table, "Are you going to the bar?"

The DJ said, "Yes."

The man asked, "Could you bring me back a gin and tonic?"

The DJ said, "Sure, no problem."

That was all he needed. There were three DJs, a dancer, a photographer, and his assistant. The man had six free drinks on a one-free drink policy. He convinced every one of them to get him a drink during the night. It was brilliant, really. The rest of the party proceeded as normally as a, *pay your own way,* party would—until it got to dinner.

After the cocktail hour ended and everyone was going to the dining room, the fiancé came over to my IT guy and said, "Here's the montage. Don't worry, I did it myself. You don't have to test it. Just start playing it when I give you the signal. Diane told me that if I just gave it to you and you didn't have to mess with it, she could waive the fifty-dollar AV fee. Are we good?"

The IT guy said, "Yeah, I guess we're good. I'll load it now and hit play when you tell me."

The fiancé said, "Great, thank you."

The appetizers had gone out without a hitch. The dinner did as well. He signaled the start, and the IT guy hit play and the montage was showing flawlessly. Everyone seemed to be enjoying the food, the company, and the montage. Then suddenly, 150 people sounded a collective gasp. My screen is huge, about ten feet by ten feet. It seems that the flash drive shuffled and froze on the screen. Right there in front of 150 guests was one hundred square feet of the birthday girl, naked on a lounge chair by the pool, taking one for the home team. In the ensuing panic, it took several minutes to get back to the montage from what had essentially become a porn movie. No one knew where to look or what to do. Intuitively, the DJ kind of saved the day by quickly playing a song to drown out any uncomfortable comments.

As all this was going on, the guy with the six free drinks called Pat over, grabbed his hand, placed seventy-nine cents in Pat's palm, and said, "You did a fantastic job!" and winked at him.

He then stopped Mario, the busboy, as he was passing the table and said, "Hey I have a tip for you as well."

Mario stopped and was standing there waiting for a tip when the guy leaned onto his left ass-cheek, lifted his right leg, and crop-dusted the entire area.

He looked at Mario, chuckled, and said, "I ran out of change and that was all I had left."

I swear to you it happened. Dessert was a rather uncomfortable affair, as you can imagine, but they did seem to all suck it up and party on. Booze and music will do that for you. I'm guessing that her fiancé must have had one hell of a tough couple of days following the event. I don't know what ever happened to them or if they even got married, but if they did, I feel for him. There's no statute of limitations on something that stupid or for being that cheap. I found out subsequently that a flash drive costs twenty-five dollars. That seems reasonable for a, *get of jail free,* card, but some folks just can't seem to part with it, consequences be damned. I firmly believe that you get what you pay for, but I'm glad those folks are out there, and I thank them for the endless laughs. It was quite a show!

BORDERING ON THE ABSURD

We were once visited by a threesome of very politically vocal, open-borders fans, one night about six months ago. We knew this because they were talking about politics all night at the table. One of the women claimed to be a sommelier and had asked to see me but not without an initial insult. I must tell you when someone tells me they're a sommelier, I'm skeptical. Sommeliers don't usually announce themselves that way. She asked the server if I was around, and the server told her that I was. She told the server to tell me to come see her if I finally wanted a good wine on my list. This is how you sell wine? I asked the server who and where this woman was. She told me the sommelier part and said she was at table twenty-five. We have four hundred wines on our list. I've tasted them all. I've approved them all. I've been tasting hundreds of wines a year for the past forty years. Do the math. I know what's good and what isn't. This, *sommelier,* and her kindergarten knowledge of wine decided to try to sell me her eight-dollar Chianti in order to save my wine list from sucking. Where do these people come from? Anyway, afterward the manager politely explained to her that I was too busy to see her unannounced in the middle of dinner service, that I'd said there was an ocean of eight-dollar Chiantis to be had and wouldn't be interested in tasting hers. Well, that apparently pissed her off, so she decided that because I had no interest in her Chianti, she would take it out on the manager. In truth, I almost never refuse to see a wine salesperson. I believe it's rude and I'm always on the lookout for good juice but to come in the middle of dinner, insult my wine list, and then hand me the condescending, *sommelier,* bit was more than I needed to blow her off. As I mentioned, there were three of them. They ordered three appetizers, one of which was a pizza. The *sommelier,* also ordered a glass of an inexpensive Argentinian Malbec, the premiere choice of sommeliers everywhere, and then called the manager to the table.

The sommelier said, "Um, we're not happy with what's going on here tonight."

The manager asked, "What seems to be the problem?"

The sommelier said, "We ordered three things and we're still hungry."

The manager asked, "What did you have?"

The sommelier answered, "A pizza, ricotta with strawberries, and an octopus."

The manager told her, "Those are all appetizers."

The sommelier said, "And your point is …?"

The manager replied, "Well, my point is that appetizers aren't a main meal or designed to fill you up."

The sommelier said, "Yeah, well, that's bullshit, pal. I don't think we should pay for what we had. We're still hungry."

The manager said, "I can take your order if you'd like some more food."

The sommelier stated, "No, we don't want anything else except for you to take our food off the check."

The manager said, "I'll have to talk to my boss."

The manager came back and explained the situation. I've been through this at least one hundred times. It's just folks trolling for a freebie for some perceived offense. We know the difference between a scene like this and a legitimate complaint.

I said to him, "Let me get this straight. They had three appetizers and they're complaining that they're not full?"

He said, "Yes."

I asked, "And they don't want to pay for the bill?"

He said, "Correct. They said that the portions are too small. What would you like me to tell them?"

Just as I said before, I think it's justifiable to fire a bad customer just as you would a bad employee. It doesn't happen often, but every so often …

I said, "Give them the check and tell them I know where there's a great diner on their way home," never thinking for a minute that he thought I meant it literally.

The manager went to the table and said, "Here's your bill. Tom said he can't do anything about that, but he does know where there's a great diner on your way home. Is there anything else I can do for you ladies?"

The sommelier looked at him and said, "Yes! You can get away from this table, you pint-sized prick!"

The manager said, "Excuse me?"

"You heard me. Pint … sized … prick!"

I must have laughed for ten minutes after he told me.

He said, "She called me a pint-sized prick!"

I said, "That's so wrong, dude. No way you're even close to being a prick."

He's five foot five, and an immigrant. I laughed until I cried. And get this: when they were on the way out, I was standing by the bar still chuckling with the bartender. As the three tolerant, inclusive, highly evolved, open-borders women were walking out they all turned around, waved to me and said, "Bye, Tom, see you soon."

You just have to shake your head. Pint-sized prick. I love it.

OPENING SALVO

One night some years back, we had a firsthand sneak preview of what was to come with the election between Donald Trump and Hillary Clinton at the bar in one of my restaurants, The Petulant Wino. A group of five showed up for some food, drinks and some friendly camaraderie. Breaking all the unwritten rules about discussing politics and religion while imbibing, they started talking about the upcoming election. They were unapologetic Trump supporters. They were saying most of the same stuff that everyone says when they're rooting for their guy or girl. Politics and alcohol are always a shitty idea, but they were bothering no one … until a Hillary-supporting couple walked in and sat at the bar. We found out about the Hillary part a bit later when all hell broke loose. They were sitting about two stools apart, and the bar at The Petulant Wino is tight, so it's hard not to eavesdrop on a conversation even when you can't tolerate the content. One of the principal Trump supporters was saying that he couldn't stand Hillary, that she's a thief and a criminal, and that she should be prosecuted like anyone else would be for doing the same sorts of things.

He asked one of the others in the group, "How the hell does someone, on a government salary, make close to two hundred million dollars in ten years producing nothing, with nothing tangible to sell? And the press doesn't even question it?"

You must admit, it's a good question. The Hillary supporter started to fidget.

Another member of the group said, "And she sold half the US uranium rights to Russia through the Clinton Foundation."

The Hillary supporter's right heel started bouncing up and down on the bar rail.

One of the women in the Trump camp said, "This stuff she sells about advocating for women is all bullshit. She says all rape victims have to be believed—except when Bill's involved, I guess. Wasn't she calling them trailer trash and liars and such?"

Courtney noticed the Hillary supporter rocking slowly back and forth but at that point she had no clue as to what for or why.

The original Trump guy then said, "Yeah, she's all about women. It turns out that her foundation pays its women thirty five percent less than the men and she's been taking money from countries like Saudi Arabia and Qatar, whose records on women's rights are horrible. She's also courting the African American vote and meanwhile she stole most of the gold from Haiti, and funneled mining contracts to her brother and relief money to investors favorable to the Clinton Foundation."

The straw that broke the camel's back, I believe, is how the saying goes.

The Hillary supporter jumped off his stool, slammed both hands down on the bar so hard that several glasses flipped over, turned to the Trump group and said, "Maybe we should make you the president since you're so well informed, you fucking asshole!"

The Trump group, all at the same time, said, "No one was talking to you!" It probably would have been able to be quelled at that point had the wives not weighed in.

Mrs. Hillary, looking at the Trump crowd, said, "Don't talk to my husband like that, you bitch!"

Here we go.

Trump woman said, "Who are you calling a bitch, bitch?"

Then the Trump guy said, "Don't you call my wife a bitch, you bitch!"

Déjà vu all over again. This is life imitating election, or vice versa—I never was clear on which one was correct, but it does sound a lot like what I expected that upcoming campaign to sound like: a whole lot of yelling and screaming with nothing of value being said. Now Mister Hillary must defend his wife and that's where it usually goes bad. He rushed the Trump guy, cocked his fist and screamed, "What did you call my wife?" He swung a haymaker and missed by two and a half feet. True to his Democrat leanings: all symbolism, no substance. The Trump guy, just like a typical Republican going to war, returned the incoming salvo, missed the jaw he was aiming for, and dislocated a knuckle on the north end of the Hillary supporter's forehead. A typical Republican: the right bomb and the wrong target. If this wasn't a metaphor for politics and the election cycle, I don't know what was. The next minute and a half looked like a WWE match gone haywire until Courtney jumped in the middle and ultimately, with the help of Wes and Kyle, broke up the scrum. They were all still screaming threats back and forth when the only sensible person in the group yelled, *"Call the cops!"* We're always reluctant to do that for fear of causing an even bigger scene and seeing that no one was really hurt, save the knot on the forehead and the dislocated knuckle, Courtney said she didn't think it was necessary given that things were calming down. My son-in-law, Kyle, who's big enough to beat up all seven of them at the same time while having a beer and watching a game, was standing guard making sure it didn't flare up again and he convinced Courtney that the cops were the right call. She called the cops and while they were on their way the Trump-sters left the bar as the two parties continued to grumble at each other. When the cops arrived, they interviewed Courtney and she gave them her version of the events. They then asked the Hillary supporter if he intended to press charges and to his credit, because he was the one who got physical, he said that he didn't but just to be clear he wanted the cop to know that the other party started it. We iced down his bruise and they left.

The policeman in charge then finally asked Courtney, "So was anyone in the right here tonight?"

Courtney said, "Nope, both wrong and both ridiculous," and the two of them had a pretty good laugh.

That was what we had to look forward to that fall. Just as the two parties at the Wino went, so went the two parties in Washington. The conservative, so-called Constitution-loving Republicans were running a big-talking, semi-liberal, New Yorker who had no use whatsoever for the document and the tolerant, inclusive, diversity-loving Democrats were backing an entitled, high-class grifter whose history condones character assassination, bearing false witness, and violence against those with whom she disagrees. It was a wild one and we had seen the coming attractions.

I DID IT MY WAY

You can see 'em coming, I swear. The waiter radar went up as soon as she sat down. The woman had to adjust the napkin, get new silverware, and change her table—the usual chain of events for folks who crave just a little more attention than the average customer. And that's all it really is. I've said it before, but it bears repeating. Writing a menu for a Long Island restaurant is a useless exercise. Instead of printing the word, *Menu,* on our menus, we should print the word, *Suggestions*, because that's all a menu is these days—merely a suggestion. We *suggest* you have it prepared like this but if you insist on rearranging the vegetables, soiling nine-side plates, replacing the starch with pasta, removing the garnish because you're allergic to rainbow greens, ordering your salmon rare and sending it back five times for more fire, deciding after consuming half of your steak that you wanted sea bass all along, giving a list of instructions for your entrée that resembles the writings of Tolstoy, and throwing a wrench into the gears of a previously well-oiled kitchen service, then by all means, have at it. But sometimes there are consequences. I have to laugh at the people who need to turn a simple task into a complicated comedy of errors that are bound to fail and then are completely surprised when they do.

Check this out: This woman couldn't eat shellfish, couldn't eat pork, and was allergic to peppers. Okay, not so bad and believe me I've had much worse. But what does she order? The clam pizza with chorizo, roasted peppers, and grilled onion. I swear I'm telling the truth.

She told the waiter, "I don't eat pork or shellfish, and I'm allergic to peppers, so I'm going to have the clam pizza with the chorizo, roasted peppers, and grilled onion."

The waiter stared at her in disbelief. "Um, isn't that going to be a problem?"

She told him, "Not at all. I'm going to have it without the clams, the chorizo, and the peppers."

He asked, "So you want the clam pizza with no clams, no sausage, and no peppers, correct? You just want a pizza with grilled onions and fontina?"

She said, "Yes."

He told her, "Okay that shouldn't be a problem."

The poor little lamb. He was so inexperienced. My question, at the risk of being obvious is, why on earth wouldn't you order something you *can* eat—and there were many items she could have had—instead of ordering three things you *can't* eat? I'll tell you. If you order something you can eat, you don't get the chance to make your waiter jump through hoops, torture three people in the kitchen, muck up the flow of the food coming out, and you don't get to send it back. Hence: not enough attention.

The waiter came to me and said, "Chef, can I get the clam, chorizo, and pepper pizza without the clams, chorizo, and the peppers?"

There's that moment where the brain doesn't fire correctly while trying to comprehend the incomprehensible, and it has a rather curious effect on your countenance.

He then asked me, "Why are you looking at me like that?"

I replied, "I'm trying to decide whether you're unbalanced or if you're messing with me."

He said, "No, that's what the lady wants."

I asked the obvious question. "Why would she want a clam, chorizo, and pepper pizza without the three ingredients that essentially make it a clam, chorizo, and pepper pizza?"

He told me, "Because she's allergic."

Next year will be my fifty-third year in this business. I tell you that to illustrate the point that after all that time, I'm still learning every day. Which means, I certainly don't have all the answers, but I do have a few.

"The answer is no."

The waiter asked, "Why? What's the big deal?"

I told him, "It's no big deal about removing the items. She's setting you up. Do you honestly think this woman is going to quietly eat an onion and fontina pizza, enjoy it, pay up, and leave happy?"

He said, "Yeah, why not?"

I asked, "How naïve can you be? This isn't about allergies, or even eating for that matter. She just wants to see how many people she can get to shower her with attention. She needs to feel fussed over and special."

The funny part is if you want to be special or different, you'd be better off ordering something that *is* on the menu because very few people do anymore. That would make you stand out.

I then told him, "Here's a teachable moment and it will only cost me two or three pizzas. I'll do it and I'm willing to bet you ten thousand dollars to your ten dollars that it comes back."

He said, "You're on."

I called the pizza out to my pizza guy. "I need one clam, chorizo, and pepper pizza with no clams, chorizo, or peppers."

The cooks reacted accordingly by giggling. Here's the problem though. I'll screw around with them when things are slow, and I'll call out orders like, *"Ordering ... two chickens with no feathers,"* or, *"I need one brownie sundae, medium rare,"* just to have some laughs. That was what the pizza guy thought when I called out the order. And who could blame him? The order was patently ridiculous. I got called to a customer at the bar and got hung up with him for a bit, so I wasn't in the pass when the order went out. Believing that I couldn't possibly be serious about the order, the pizza guy made the pie with the clams, chorizo, and the peppers, and the runner brought it to the table. It was perfectly understandable.

The lady went nuts. "How could you bring me a pizza like this? I asked for no clams, chorizo, or peppers! Are you trying to make me sick? Get this off the table! Now!"

This is where, I believe, she started to enjoy her meal. She was the center of attention and had the three other guests consoling her, a frantic waiter trying to right the wrong, an, *in the weeds,* pizza guy making a second pie, and a snickering chef who was ten dollars richer. It couldn't have gone better for her.

The waiter said, "I'm not paying you. That was the kitchen's fault."

I told him, "Okay, you're right but the bet's still on."

The second pizza went out to the table. I like onions and I like fontina cheese, but the combination isn't exactly tea and crumpets. Have you ever been in line at a deli and had the person in front of you order an onion and fontina hero? Me neither, but this is essentially what she was getting. The only difference was that it was hot. I looked out into the dining room and saw the runner with the onion and fontina pizza scurrying back to the kitchen.

I asked him, "What's the problem?"

He said, "I don't know but she doesn't want it."

I said, "Get the waiter to the table."

The waiter came back to me and said, "She doesn't like it. It's disgusting."

I asked him, knowing full well what the answer would be, "What does she want instead?" He started to answer me, but I stopped him and said, "I'm going to take a wild guess. She doesn't want anything, correct?"

He said, "Yup, she doesn't want anything. How'd you know?"

I said, "They never do. They don't come to eat. They come for the sport, and you owe me ten dollars."

Poor little lamb.

EVERY PIG HAS ITS DAY

I was recently contacted by someone who was getting married at one of the vineyards on The North Fork. They told me they were on a limited budget and price was a consideration.

"Price is always a consideration," I told them. "And we can usually make a menu that will fit almost any budget."

I stress the word *almost* because, hey, it's a wedding and there are certain cost realities associated with weddings.

When we first met, the bride told me, "Tom we'd like to do a backyard type of wedding. We don't need anything fancy. I know you're used to doing these elaborate parties but we're not into it. We're very low maintenance and believe we can have just as nice a wedding as if we went nuts and spent a lot of money."

If I could inject a thought here. I know most people who say that mean it at the time and I agree that those types of down and dirty weddings can be great and an awful lot of fun, but what usually happens is that other family members, friends, in-laws, and moms get their two cents involved and stress the principals into rearranging the whole thing, trying to make the proverbial sow's ear into the silk purse. They were right on cue.

They decided on a barbeque. The menu was essentially ribs, chicken, salmon, hamburgers, hot dogs, a bunch of cool salads and sides, assorted cookies, brownies and blondies, and a wedding cake. They got a very good price and that's perfectly okay. It was when the shenanigans started that I may have lost my patience. She asked me a couple of days later if, because they were getting married on a Friday and not a Saturday or Sunday, I could make the price a little fairer. I said I could if it was a Monday and that Friday counts as a weekend, the barbeque menu notwithstanding. Sometime later, the call came in for a *wedding tasting*. Customarily, the bride and groom will sit for a tasting to check out the food from a potential caterer. It gives the couple an opportunity to look at plate presentation, taste some of the dishes that are to be served, and converse with the caterer as to how they see the wedding playing out from their perspective. It also gives the caterer a chance to get to know the specific tastes of the couple and how they see their wedding from the food and service aspect. I admit I was a bit surprised when the call for a tasting came in. You saw the menu.

The event planner called me and said, "The bride and groom called me and said they'd like to come for a tasting."

I said, "They what?"

She said, "They called and told me they'd like a wedding tasting. They said that when you first sat down and talked with them you told them that you do tastings before the weddings, and they'd like one."

I told her, "I do representative menu tastings for weddings so the couple will know what kind of food we do but they're essentially having a barbeque. I don't do barbeque tastings; I do wedding tastings."

She then asked me, "So what do you want me to tell her, Tom?"

I said, "Tell her to have dinner at Famous Dave's and she'll get the general idea."

She said, "I'm not telling her that. Look, she's been a pain in the ass through this whole process. You should have been involved in the rentals. It was a nightmare. Just do it, please."

I said, "Doesn't everyone know what a hamburger tastes like?"

She said, "I'm booking it for the following Sunday."

Sunday came and I had, frankly, forgotten about it.

About an hour before, the event planner called and said, "You set for the tasting?"

I asked, "Oh shit, is that today?"

She said, "Yes, at 4:30."

I told her, "I never ordered the stuff."

She said, "Well, you'd better go get it."

I said, "This is the most ridiculous thing ever. I'm doing a rib and burger tasting for a wedding."

Fifteen minutes later, I was at Stop and Shop with a basket of goodies at the checkout line behind a woman in a pair of oversized Coach sunglasses, oblivious to the world around her. Her bill was something-something and eighty-six cents and despite all evidence to the contrary, and a growing line of annoyed patrons behind her, she was determined to find the exact change that she was certain she had, in a pocketbook that could have housed a Maserati. She was at fifty-five and still counting.

I asked, "Need some change?"

She said, "No, I think I have it," missing the sarcasm.

What is it with women and exact change, anyway? I remember thinking, *"A jury of my peers will be all men; they'll understand."*

I finally got back five minutes before the couple showed up with the parents in tow and the tasting began. We usually send out ten to twelve mini courses like a tasting menu you would order in a restaurant, and we announce each dish as it's served, but it's impossible with those menu items. I can't picture myself saying, *"Here you have a hamburger, which we cooked to death because Princess E. coli over here can't eat medium rare beef due to a random report of an outbreak, with Heinz Ketchup, B&G pickles, and locally sourced Ore-Ida French fries."* It doesn't really flow, if you get my drift. And how the hell do you artistically plate baked beans? The whole tasting was tragic. Then, much to my disappointment, they gave me a deposit.

About a week later the event planner called and said, "The bride wants to know if they could have baby back ribs instead of the St. Louis ribs. They prefer those."

I said, "They're a bit more expensive. I'll have to upcharge."

The event planner said, "No, please, this woman is a nightmare. I'll pay for them myself because I can't go through much more with her. It's at every level. Just make the switch. I'll pay for it."

I said, "All right, but that's it."

She said, "Thank you," and we left it at that.

A few days later, the bride called and asked me, "Tom, what kind of meat do you use for the burgers?"

Tongue in cheek, I answered, "Beef."

She said, "No, I know they're beef, but do you use a special cut of the beef?"

I said, "No, just plain old eighty-twenty. Eighty percent beef, twenty percent fat."

She asked, "Could you use ground short rib?"

I answered, "Yes, but there's an upcharge"

Annoyed, she said, "Then forget it."

The questions kept coming from the soon-to-be Mrs. Low Maintenance.

"Are the hot dogs all beef?"

"Yes."

"Is the salmon wild or farm raised?"

"At that price, farm raised."

"Are the chickens free ranging and are they raised without hormones and antibiotics?"

"I have no *(fucking)* idea."

"Whose barbecue sauce do you use?"

"Tommy's famous."

"Can you make brownies without gluten for some of our guests?"

"Yes, but there's an upcharge."

"Then forget it."

This simple *backyard barbeque* was turning into the Godfather wedding, and I was having second thoughts when, on a beautiful spring morning, the event planner walked into my office and said, "I'm not quite sure how to ask you this, but the bride wants to know if you buy the hot dogs premade, or do you make them fresh yourself?"

I thought about it for a second and then gave her my answer. I said, "I see. She's a bit uppity about her puppies, is she? Not to worry. Tell her that the day of the wedding we'll procure a Mangalista pig from a farmer in the Midwest. As they're exchanging their vows, we'll free the pig on the winery property. While everyone else is congratulating them on the receiving line, I'll chase down the pig, beat the living shit out of it and drag it back to the cook tent, where we'll finish off the bastard humanely, inducing a heart attack by showing it the rendered bacon fat for the spinach salad. As they're being announced for the first time as Mr. and Mrs. Low Maintenance, I'll butcher his ass up and by the time she's stepping all over her father's shoes, dancing to *Daddy's Little Girl,* we'll have those babies stuffed and ready to go. Would that work?"

We were howling in the office. How ridiculous can you get? Hot dogs made to order for a wedding? Where does it end?

OUR WEDDING NIGHT

Last year, we booked a wedding at one of the vineyards on the North Fork. These are usually very civilized affairs—usually—but you really can't be sure until they get rolling. This was, we thought, a very nice couple. The preliminary conversations are where you normally find out about the personalities of the participants and make your judgment accordingly. Obviously, some people are easier to deal with than others and more, or less, maintenance is required while guiding them toward their big day. This couple was easy, but they wanted specific things; expensive specific things and they wanted us to pay for them. Everyone has a vision of what their wedding will look like, and our job is to help them achieve that look. The trouble starts when a person's vision starts to outrun their finances. We must try to reel them in and show them where they can cut back or reduce extraneous items. You can have just as much fun and a very cool wedding in a backyard without spending like Diana and Charles. I'm not sure these two got the memo. Aside from the usual cocktail hour, passed appetizers, salad, entrée, dessert, coffee and tea, and a five-hour open bar, they wanted a special, *welcome to my wedding,* cocktail customized just for them in a special glass. They wanted a pasta course served in between the appetizer and the entrée. They wanted an upgraded liquor package including cognac and after-dinner cordials. They wanted the bar open for an extra hour and a half because, *"We like to party."* They wanted a dessert buffet instead of one plated dessert, sliders and various types of bar food served at midnight. There was one slight problem: they were only willing to pay for the extra hour and a half that the bar would be open.

We said, "You want us to throw all this in?"

The bride said, "Yes. We're spending a lot of money with you."

We said, "We can't do that."

She said, "Why? You're not making enough on this wedding? Is it really that big of a deal?"

When I'm in these conversations—and I've been in many—it always occurs to me, *"If it's not such a big deal to you, why don't you just pay for it instead of panhandling me?"* We let her know that we would work as closely as we could, but we couldn't do it for free. She politely declined. If you're a reader of Yelp, the literary equivalent of twerking, you'll notice a pattern. As you read through the not so stellar reviews, the phrase, *"It wasn't worth the money,"* seems to surface more often than not. My theory is that some folks are comfortable spending a certain amount of money on dinner and when they go above that mark their expectation levels rise in direct relation to their anxiety. You will never get a Yelper to write a good review of a restaurant they can't comfortably afford no matter how good it may be. I've seen bad reviews of Le Bernadin, Bouley, and Masa—all great restaurants—and it always gets down to the price. Anyway, the couple seemed disappointed and dispensed with the extras rather than pay for them. We assured them that their wedding would be incredible. And it was—incredible, that is.

My first anxious moment came with the arrival of the bridal party. They literally fell out of two limousines and the maid of honor announced their arrival with, "They fucking did it!" with the entire bridal party clinking champagne glasses.

It resembled an outtake of the first season of The Jersey Shore. Cocktail hour started and three minutes into it I got a call to refill the Tuscan Table. This party was to pork products what Hillary Clinton is to emails.

One of the aunts announced at the top of her lungs, "They ran out of salami!"

I told the server as I was getting the second one ready, "We didn't run out; it was deleted."

Panic ensued. Twenty people, including the bride, rushed the cook tent asking for more salami. I'm under the impression that salami is a synonym for prosciutto, coppa, sopressata, and the like. We sent out more … lots more.

Things calmed a bit and just when I thought, *"Maybe this will be okay,"* a different aunt popped the last crab cake off one of the passing trays into her mouth, and screamed while spitting crabmeat all over her dress, "They're out of crab cakes!"

Twenty people including the bride rushed the cook tent once more. We sent out more crab cakes … lots more. It was very hot out that day and not everyone was drinking all that much, except for the bridal party, who were making up for the others. They were inside doing shots of tequila and taking selfies—which is never a good idea mind you—and talking about the ALS ice bucket challenge. I've had shots of tequila. The combination of tequila, an idea *(any idea, for that matter),* and the resultant flawed decision process, can make for an interesting evening. I once found myself on an unscheduled flight to San Juan at six in the morning but let's not lose track here. Someone came into the cook tent looking for ice and a bucket. We gave it to them. They kept asking and we kept giving. We're good like that. I believe they raised over one thousand dollars before the cocktail hour was over and I had to send a server out for more ice.

As I was telling him where to get it, the aunt wearing the crab cake must have overheard me and yelled, "I just heard him say they're out of ice!"

Geez! Finally, the cocktail hour ended, and everyone went inside. You had to see the bridal party as they were announced; it looked like a wet T-shirt contest.

The rest of the wedding was almost uneventful until the full effect of the alcohol kicked in about an hour before the wedding ended. It started when one of the groomsmen was refused a shot of tequila, largely because he couldn't pronounce it.

We told him we were out of tequila—for his own good of course—and someone said, "They're out of tequila!"

There was a riot.

The bride called Courtney over and said, "You people are stealing our liquor."

Courtney answered, "You mean the liquor we brought? And we didn't steal anything. We told him we were out because we didn't want to tell him he was too drunk to be served."

The bride said, "You can serve him. We're taking limos home."

Courtney said, "I'm not worried about him getting home. I'm worried about him getting to the limo."

That escalated the whole thing. Ten minutes later another very well-oiled groomsman couldn't find his sunglasses and accused us of stealing them. Five more groomsmen followed suit. None of them could find their sunglasses, so they thought we must have stolen them. I'm assuming climate change is responsible for needing sunglasses at 10:00 p.m. Another one came over and said that someone had stolen his sneakers. They accused me of not feeding the band and the photographer, which was ludicrous. The most dangerous place in the world is between a musician and a buffet. They said that Courtney cursed out the photographer, who happened to be a friend of hers. It never happened.

The best man said, "I'm going to search the server's pocketbooks!"

Courtney said, "No, you are not!"

A standoff formed on the dance floor. A crowd of about a dozen people literally surrounded Courtney calling her names and threatening her.

The manager of the vineyard was about to intervene when another aunt yelled, "They stole the flowers too!"

You wouldn't have believed the scene. Thank God I was in the kitchen at the time. The vineyard manager pulled the bride and groom aside trying to talk some sense into them and they turned on him. They accused his staff of taking their stuff and screwing them. It was surreal. The wedding was to end at 11:00, and finally at about 10:55, the bride said it. We'd been waiting for hours when she finally said it.

She said, "You need to take something off the bill. You people are thieves and I want something taken off the bill. And you"—she pointed at the vineyard manager— "had better take something off also."

It always comes to that in the end.

The next day, the bride called in the early afternoon. She said, "Can I speak to Courtney?"

I said, "Courtney's not here."

The bride asked, "Do you know where she is?"

I said, "Yeah, she's at the beach. You'll recognize her immediately. She's the one wearing men's size twelve sneakers, holding a bouquet, and sporting nine pairs of Ray Bans. She's hard to miss."

I never heard from them again. Hopefully they were sufficiently embarrassed. It all came down to drinking too much. After all, it was ninety-two degrees that night. Climate change.

TENACITY

There's a case to be made for tenacity. And then there's …

A couple came into the restaurant for dinner one night this past fall, on a first date. They looked normal enough, but then again, so did Jeffery Dahmer. The strangeness started after dinner. When they were leaving the gentleman went to get the car and the lady sidled up to the hostess desk.

She said, "I'd like to speak to a manager."

Diane said, "I'm the manager. How can I help you?"

She said, "There was a problem with my steak."

Diane asked, "What was wrong with it?"

She said, "It was undercooked."

Diane asked her, "Did you send it back or tell your server?"

She said, "No."

Diane asked her, "Why not?"

She said, "Because I'm on a first date and I didn't want him to think I'm a complainer."

Diane told her, "That's not really complaining. If it wasn't served how you ordered it, we would have been happy to cook it a little more for you."

She said, "I was trying to make a good impression. I've been single a long time."

Diane asked, "How did you order it?"

She answered, "Medium rare, but it came out medium rare to the rare side. And my date got three more carrots than I did."

Diane asked, "Three more carrots?"

She said, "Yes, I counted them; three more carrots. Is that normal?"

Diane informed her, "I don't think the kitchen counts the carrots. I think they just give what they think is an equivalent amount to each person. The carrots are different sizes, so they guesstimate."

She said, "Well they guesstimated wrong on our table. Is it because I'm a woman that I got three fewer carrots? Because that's bullshit! I should get the same number of carrots as my date."

Diane, sensing that there was a facility that was one inmate short of a full bed check said, "Okay, we want you to leave happy. How about I send you a gift certificate for the next time you dine with us? Would that make you feel better?"

She said, "Yes, it would."

Diane said, "Okay, let's do that. What's your name and address?"

The woman said, "Brooke Anthony, and I live at such-and-such address."

Diane said, "Okay, I'll get that off to you tomorrow."

Brooke asked, "Are you sure you're going to send it? Why don't you just give it to me now?"

Diane responded, "I can't. I have to check with my boss on the amount, and I won't see him until tomorrow."

Brooke asked Diane, "Why don't you call him while I'm here? The phone's right there."

Diane, becoming annoyed, replied, "Because it's his day off. There's no reason to annoy him with this and unless you're planning on using it before ten tonight this can wait until tomorrow."

Brooke, "Do you promise you'll send it?"

Diane answered, "Only if you stop asking me and go home!"

Brooke said, "Okay, but don't forget. You have my information, correct?"

Diane told her, "Brooke, you have to leave now. Good night."

Brooke walked out the door at 9:10 p.m. The phone rang at 9:50. Diane answered, "Hello, Jewel, can I help you?"

The caller said, "Can I speak to Diane?"

Diane said, "This is Diane."

The caller said, "Diane, Brooke Anthony here. I lost an earring in your parking lot, and I need you to go out and find it."

Diane, "What?"

Brooke aid, "I lost one of my earrings. It's a gold hoop with a stud. I need you to go look for it."

Diane, "Brooke, I'm busy at the moment. I'll send someone out there in a while and see if we can find it for you."

"Okay. You're not just telling me that, are you? You know, so I'll get off the phone and you won't really look for it."

Diane said, "Brooke, I'm busy here!"

Brooke told her, "Okay, call me back and let me know."

Diane hung up. At 10:15, the phone rang. Diane answered, "Jewel, can I help you?"

The caller said, "Diane? Brooke Anthony. I forgot to mention that our server never read us the specials. I heard her telling the table next to us, but she never read them to us. Why is that?"

Diane answered, "I don't know, Brooke, but I'll look into it."

Brooke told her, "Okay, but make sure you tell your boss, because there should be something extra on my gift certificate for that."

Diane rolled her eyes and said, "I'll be sure to let him know."

Brooke said, "You're not just telling me that to get me off the phone, are you?"

Diane patiently told her, "Good night, Brooke." At 10:20, Diane hung up the phone. She asked the waitress if she read the specials to the couple at table twenty. The waitress explained that she was about to when they stopped her and told her that they knew what they wanted, and that it wouldn't be necessary to hear the specials.

At 10:31, the phone rang. Diane answered, "Hello, Jewel, can I help you?"

The caller said, "Diane, please."

Diane said, "Brooke, what is it now?"

Brooke told her, "There wasn't enough whipped cream on my bread pudding either. Make sure your boss knows that."

Diane said, "Brooke, if you call me once more tonight, I'm not sending it."

"Just make sure he knows that I expect to be compensated."

Diane said, "Good night, Brooke."

"Don't forget."

"Good night, Brooke!" At 10:36, Diane hung up the phone. At 10:50, the phone rang.

Diane answered and said, "Hello, Jewel, can I help you?"

The caller said, "Diane, Brooke Anthony again. How much do you think he'll send me?"

"Brooke, I promise you if you call once more tonight, I'm not sending anything. I'm serious!"

Brooke said, "Do you think it'll be more than twenty-five dollars?" Diane hung up the phone at 10:52.

The next morning, I came in, and Diane explained the situation over a good laugh. I told her to send her a gift certificate for twenty-five dollars to get her out of our hair.

Diane said, "I'd like to shove it up her …"

I cut her off and said, "You have to admit it, she's nuts but at least she's entertaining."

Diane said, "Really, you think so? Fine, you take the calls."

At 11:35 a.m., the phone rang. The hostess answered," Hello, Jewel, can I help you?"

The caller asked, "Is Diane there?"

"Yes, who's calling, please?"

The caller said, "Brooke Anthony."

Diane picked up the phone. "What is it, Brooke?"

"Did you send it?"

"Not yet, Brooke. I just spoke to my boss. I'll send it this afternoon."

Brooke asked, "How much did he tell you to send me?"

"Twenty-five dollars."

Brooke, "That's it? Did you tell him about the specials and the whipped cream?"

"Listen, Brooke. I've had it. You're lucky I'm sending anything. We're trying to do something nice for you but you're becoming a pain in the ass. I'm hanging up, and I'll send it today. Don't call me anymore."

Brooke said, "Do you think he could make it fifty?"

"No!"

Diane hung up at 11:38. I was getting dribs and drabs of the conversations and was enjoying it immensely. Diane was having fun with it too because it's not every day you get one quite this affected. Diane mailed the gift certificate and told the hostess that if Brooke Anthony called, tell her she wasn't in. We thought that would be that.

We were mistaken.

At 11:39, the phone rang.

The hostess said, "Hello, Jewel, can I help you?"

The caller said, "Is Diane there?"

The hostess asked, "Who's calling?

"Brooke Anthony."

The hostess told her, "I'm sorry, she's unavailable at the moment. Can I take a message?"

The caller said, "No."

At 11:40, the phone rang. The hostess answered and said, "Jewel, may I help you?"

The caller said, "Is Diane there?"

The hostess asked, "Who is calling."

The caller said, "Sandy Duncan."

Diane picked up and asked, "Can I help you?"

The caller said, "It's Brooke Anthony. Did you send it yet?"

Diane said, "Listen, Brooke, you're driving me crazy. I sent it, okay? I sent it today, okay? It's in the mail, okay? You should get it shortly, okay?!"

Brooke replied, "I don't know why you're yelling at me, but you're not lying to me, right?"

At 11:42, Diane hung up the phone and all was quiet for the rest of the day. The following day, the phone rang at about 1:30 in the middle of lunch.

The hostess answered, and the caller said, "Diane, please."

The hostess asked, "Who is calling?"

The caller said, "Marlo Himmelfarb."

Diane picked up the phone, and the caller said, "Diane? Brooke Anthony. I didn't receive it yet. Are you sure you sent it?"

Diane slammed the phone down at 1:31. In the interest of space, this went on for about a week and a half. Every day, Brooke would call two or three times under an alias and bug Diane about the gift certificate, saying she never received it. It all came to a head about a week later. The phone rang at about 4:30 in the afternoon.

The hostess answered, and the caller said, "Is Diane there?"

The hostess asked, "Who is calling?"

The caller said, "Sister Betrille, from the Daughters of Charity."

Diane asked me, "Are we still doing donations? There's a sister or someone on the phone. I think they're probably looking for a donation."

I said, "Give them a lunch for two."

Diane picked up the phone and said, "Hello?"

The caller said, "Diane, it's Brooke Anthony. I didn't get the gift certificate yet."

Diane told her, "Brooke, this is now what's known as stalking. If you call me one more time, I'm calling the police." She slammed the phone down at 4:32.

She came into my office, laughing, and said, "You have to do something. This freak keeps calling me about this gift certificate. She said she never got it, it isn't enough, and she wants another, blah, blah, blah. This has been going on for a week and a half, and I can't take it anymore. She's a head case."

To hear Diane, who is a recovering head case herself, telling me about a head case, nearly sent me into convulsions.

As hard as we were laughing, she managed to tell me, "No, seriously, you have to take care of this. This woman is sick. I'm starting to get worried."

I said, "Don't take the calls."

Diane told me, "I wasn't, but now she's calling and using aliases to get me to the phone. I'm telling you, she's wacked."

I said, "Okay, if she calls again, give me the phone."

At 5:10, the phone rang. The hostess answered and the caller asked, "Is Diane there?"

The hostess asked, "Who is calling, please?"

The caller said, "Bridgette Jones."

The hostess called down to the office and asked, "Is Diane there? She has a Bridgette Jones on the line for her."

Diane turned to me and said, "That's her, I know it. She's crazy. She just called here twenty minutes ago. I'm telling you, it's her."

I picked up the phone and said, "Hello?"

The caller said, "Diane, it's Brooke Anthony."

I said, "Brooke, it's Tom, Diane's boss."

She said, "I need to speak to Diane."

I said, "Diane's done speaking with you. You've been harassing her for two weeks. We're done with this. We're done with the phone calls, the gift certificates, the aliases, all of it."

She asked, "Does that mean you're not sending me my gift certificate?"

I said, "Ms. Anthony, you are certifiably nuts! The fact that you were here already frightens me out of my wits. I don't want you here again. You are not welcome back. You are banned. You need counseling and medication, not a gift certificate. Go get yourself some help, for God's sake."

I hung up the phone at 5:15. I turned to Diane and said, "Well, that should do it."

At 5:45, the phone rang. The hostess answered, and the caller said, "Is Diane Flynn there? This is an emergency call!" The hostess told Ann, and Ann came running to get Diane, who was in the kitchen with me.

Ann said, "Someone's on the phone, and they say it's an emergency."

Diane said, "Oh, my God! I hope it's not my son or my dad!" She raced past me to the office, picked up the phone, and said, "This is Diane Flynn!"

The caller said, "Diane, it's Brooke Anthony."

Did I mention that she said she's been single for a long time?

MIXED(-UP) MARRIAGE

Many years ago, I was working at a country club that shall remain nameless for the all the right reasons. It was a very toney club with an exclusive membership, a great golf course, and a pain-in-the-ass French chef. This was the early seventies, and I was working as a sous chef trying to hone my chops. We used to do a fair amount of catering, like most clubs do, and I worked most of those affairs. When the schedule went up for June, I noticed that one of the more prominent families had a wedding booked for a Saturday night at the end of the month. This family had three beautiful daughters in their mid to late twenties, the middle of which was engaged to one lucky bastard I'd known for several years. I'll call him John. He was someone I knew from growing up and was a few years older. You've heard the expression,

"He's not playing with a full deck?" This boy was missing the whole suit of hearts.

My hometown was a fun place to grow up … if only that had happened. I refer to it as the home of the forty-year-old teenager because it seems like no one I know has ever been able to avoid the arrested development that seems prevalent there. When we were in grammar school, they told us that they fluoridated the town water supply which was supposed to be good for your teeth, I'm guessing. I'm not sure they were telling the truth. Something was in the water, for sure, but I don't think it had much to do with dental care. One hour on a Halloween night, in the sixties in my hometown, would be all the convincing you would need. It was total madness, and madness or genius is what we do in my hometown. It was always one or the other. For one square mile, it has produced some of the most memorable characters I've ever known.

John was on the madness side of the ledger. That was what was so hard for me to get down when I saw the catering schedule. He was getting married to this privileged woman and everyone who knew them knew it was a bad idea. Here was this beautiful, Hermès-wearing, Protestant, blonde debutant marrying, uh, John. And the best part is that it was her idea. In fact, the pressure she put on him was enough to turn a piece of charcoal into an engagement ring. There were always different crowds growing up in my hometown, as I'm sure it is everywhere. You had the jock athlete types like John, the smart and studious types, and the biker rock-and-roll guys. Although we all pretended not to like each other everyone basically got along. The main difference was that the biker types got into things they shouldn't have much earlier than the other groups, but they got out earlier as well. The jocks were late bloomers and the reason I bring it up is because at that time John, the jock, was blooming his rear end off into his late twenties. Like I said, those of us who knew them as a couple weren't very optimistic about their chances. I don't think her family was very happy about the union either, but they all put up a good front for the daughter's sake.

The father was concerned about John's friends drinking themselves stupid at the reception and said to the manager, "Have your bartenders keep an eye on my son-in-law and his friends. They tend to get out of control."

The manager said, "Don't worry, sir, we'll watch them."

That Saturday was a beautiful day for a wedding: bright blue sky, not a cloud to be seen, a high of seventy-eight degrees. The limos started arriving at around 5:45. The cocktail hour started at 6:00.

At 6:05, a waiter came to me and said, "Someone is at the kitchen door looking for you."

I said, "For me? Who is it?"

The waiter said, "I don't know, but I think he's in the bridal party."

I walked over to the kitchen door to find John, half shitted, leaning against the jamb. He said, "Hey, T. I just got married."

I said, "Congrats, John. Are you okay?"

He was giggling as he said, "Yeah. I promised Missy I wouldn't get banged up, but you know these guys."

I said, "Yeah, I know but pace yourself, dude. You've got a long night ahead of you."

He said, "I will, I will. But listen, I need a favor. My father-in-law told the manager, *'No Heinekens at the bar,'* because he was afraid we'd go nuts, and all they have is shit beer out there.

I can't drink it, man. So listen, I need you to smuggle a few of cases of Heineken out to us."

I said, "John, are you out of your mind? I can't do that. Besides how are you going to explain fifty green beer bottles lying all over the place?"

John said, "C'mon, man. For me. Do it for old times."

"Can't do it, John. Tough it out. One night won't kill you."

"All right, man. I gotta get back in there. Thanks anyway. See you."

I answered, "Cool, and congratulations by the way."

He yelled, "Thanks," over his shoulder and went back inside.

I knew the crew he was running with and made a mental note to have the waiters keep me up to speed on the antics. It was quite the group. This was the early seventies and the weddings still adhered to the traditional father of the bride speech, the best man toast, dances with Mom and Dad, the couple's first dance together, and flying garters and bouquets. From my server reports, John and the boys were fairly well behaved except for the best man toast, which was more roast than toast, but that was to be expected. About two and a half hours into the party, one of the servers came to me and said that a couple of the guys were acting a little *off.*

I said, "What do you mean, *off*?"

He said, "I don't know, just *off.* Their eyes are all googly and they're laughing uncontrollably at nothing."

I started to chuckle and said, "Oh, shit." Then I asked the server, "Could you get one of them back here?"

He said, "Sure."

One of the groomsmen came back to the kitchen door.

I said, "Hey Steve, what's up?" We'd known each other our whole lives.

He said, "Good man, and you?"

I said, "Good. Hey, the server told me they're getting a little strange out there."

Steve said, "Yeah, you know John. He sent one of the guys to go get some Heinekens, which they stashed downstairs, and they're going through them at Olympic pace. Then one of those knuckleheads broke out some mushrooms and now five of them are tripping—including John."

Laughing, I said, "I don't see that working out so well."

Steve replied, "Nope, me either."

I said, "Well, try to keep an eye on them."

Steve said, "Yup, wish me luck," and he went back inside.

Another hour went by, and it was time to wheel out the cake for the cutting ceremony and we would have if we'd had a groom. We did not.

It started with the bride and a question: "Where's John?"

Then the bride's mother: "I wonder where he could be, honey?"

Then Dad weighed in. "Will someone go find that idiot!"

It escalated into a full-blown APB. They couldn't find him anywhere. We even had servers searching the grounds because we thought maybe he'd passed out. This went on for about twenty minutes and the families were starting to panic.

Finally, one of the busboys came up to me and whispered, "I ting I fown you fren."

I asked, "Where is he?"

He said, "I ting his asleeping on dee dybing bore."

I asked, "What? By the pool?"

He said, "Jess, by dee pool."

I said, "Oh, shit. Let's get him up to the kitchen and try to straighten him out."

The kitchen and dining room were on the second floor and the pool was on ground level under the wall of dining room windows. Sometime between the busboy finding him and us getting to the pool area, John woke up and decided to try to sober up by taking a dip. His timing could not have been worse. As we got to the bottom of the stairs, I looked out to see a stark-naked John standing on the diving board. With both hands extended parallel to the ground for balance, he began slowly navigating the walk to the end of the board. About halfway there another busboy, who was diligently searching the grounds, hadn't seen him yet and decided to flick on the floodlights to illuminate the pool area. Did he ever. Two hundred twenty-two wedding guests were illuminated to what the bride had just signed on to, for better or worse. John looked up, smiled, waved to the crowd, and jumped into the pool with his hands cupped over his crotch. The father of the bride had to be physically restrained.

HAPPY BIRTHDAY

I've always said that I've never seen or heard one well-sung *Happy Birthday* performance in the years that I've been at this. For a simple song with a 1-5-4 progression, it stumps a lot of aspiring Bocelli's. It never stops people from belting out the obligatory ditty, but I think it's high time we ban the custom. A sparkler in a slice of cake with the Beatle's song, *Birthday,* blaring through the sound system should be sufficient acknowledgment that you've completed another trip around the sun. That being noted, I have to tell you this one.

A Japanese restaurant I was eating at years ago had devised a solution to all the bad *Happy Birthday* celebrations they'd obviously suffered, and it would have been close to brilliant had the waitstaff not messed it up in such spectacular fashion. About forty years ago, I witnessed one of the funniest *(unfortunately not for the birthday girl)*, most embarrassingly bungled, and most unforgettable birthday celebrations to ever grace a restaurant table. It was called the *Bonsai!* Not the restaurant, the celebration.

Let me explain.

There was this Japanese restaurant that I used to frequent when I was spending a lot of time in Boston in the early seventies. One of the chefs used to make this green tea flavored cake that the clientele grew to love. It was essentially layered crepes with green tea frosting between the layers, and he would serve a slice with a strawberry sauce and some whipped cream. They sold tons of them so there were always extra cakes on hand. I don't know this for certain but I'm guessing that he, like many of the rest of us in the business, was sick of hearing all the mangled *Happy Birthday* celebrations in the dining room and came up with a solution. What they would do was bring a whole green tea cake to the table with a lit sparkler in it. They would first set the cake down in front of the celebrant. Four or five servers would then gather around the table and say—not sing—in unison, *"Happy, happy birthday, happy, happy birthday, happy, happy birthday, happy birthday to you!"* Then one of the servers would go behind whose ever birthday it was, grab them by both wrists, say whatever they said in Japanese *(I guess it was a good wish, or a toast, or something),* and then yell, *"Bonsai!"* at the top of their lungs while yanking the person's hands in the air three times. A quaint little ritual, I must admit, and I have to tell you that alone brought in a lot of business. On any given night you would see eight to ten of these celebrations going on. Word got out and people would dine there specifically on their birthdays to get *"Bonsai-ed"* and have the requisite celebration ritual. It was a bonanza that would turn out to be short-lived. That night, the Bonsai cake would become a casualty of the seventies.

I was sitting at a table for two with my girlfriend at the time when a party of six birthday celebrants sat down at an adjacent table. These six women were all fired up and looking forward to a fun night of pillow fighting and discussing boys. A Bonsai cake came out to a table across the room. It was my girlfriend's first time at the restaurant. She watched the ritual and asked, "What's going on over there?"

I replied, "Oh, they're having a Bonsai cake. It's someone's birthday. They do it for everyone. It's kind of why a lot of people celebrate here."

She said, "I've never seen it done like that. Is it a Japanese custom?"

I said, "I don't know, but I prefer it to five waiters singing off-key in broken English."

She then asked, "What are they saying before they yell Bonsai and yank the person's hands up?"

I told her, "I don't understand Japanese, but I suspect it's some kind of toast."

She said, "That's fun. I would totally bring someone here for their birthday."

We had a leisurely dinner and some wine and talked for a couple of hours. As we were just about to get our bill, a Bonsai cake came out to the table of six women adjacent to us.

It was the last one ever served.

I told you that the Bonsai cake was a casualty of the seventies, and it was for two specific seventies reasons: a halter top and a braless woman. Five waiters brought out the Bonsai cake with its glowing sparkler and placed it in front of the birthday girl. With military precision, the servers said, "Happy, happy birthday, happy, happy birthday, happy, happy birthday, happy birthday to you."

And then it all went to shit.

The lead server slid behind the birthday girl, took one of her wrists in each hand, and screamed something in Japanese that sounded like, *"Suzuki, Yamaguchi, Takamoto!"* and then … *"Bonsai!"* As he was yelling *"Bonsai!"* and simultaneously yanking her hands in the air, her halter came flying up at the same rate of speed as her hands and flipped inside out, landing across the bridge of her nose. All you could see of her face was her wider than normal eyes and a rapidly reddening forehead resembling a sunburnt, topless bank robber. As bad as the situation was, two mitigating circumstances were about to make it worse. The first was that Bonsai boy was so into this role in the celebration that he didn't notice what had happened and he was sporting a pair of glasses so thick they could have been used for burning ants. The second and more pressing problem was that there were two more Bonsais on the schedule. The second Bonsai was a masterpiece. Gravity found its way into the mix. The birthday girl was rather endowed. Bonsai boy revved up for number two. He screamed something in Japanese that sounded like, *"Nagashima, Sukiyaki, Yellow Tail!"* and then … *"Bonsai!"* But as he was trying to yank her hands in the air a second time, she was fighting for her dignity, yanking them back down. This push-pull struggle combined with gravity and the weight set the girls in motion, looking like two out-of-control Volkswagens sliding down an icy incline. You have to understand that all this happened in a matter of seconds. As it was unfolding, it was so surreal, and everyone involved was so stunned that it took a few seconds to process. Our hero readied himself for number three. He never made it. He screamed something in Japanese that sounded like, *"Kawasaki, Edamame, Spicy Tuna Roll!"* and then … *"Bonsai!"* But as he started to yank on her hands, she stood up and faced him. I can't imagine what her chest looked like through those glasses. As he stood there with his mouth open, she ripped her right hand from his grasp and round-housed his ass right on the button. His legs buckled and one of the other waiters caught him on the way down and got him to a chair. She pulled her top back down and adjusted it into place. It took the other three waiters to keep her from killing him.

Standing over him trying to get her hands around his neck, she said, "You fucking idiot! Didn't you see my top was off?"

Considering the glasses, it was a silly question—hilarious, but silly. Through his haze, he whispered an explanation. It was something in Japanese that sounded like an apology that ended in *bonsai*. I guess she bought his version of the events because she calmed down, went back to her table, and had a piece of Bonsai cake. God knows she earned it. There were all manner of apologies and a whole bunch of bowing, but all involved seemed to have gotten over it by the time the ladies were ready to leave. It was the last Bonsai cake I ever saw served there, and out of the fifty or so I'd been a witness to, that one was like hitting the Bonsai lottery. It was one of the most insane restaurant moments on record.

As they were walking out my girlfriend asked the birthday girl as she passed our table, "Are you okay?"

She replied, "Yeah, I'm fine. Mortified, of course, but I'll be okay." Then she looked at me, shook her head, and said, "Do you believe that guy?"

I said, "I didn't see a thing."

She lowered her head, raised her left eyebrow, smirked at me, and left.

A MAD DASH FOR LOBSTERS

A while back, I was in a restaurant and on the inside front cover of the menu was a little vignette about the chef and his beliefs. It went something like this.

Chef Peter Purity believes in serving local, organic vegetables, harvested at the peak of flavor, according to Rudolf Steiner's personal timetable, in a biodynamic, pesticide-free environment. He buys only from farms employing humane animal husbandry, resulting in less stressed animals, an unrivaled level of mental health, white teeth, a smooth and shiny coat, and a college education. He uses sustainable fish, wild harvested from rose-scented salt water, without the use of hooks or nets so as not to injure them or hurt their feelings.

Admittedly there's some artistic license there, but exactly whom is he preaching to? I was thinking, *"Chef Pete, could you just shut up"*? Don't we do this as a matter of course? There's never been this level of awareness in our industry about food, how it's cooked, and how it's raised but for all the good it's done it's also fueled an unprecedented neurosis on the general public. May I say a few words about local, sustainable, vegan, genetically modified, organic, gluten-free, biodynamic, anti-meat, anti-lactose, and anti-preservatives? We're all trying to do the right thing, but I don't fret much about it all. I really don't. My job is to buy great ingredients, hopefully make them taste good, sell the dish at a fair price and try to garner a profit. That's pretty much it. I believe the rest of it to be silly at best and elitist, vanity preening, at worst. Thomas Keller once wrote a very insightful article about the *local* movement. In essence, his position was that as a chef, his responsibility to his clientele was to put the best possible ingredients he could find on the plate. If those ingredients came from within three hundred miles, great, but if they didn't, oh well. You must admit, he has a strong point. I try to support my *local* purveyors as much as possible and I'm sure that the Long Island farmers and wineries will attest to that. But to be *locally* pure, I would have to have twenty menu items with cauliflower on them from December to April, which is obviously a bit of a problem. What I find amusing about the movement is the militancy with which its beliefs are forced upon us. It's even getting crazy with wine. I have a buddy who grows his grapes biodynamically. He's very excited about it and they do a very good job at the winery. Great, but I don't care. It's a nice little backstory that I could probably use to sell their wine to some Oregonian couple, he driving a Prius and she with braided armpits, but I can tell you for sure that the general public doesn't really care. He's very proud of the fact that he doesn't spray with pesticides … but his neighbors do. So, in the end, what? Ever hear of wind?

Even my salespeople give me the *organically grown* or *biodynamically farmed* speeches when selling me wine and when they're through, I tell them, "That's nice, but I'm primarily concerned with the color, the nose, the taste, the finish, and the price because that's all my customers are concerned with."

No one's ever asked me, *"Hey, T, what was the organic approval index at the time of the harvest?"* Or *"Were those grapes sprayed, and what was the brix level when they were picked?"*

No one cares, trust me. A little less sanctimony and a little more fun would be a lot more refreshing. We're not saving lives here; it's only dinner, so relax. But some people just don't have the ability. As we've clearly established, there are folks out there who need to turn dining rooms into triage centers. My research tells me that about twenty percent of alleged allergy sufferers actually sneeze, break out, or worse, and eighty percent just don't like an item and feel they'll receive a higher priority of attention to their meal after copping the allergy plea. Think I'm kidding?

Two couples arrived for dinner one Friday night straight from what had to be an allergy support group. From Memorial Day to Labor Day, we have a lobster special on Friday nights. When they arrived, they inquired of the hostess about the lobster special. The hostess assured them that it was in full swing. They told her that, in their experience, some restaurants would advertise a special just to get folks to come and then not have it. I don't know what restaurants they'd frequented, but we assured them that they were safe with us and that we had plenty of lobsters. Thank God we did.

The server came over and asked them, "Can I get anyone something from the bar?"

One of the women responded, "We know Tom really well. We eat in all of his restaurants, and we would like the lights turned down."

The server said, "Okay, I'll see what I can do. Would anyone like a drink in the meantime?" There was a collective shaking of heads at the table and the other woman said, "We'll just have water, and can you make sure to turn the lights down? They're hurting my eyes."

Often this age group asks for the lights to be turned up, not down, so we thought the request a bit unusual. I made a mental note because after so many years of doing this you get that feeling about people. I wasn't at the table, so I'll give you this from my perspective at the expediter station.

The server came to me and said, "That table, the ones that wanted the lights turned down, are now complaining that they can't read the menus."

I said, "Okay, turn them back up and then leave them where they were in the first place."

Five minutes later, the server came back and said, "I went to take their order and the woman told me that she has a severe allergy to bergamot. She wants to know if you use any bergamot in your cooking."

I said, "Congratulations, you've brought me another bergamot allergy. I didn't think it possible to find more than one person suffering the affliction, but there you go."

The server asked, "What should I tell her?"

I said, "Jenna, I don't even know what bergamot is, let alone cook with it."

Jenna said, "So we're safe here?"

I said, "Yeah, I think it has something to do with oranges. Just tell her to not order anything with oranges, and she'll be fine."

Pardon my skepticism, but if everyone who told me they were allergic to something sneezed at the same time, Mount St. Helen would be a footnote in history. I'd be curious to know just how many bergamot-related deaths happen in the United States every year. I would imagine the majority of them would have to be concentrated in Florida. I think the governor should issue a warning to all the bergamot allergic souls in that state like the ones the drug companies are forced to do on TV. *"If you experience any of these symptoms—better skin, normal blood pressure, faster healing, improved heart function, an absence of common colds, a boosted immune system, healthy gums, or an erection lasting less than four hours—stop taking bergamot and see your psychiatrist immediately."*

It's vitamin C, for God's sake. And what's the test for it? Eat a case of oranges and wait for a reaction? The server came back and told me that they'd decided to order a bottle of wine but sent it back.

I asked, "Was it a bergamot issue?"

The server told me, "No, it had a screw top. They said that they don't drink screw top wines because they're cheap."

I said, "Them, or the wine? A twenty-dollar bottle of Pinot Grigio, and they're worried about the screw-top cheapening the wine?"

"That's what they said."

I asked, "What do they want instead?"

She answered, "They didn't see anything else in their price range, so they decided to pass."

I can't say I was shocked.

Our lobster special had a choice of three preparations: steamed, butter poached, or a sushi roll. The group ordered one sushi roll, one butter poached, and two steamed. Three came back. These things always start the same way, slowly, and then they build into frenzy. I think it has to do with the elevated amount of attention that the first complainer gets. It becomes contagious and spreads to the rest of the table. Funny—no one is allergic to attention.

The server brought the first one back and said, "Um, he can't eat the lobster sushi roll—and you're going to love this—because it has rice in it."

I said, "He can't eat the *sushi* roll because the *sushi* roll has *rice* in it? You're shitting me, right?"

She said, "Nope, sorry. He wants the butter poached."

I said, "Could you please explain to Nostradamus that he needs to prepare himself because there's going to be butter in the butter poached lobster. Just so we're clear."

She said, "I'll let him know."

Two minutes later, she came back with the second lobster, one of the butter poached ones that had gone out.

I asked, "What is it now?"

Jenna told me, "She says there's no way that this is a one-and-a-half-pound lobster."

I can't tell you how many times this happens. Again, I find myself saying, "Once a one-and-a-half-pound lobster is removed from the shell, it doesn't weigh one and a half pounds anymore. What's so hard to understand?"

I told Jenna, "If she wants all one and a half pounds, then she'll have to have the steamed one."

Three minutes later, Jenna came back and said, "All right, she'll have the steamed," holding the third lobster in her hand.

I asked, "What is wrong with that one?"

She said, "You'd better sit down. There are two problems with this one. The first problem is that it seems she's allergic to Mrs. Dash and because she forgot to mention it earlier, she's afraid there may have been some use of Mrs. Dash in the steaming process. But that's really a moot point because she said her lobster's burned."

I thought my head would explode.

I asked, "What the hell is Mrs. Dash and how can you burn a lobster in boiling water?"

Jenna told me, "Mrs. Dash is some kind of seasoning mix, and I know nothing about cooking lobsters." She placed the lobster plate down in front of me and pointed to a black mark on the lobster's claw, which is completely natural and very common, and said, "She pointed to this black mark and said that her lobster was burned, and she isn't going to eat it."

We looked at each other, started laughing and said, simultaneously, "Mrs. Dash?"

Have you ever longed for an early death?

HEY T., PHONE HOME

Ever notice that there are acute similarities between politics and the restaurant business? The more you think about it, the more examples come to mind. Here's what I mean. We in the restaurant business are in the business of feeding people for money. We put out signs, take out ads, give out coupons and beg on the social media sites to get folks into our restaurants so we can feed them, charge them for the service, and hopefully make some money. It rarely works out. Politicians are also in the business of feeding people for money. They put up signs, take out ads, and create programs. They give out stamps and vouchers so people can eat, vote for their benefactors, and put them in a position to make a lot of money. It always works out. Restaurant owners have a tendency toward mendacity. Ask any restaurant owner how many dinners he did the night, week, or year before, and there's not a chance he'll tell you the truth. Politicians lie too. In fact, they've made it legal. Did you know that if you lie on the Senate floor, you're good? It has to be the irony of all ironies. With all the bullshit that's thrown around in the Senate no one can be called out for lying. Another thing we have in common is that usually everyone who is in politics has failed at something else first. Washington is the Hall of Fame for incompetent lawyers. The restaurant business is littered with souls who've tried just about every other way to make a living and just couldn't succeed. How about economics? Cite me any other business, profession, or undertaking that spends tenfold more than it takes in. It's only restaurants and government. The difference is that restaurants are held accountable. That's the main reason for the 90 percent failure rate. Politicians get to borrow indefinitely, print money as they need to, tax your ass into compliance, and lie about the losses. That's the main reason for the 90 percent incumbency rate. Flowery prose? Communication is just one more thing that we have in common. We get to say things like, *"Line caught yellow fin tuna, with first of the season ramps, tiny marble potatoes, organically grown heirloom tomatoes, pickled mustard seeds, and pureed seaweed, gathered by a guy with locally made waders who happens to live right down the block,"* on our menus. Politicians are wordsmiths also and can push the bounds of meaningful elocution at the drop of a television camera, but when it comes to naming a military shenanigan, they're at their best! Early on, in previous wars, we had simple code names like—and this is true—Operation

Larry. I'm assuming it was named after the guy who incited the mischief, so they knew whom to blame when the whole thing went sideways. Then they later decided to be more colorful and fun—you know, to kind of make light of what was really happening so we wouldn't have to think about it—and we were given Operation Slapstick. I kid you not. I'm not sure if that name was because of the folly of the mission or if they happened to squeeze in Operation Moe and Operation Curly between the two incursions. It's hard to keep up with the adventures. But now we have names like Operation Enduring Freedom, Operation Inherent Resolve, and Operation Productive Effort. Admittedly, the last one's a knee-slapper but who can't get behind names like that? If you had names like Operation Let's Bomb the Shit out of The Iraqis, Operation We're Going to Blow You Bastards to Smithereens, or Operation Let's Fuck Up the Entire Middle East, it might just make for a more sobering discussion and maybe a little less intervention. I'm just saying.

Now that we're clear on that, I'll show you why communication isn't all it's cracked up to be. Other than a new tax or regulation every twenty minutes or so, political correctness is one of the biggest problems for anyone in business today. Do you know that you are not allowed to yell at, reprimand, correct, or dismiss an employee without eight previous written warnings, five witnesses, a sensitivity training class diploma, and legal counsel? Think I'm kidding? Try it—I dare you. When you've been giving blue ribbons for coming in ninth and have replaced reading, writing, and arithmetic with self-esteem, you've pretty much finished off a generation. God forbid you correct or reprimand anyone who has been told that they're perfect their entire life. I promise you that by the end of this story, you'll be convinced that I'm lying but like I've often said before, you can't make this stuff up.

We had a woman in her mid-twenties apply for a hostess position. She had a graduate degree in whatever subject that made it impossible for her to get a job, so she landed at our front desk. The hostess position is harder to fill than it would appear because it requires one to be able to answer the phone, say hello, take a message or reservation, escort the guests to their table, and spell the word *food*. You may be asking yourself, *"What's so hard about that?"* And had I not had so much trouble finding someone with that skill set I might agree with you. The saying *"Needle in a haystack"* comes to mind, and just like finding a needle in a haystack, you need to keep sifting the hay through your fingers until the needle is stuck in your palm. It's a painful process and so is finding a hostess. We thought we had one, with a graduate degree and everything, and we trained her for several days and then gave her a schedule. She was doing an adequate job for about a week or so and then for whatever reason she began to stumble. The messages she took were illegible, phone numbers were wrong, reservations were getting screwed up, and there was a general air of incompetence at the desk. I was crushed. She had so much unrealized potential so we were trying to hang with her hoping she would improve because the devil you know is better than the devil you don't, right?

One day after lunch, I was coming up from the office downstairs and into the dining room when I heard the phone ring. When it's your business you tend to be much more aware of your surroundings than your employees are. I see napkins on the floor, dust in the vents, crumbs on the carpet, wrinkles in the uniform, and I hear ringing phones. Most of my employees do not. I've often said that if I left one of my restaurants for a two-week vacation and turned all the artwork upside down, it would be in the exact same position upon my return. It's just the way it is. I honestly don't mind picking up a cocktail napkin or whatever from the floor, straightening a chair or tablecloth, or adjusting the lights or the music but I'm bewildered by the fact that very few of my employees share my concerns. That said, the one thing that absolutely chafes me is when the phone rings more than three or four times, and no one answers it. It drives me nuts. I heard it as I entered the dining room. Once … twice … three times … I looked at the front desk and saw no one there. We have about seventy-five employees and granted they don't all work on the same shift, but you would think that one of them would pick up the phone. You would be wrong.

I ran to the desk. When I got there, I picked up the phone and gasped into the receiver, "Jewel, can I help you?"

The man didn't acknowledge me and simply asked, "Do you have anything on your menu without garlic?"

I answered, "We do."

He asked, "Are you sure?"

Tongue in cheek, I answered, "Reasonably sure, yes."

He asked again, "Are you positive? Because I have friends who are highly allergic to garlic and if you don't have anything on your menu without garlic we can't come there."

Forgive me, but I'm a bit cynical on the, *"I'm allergic,"* bit because so many people use it instead of, *"I don't like it,"* and although I guess there could be a few unfortunate souls who are allergic to garlic I don't imagine it could possibly rise to the level of peanut or shellfish allergies. In the fifty plus years I've been in this business I haven't heard of one throat closing, hospitalization, or spontaneous death caused by the ingestion of garlic. If garlic was dangerous, Emeril Lagasse would be on death row. And what restaurant has he, or anyone for that matter, ever been in where every item had garlic in it?

Again, I reassured him, "We have plenty of items without garlic."

He hung up and I turned my attention to the hostess coming out of the ladies' room. I said, "Could you please get someone to cover you when you're away from the desk?"

She assured me she would. My skepticism was based on experience.

I went to the office, explained to Diane what had happened and said, "If you want to save me countless dollars in therapy bills could you please tell Brenda to take the phone with her when she leaves the desk? It's perfectly okay to go to the ladies' room but take the phone. Go have a break and a cup of coffee but take the phone. She can go to the mall for all I care—just take the phone!"

Diane asked, "I'm assuming you want that word for word?"

I said, "Whatever, but I don't want the phone going unanswered. This shit isn't that hard."

Sometimes Diane will, *"yes,"* me to death and use discretion when relaying my messages and it's probably for the better, but I knew she relayed this one verbatim and here's why.

Two days later I was sitting in the office and Brenda came in with the phone in her hand. Not the cordless phone—the real phone. Yup, it was detached from the wire, with all the switches and buttons, sitting there in her hands.

Thinking it was broken or there was some other problem, I asked, "What's with the phone?"

She asked me, "What do you mean?"

I said, "The phone. What's wrong with the phone?"

She replied, "There's nothing wrong with it, why?"

"Then why did you bring it down here?"

With considerable attitude, she said, "Diane told me that you said that I have to take it with me whenever I leave the front desk."

It took a moment to process. I placed an elbow on each knee, lowered my head, and said, "Can I ask you a question?"

"What?"

I asked, "Has it been ringing?

She said, "No, it's been a little quiet."

I said, "Hmm, yeah. It's probably the time of year."

She asked Diane whatever it was she needed to ask her and went back upstairs to the front desk, and I'm assuming she plugged it back in because it started ringing again. Diane and I looked at each other and cracked up.

When I could finally speak, I asked her, "What college would give her a master's degree?"

Diane answered, "Maybe her father donated a wing?"

Laughing, I said, "And what could she have possibly been studying?"

Diane suggested, "Communications?"

WINE-KNOW

I had a party of six in Jewel one night several months ago. Four were normal, one was the designated driver, and one was the self-anointed wine expert. I can't tell you how many of these Saturday night wine wizards I've experienced in my years doing this because I've misplaced my abacus. Suffice it to say there have been many and I want you to be aware that I'm not roaming the restaurant looking for a fight. For some reason the people who know the least about wine are the loudest with their opinions. Ignorance begs silence, education, and an occasional question pertaining to the subject at hand, not condescension, pontification, and blather. I know a lot of people with a lot of wine knowledge and experience, and I've never seen one of them cop an attitude with a server or a sommelier. If you know the material there's no need, and if your palate is educated you can always find something to drink, even if its beer.

I was standing by the bar yapping with a friend when the wine expert came up to me and asked, "Are you Tom?"

I replied, "Yes, what can I do for you?"

He said, "My friends and I are having dinner here and I'm enjoying it very much, but I have to tell you one thing: your wine list sucks."

I said, "Yeah, and your mother's fat."

He stared for a moment, then we both started to laugh.

I said, "It sucks? Sucks?? There are almost over four hundred selections there and it sucks? What are you looking for?"

He responded, "It's all that Long Island garbage. I can't drink that stuff. It's terrible."

I asked, "What's your name?"

He said—and I'm not kidding— "Dick. Dick So-and-So."

A question: who takes the name Richard, shortens it into the word for male genitalia and proudly admits to being one? I hope he didn't marry Connie.

I then said, "Okay, Dick, when was the last time you drank Long Island wine?"

He said, "I've had them. Probably fifteen years ago. I hated them. They can't make wine out there."

I said, "Different game now, dude. That was a long time ago. What do you usually drink?"

This is the key question if you want to find out who you are dealing with. A real wine person will tell you the grapes they like; the faux wino drops a name.

And just as I suspected, he said, "Screaming Eagle."

Screaming Eagle is a cult wine from the Napa Valley that has a small case production and commands up to three thousand dollars a bottle. The allotment for all of New York is a few cases. Trust me; No one *usually* drinks Screaming Eagle.

I said, "Okay, spare me the Screaming Eagle speech; I've heard it. And please leave out Harlan and Dalla Valle; I've heard them also. You like California Cabs? I have many. Pick one. You want a big Cab like you're used to? I happen to have a 2003 Abreu, Madrona Ranch. It's eight hundred dollars. Shall I bring it over?"

He said, "Uh, well, um, I … I don't know if the others will like it. Um, let me check with them."

I said, "Just for the record, I taste roughly five hundred wines a year and have been doing so for about forty years. Do you really want to talk wine with me or put your palate up against mine?"

He said, "Well, no, but you know, well … Okay, um, pick me a California Cab that you think is nice for about fifty dollars, and we'll drink that."

I said, "Okay, I'll be happy to do that for you."

He went back to his table, I picked him out a nice juicy fruit Cab and both of us were happy. The whole bit could have been avoided if he'd been a little more polite in his approach. I might have hurt his feelings just a bit, but he also hurt mine. I like to think he learned something, but I suspect he'll find a way to make an ass of himself at some point in the future. Those guys usually do.

GOLF BALLS RATED R

Golf is life. It really is. I think the reason for its popularity is that every human emotion is experienced playing a round of golf, squeezed into eighteen holes, over a period of four hours. It's the quintessential emotional roller coaster. Years ago, whenever I had to do any kind of business deal with someone I didn't know well, I would either take them out and get them drunk or take them golfing. The same person shows up to either show. Neither endeavor changes who you are; it simply brings out the real you. If you have a penchant for lying, cheating, stealing, or profanity, just like when you're drinking, somewhere in those eighteen holes it's going to show up. Golf brings it out of you, I swear, and these are good things to know about a prospective business partner. On the other hand, I've had some of the most fun in my life and some of the hardest laughs on the golf course. The combination of the fact that almost no one is good at the game, the ability of the mind to comprehend that fact and try to remedy the situation, the cognitive reality of the hopelessness, and the ultimate resignation, make for some extremely funny moments, mostly at the expense of your playing partner.

Years ago, I had a customer I'll call *Jimmy*. I met Jimmy one evening when he barged into my kitchen and yelled, "Where's the chef?" He went on to critique his entire meal in the middle of service. I looked over to see this guy who appeared as though he'd just stepped out of central casting for The Sopranos. In all the years I knew him, and with all the time we'd spent together, I was never really sure whether or not he was a gangster, and I suspect not, but he played the part to a tee. He had the clothes, jewelry, lingo, and attitude down pat, but he also had a redeeming, self-deprecating humor that kept him from being an insufferable ass. And I believe that the only *contracts* he'd ever executed were on the English language. Those two qualities kept me laughing for nearly fifteen years. I could tell hundreds of Jimmy stories but this one is a classic. It's not for the fainthearted or the hypersensitive but it's a classic, nonetheless. Be forewarned.

As I came to know Jimmy, he decided to take up golf. He had zero patience, very little time and even less talent. He asked me to teach him, and I took him to the range a few times, but it was hopeless.

One day, after taking seventeen swings at the ball without once hitting it, he said, "Okay, I know I'm not an *"attalete, (his pronunciation of athlete)* but what the fuck am I doing wrong?"

I answered, "You're not hitting it."

Jimmy said, "What are you, some kind of smart-ass? A comedian or something? You think you're funny? I don't think you're funny. There are a thousand golf teachers on Long Island, and I wind up with *"Shacky"* Green."

I said, "I think that's Shecky."

"What?"

"It's Shecky Green, not Shacky."

Jimmy said, "Now you're an English teacher? I don't give a fuck if it's Smucky. Knock it off with the funny shit and teach me how to hit this fucking ball!"

I said, "All right. Adjust your feet. Loosen your grip and turn your right-hand in. Take it back slowly and not as far this time either. Then swing through the ball and finish high."

You had to see it. He swung four or five more times before he finally shanked one off to the right.

I told him, "Look at what a quick study you are."

Jimmy looked at me for a minute and then finally said, "This ain't *woiking* out too good. I gotta get a real teacher because I can see this is going to impinge on our friendship. I need to see a professional for two reasons. One, because you obviously suck as a teacher and two, because you will be deceased by the end of the day if I hear one more crack outta you."

Thankfully, Jimmy got to a professional and I'm still here. About a year went by and Jimmy became the ultimate golf nut. Every time he would come for dinner, he would fill me in on his game, hole by bloody hole. He was taking major golf vacations with his buddies playing all over the country. The only problem was that he had yet to break 120.

He told me, "We gotta play, you and me and two of my crew, Sal and Johnny. I'll set it up."

I asked him, "How's your game?"

He said, "It's getting better. I finally broke 120, but I'm losing about two thousand dollars a week."

I asked, "You're what?"

He told me, "Yeah, two large a week playing this stupid fucking game."

"Jimmy, you need to either change your playing partners or get better … fast."

He looked at me and said, "That's where you come in. I got a match set up with you and me against Johnny and Sal. I told them that you were a fifteen handicap, so we'll kick their fucking asses and I get my money back."

I said, "You got this all figured out, huh? What happens when they find out I'm not a fifteen? Do I go into the Witness Protection Program? I'm not doing it."

He said, "You gotta do it. I got it set up already."

I responded, "No, it ain't happening. I don't play golf for money, especially with people I'm afraid of."

He laughed and said, "You watch too many movies. Nothing's going to happen. Just be there on Wednesday."

I told him, "I'll come on Wednesday, but I'm not playing for money."

That Wednesday I showed up at the club and I could tell Jimmy was anxious.

He came running up to me and asked, "How's your game? You been playing okay? You feeling good? Get any sleep last night?"

I asked him, "What does it matter? I'm not playing for money, remember?"

Jimmy says, "I know, I know. I'm just concerned about your emotional well-being. You playin' okay?"

I answered, "My emotions are fine; it's my game that sucks."

Panic set in, and Jimmy said, "Your game sucks? Whadda you mean, your game sucks?"

I told him, "It's my driver. It's killing me. I'm not hitting it very well. I'm thinking about getting a new one."

His eyes lit up. "A new driver? What kind of driver?"

I said, "I don't know. I'm leaning toward the new Ping, but I've got to hit a few before I decide."

He said, "Yeah, I heard the Ping is great."

Jimmy then went to the clubhouse, and I went to the putting green. Fifteen minutes later he showed up with a brand-new Ping driver and handed it to me.

I asked, "What's with the driver?"

He said, "It's a gift from me to you. It's for all the great meals you made me."

I said, "Jimmy, you're full of shit. How much money is on the line here today? I'm not taking this. And besides, it's the wrong loft and the wrong shaft. I'll be popping up drives all day with this thing. And I'm not playing for money."

With a hurt look in his eyes, he told me, "I can't believe you *dink* I have a *nefaranus* motive. *Dat* was a gift from my heart."

I said, "That was a gift from your wallet, and I'm not playing for money."

Exasperated, he said, "Okay, okay, you ain't playin' for money. Then let me *axe* you a question, Mr. Goody Two-Shoes. Can you play for pride? You got any of *dat*?"

I told him, "Jimmy, golf's always about pride. It's what makes it so painful when you play shitty."

Jimmy said, "Yeah. But you ain't gonna play shitty today, right?"

"I have no idea."

"Listen to me! That fucking guy Johnny thinks who da fuck he is. I need you—excuse me; it would be wonderful for me to see you beat his ass, for me, this one time, here, today. Capice?"

I said, "Yeah, Jimmy, I capice."

We drove up to the first tee box, and after he introduced me to Sal and Johnny, the negotiations started.

"Okay, it's a five-hundred-dollar Nassau, automatic presses, fifty dollars for junk including sandies, boidies, greenies, and barkies. One hundred dollars for an offshore, and two hundred for a Super Storm Sandy."

We needed an attorney.

I've been playing golf since I was five and have never heard anything quite like it. Yeah, sandies, birdies, and greenies, but barkies, offshores, and Super Storm Sandys? I had to ask.

In my politest tone, I asked them, "What's a barkie?"

Jimmy told me, "It's when you hit a tree and still make a par."

I say, "Oh, and that's happened to you?"

He said, "No, not yet, but it could."

"And what are an offshore and a Super Storm Sandy, pray tell?"

He told me, "An offshore is when you sink a shot from off the green, and a Super Storm Sandy is when you make a par from a sand trap that's not even on your fucking hole."

I said, "I can't believe I'm doing this. What about an eagle? What does an eagle pay?"

Jimmy said, "A quarter."

I say, "A quarter for an eagle? A quarter?"

In his best sarcastic tone, Jimmy said, "Yeah, a quarter. You're the only one here capable of making an eagle and you only play for the purity of the game. I wouldn't want to upset you by making you take any money. You can use it as a ball marker."

We all teed off. There were only two things Jimmy ever talked about and they were sex and money. So, there we were walking down the fairway with Jimmy yapping about some conquest or another, keeping Sal and Johnny thoroughly amused. I was mortified and tried to let the caddies know that this wasn't my regular group. Don't get me wrong; I loved Jimmy, but he didn't have a filter and could be brutal in mixed company … hilarious, but brutal. There must have been a lot of money riding on the match because whenever I hit a poor shot, and it happens relatively often, he would run over and ask if I was all right, did I need water or a beer, a new iron perhaps, or grips. Sal and Johnny weren't very good players so I'm sure Jimmy's match was never much in doubt, but I wasn't aware of the bet, the amount, or the number of strokes that were spotted. Occasionally I would hit a terrible shot on purpose just to drive him nuts and watch him react. I think it was on the fifteenth or sixteenth hole when I deliberately ran a putt about twenty feet past the hole.

Jimmy looked at me and said, "What *da* fuck? What *da* fuck was *dat*? You want my glasses? You ran *dat ding twenty-tree* feet past the fucking hole. What da fuck? You got no fucking deception, my friend!"

He meant depth perception but couldn't quite come up with it. I thought he just blew the phrase out of frustration until I heard it the second time.

As I was standing over the comeback putt he turned to Johnny and Sal and quietly said, "Did you see *dat* putt? What da fuck? I think he's got a deception problem."

Have you ever tried to make a *twenty-tree* footer with tears in your eyes?

As we got back in the cart, Jimmy said to me, "You know, you should have your deception checked. *Dat* was one fucked up putt."

Still laughing, I said, "I'll look into it."

He thought I was laughing at the putt. We finished the round, and Jimmy must have made a lot of money because he was nearly making out with me when it was over.

He said, "Hey, Goody Two-Shoes, you want half?"

I said, "No, I was serious. I have no interest in playing for money."

Jimmy, reveling in victory, said, "Okay, then let me buy you dinner."

I told him, "That's fine, let's go. But we can't go to an Italian restaurant."

Jimmy asked, "Why not?"

I replied, "Because every time one of you guys gets it, you're staring down at a plate of spaghetti. I'm not risking it. How about sushi?"

He said, "How about you're an idiot. I told you, you watch too many movies."

That night Jimmy and I walked into the restaurant, and he was a sight to behold. His outfit was a cross between RuPaul and Liberace. He was a vision in maroon, light on the top and darker on the bottom with enough gold chains to record a rap CD. Johnny met us there and Jimmy had called and invited his then current girlfriend and a friend of hers to join us. It didn't take long. Jimmy, in an Irish whisper, started telling a story about throwing a bachelor party for his friend, Louie the Meat Guy, in the private room of a club in Florida. I've heard Jimmy's stories before, and he rarely holds back. That, combined with his inability to be discreet has made for some embarrassing moments for me over the course of our relationship.

Holding court at the table, he announced, "I gotta tell you what happened at Louie's bachelor party in Florida. You'll piss yourselves."

I looked around for the exits.

He continued. "I decided to *trow* Louie a bachelor party, 'cause he was getting married and I hired *deese* two broads to dance."

I was thinking as I sank farther down in my seat, "*Oh my God, this is not going to go well.*"

Jimmy plowed on. "So, *da* broads are dancing but *day* ain't really doing anything, so I *sez ta dem,* "Hey, *dis* is a bachelor party for a guy we all have a tremendous amount of respect for. *Youze* two gotta do something here. There's a couple large in it for both a *yiz,* but *yiz* gotta do something special for Louie. Could *yiz* make out or something? Something, anything. He's getting married over here."

By this point, I knew we weren't the only table with a ringside seat to Louie's bachelor party. As I looked around the dining room there were two camps: one that couldn't wait to hear what happened next and one that couldn't believe their ears. Jimmy was on a roll, and I feared the worst.

Jimmy said, "So *da* two broads started goin' at it and Louie gets himself so excited, and thinking they're pros, he drops his pants and what do *youze* think he's got?"

I was looking around the table to see if anyone else was horrified. They weren't.

The other woman said, "Tighty-whiteys?"

Jimmy said, "Nope," and to his girlfriend he asked, "Jen, you want to guess?"

She said, "I don't know. Just tell us."

Jimmy said, "Johnny, what do you *dink* he had? C'mon, Johnny. Whatta you *dink*?"

Laughing, Johnny said, "*Underwears* with hearts on 'em?"

Jimmy was howling by this point. "Nope. Hey, Goody Two-Shoes, you wanna take a shot at it?"

I didn't know what to do. Frankly, I wanted to run from the building screaming, with my fingers in my ears, but ridiculous situations require ridiculous participation.

I said, "A vagina?"

There was a moment of dead silence, and then everyone but Jimmy completely lost it.

He glared at me and said, "No, you idiot. Louie's a guy."

I thought that would be the funniest thing I would hear that night, maybe even in my life.

I was wrong. Jimmy shook his head disapprovingly at me, turned to the rest of the table, started to giggle uncontrollably and then issued the showstopper. "He had cow balls!"

At first, I wasn't sure I heard him correctly and I asked, "What?"

Jimmy, starting to lose it now, spat out, "Cow ... ha-ha ... balls. He's got balls like a cow!"

I looked around the table to see if anyone else got it. It was immediately apparent that I was the only one who knew that a cow was a ... she.

Desperately trying not to laugh, I said, "Jimmy, I think it's a bull."

Jimmy looked over and said, "Hey, it ain't bull, okay? I saw it with my own two eyes. He's got balls like a cow!"

Have you ever laughed so hard that had to hop repeatedly from one foot to the other? And no one else at the table got it which made it twice as funny, if that's possible. It was nearly an hour before I could compose myself. I spent the majority of that time in the men's room. When I could finally go back to the table, dinner was already there. I ate as fast as I could, excused myself, and laughed all the way home.

Two days later I went to work and when I got there, the manager told me someone had left something for me, and she had put it in the office. It was a brand-new Ping driver with the wrong shaft and the wrong loft. It was obviously from Jimmy. I popped twelve drives straight up in the air with it and retired it to the driver graveyard in my garage ... across from the putters.

The note on it said, *"Hey Goody Two-Shoes, thank you for a profitable day and all the laughs."* No, thank *you*, Jimmy.

Sadly, Jimmy has left us, but the club is still sitting there. I cherish it.

THERE'S MORE THAN ONE WAY TO SKIM A COW

I've learned that there's a direct relationship between stealing and shame, provided you're capable of the latter, where the one keeps you from exploring the fruits of the other. Getting caught and the resultant embarrassment is what removes the temptation of grabbing somebody else's stuff—for most of us. But for there to be a majority there must be a minority and it's that minority that is able to circumvent the emotion or is not able to process the requisite shame. I once had an employee who used to brag about her ability to steal things and her ability to deny her way out of getting caught. Not to me of course, but to the other employees, who eventually snitched. Her two greatest heists, according to my employees, were an extra turkey in a Shop Rite Supermarket at Thanksgiving and a blouse from Macy's. Maybe the five-finger discount on the blouse was too tempting to pass up, but boosting a bird does not make you Bonnie Parker, and admitting it makes you look even more foolish than taking it. Can you picture the family gathered around the Thanksgiving table, heads bowed in prayer and her saying the following? *"Thank you, God, for bringing our family together today, and for this beautiful banquet, some of which we stole and some of which we reluctantly paid for, because even though the blouse was a size sixteen, I couldn't get the second bird, me, and all the vegetables under there without security noticing. Amen."*

If I'm going down for stealing, it isn't gonna be poultry. Steal big, steal millions. I wouldn't do it, but I certainly understand it. Selling your character for a turkey gives one all the insight one needs to know about the individual. And wouldn't you know it,

I wound up firing her for … yup, stealing. The grand total was about twenty-four hundred dollars plus untold quarts of cheap rye. The crew and I have had at least twenty-four hundred dollars' worth of laughs at her expense since then, so I guess we're even. The rye is on me.

That said, one of the most fun things to witness is to watch someone whose inherent thrift will not allow him or her to pay the proverbial going rate for a product or service. The sweating, labored respiration, and clammy palms are the telltale signals to keep an eye peeled for the impending larceny. Where this comes from, I'm not sure but the lengths some people will go to save a relatively paltry sum is hilarious. A case in point: we have a South Asian fellow who frequents one of the restaurants on a regular basis. I'm not sure what country he's from, not that it matters all that much, but I'm guessing Pakistan. That guess is because, as I have described in a previous tale, the accent makes me giggle. I'm sure it's the *wee's* and the *wubble-u's* that seal it for me, but I turn into a giggling child as soon as I hear more than three words inflected like that. Armed with that knowledge, I feel compelled to warn any of you who happen to be hypersensitive, a dyed in the wool political correctness freak, an immigration grievance monger, any number of Hollywood types, or a guilt-ridden elite, that what you're about to read may just rankle your ass. I apologize in advance, kind of.

This gentleman came in one night with his wife and child and sat down to have dinner. As the server came over to take a drink order, he said to her, "Bardon mee, my vife and mee vood werry much like doo have doo cups dee."

The server asked, "Would you like flavored tea or plain?"

The man said, "Vee vood much like doo brefer blain dee. And vee vould like werry much, doo mealk. Tank you."

The server replied, "Okay, two teas with two pitchers of milk. I'll be right back."

It all seemed innocent enough but then a curious thing happened. We started to hemorrhage milk.

No one knew it at first. It just started with the request for an extra cruet, but then he asked the busboy, "Bardon me, vood yoo bring vun more mealk?"

The busboy said, "Chure, I bring eet right ober to chu."

As the hostess went by some time later, he asked her, "Bardon me, ven you get chance, vood yoo tell vaitresss doo bring vun mealk here?"

The hostess replied, "Sure, I'll have her bring it right over."

I'm not sure how many cruets of milk he had that night, but it was over six.

No one had a handle on it until after he left, when one of the busboys said, "Holy chit. Dat mang drinky lotta milk. I bringy fy time."

The waitress heard him and said, "I brought him two pitchers myself."

The hostess chimed in, "I brought him one also."

As they were talking, Diane overheard them and said, "I've waited on him before, and he always drinks tea with extra milk."

The others were telling her just how much extra milk he had asked for, but they couldn't think of what he could be doing with it because he only had a cup or two of tea. They all eventually gave a shrug of the shoulders and put it off to quirkiness, which as you might have guessed by now is a common affliction. Fast-forward three weeks, and our South Asian friend returns with his wife and son. They sit down for dinner, and Diane goes to the table to wait on them.

Diane said, "Can I get you something from the bar?"

The man replied, "No, my vife and mee vood like doo cups dee, vit doo pitcher mealk."

Diane, noting the amount of milk they went through the last time, asked, "Would you like me to bring you a glass of milk?"

The man asked, "Ow much cost dee mealk?"

Diane, "Three seventy-five."

The man, "Three sewundy five? Dat is a robbery of dee hy-vay. No, I take doo pitcher. Vy doo I buy glass ven pitcher come free? I take doo pitcher."

Diane brought him the tea and the two cruets of milk and went about her business.

The man flagged down a busboy five minutes later and asked, "Sir, vood yoo get for mee doo more mealk?"

The busboy said, "Chure, I getty ri now," and brought it to him. He told the hostess, "Dat crazy mang hoo drink all di leche ees ober dere ageng. He asky me for more ri now."

The hostess said, "It's okay, just get it for him."

This went on for a while and I believe it was the third request that sent the busboy into a tailspin because he went to Diane and said, "Okay, dat mang on table teng, he yust asky me for leche ageng. Three tines to-nigh he asky me for di leche. I berry beesey. I gonna tell hing I gonna chub the leche upa heese culu. I gonna tell hing!"

Diane, laughing, said, "Stay away from the table, and no *chubbing*. What the hell is he doing with all that milk?"

The busboy, "I no know. Nex tine he aks me, I tell hing I no hab no more, or I going to chub it upa his ass."

As Diane decided to investigate, he called her over yet again and said, "I vood like vun more pitcher milk."

Diane went to get it, served it, and then watched from around the corner as the man and his son shared the milk, shamelessly drinking from the pitcher. Then she exploded in a fit of uncontrollable laughter. Got milk?

◈

EMPLOYEES

I f you've ever spent any amount of time as a boss or supervisor, or even worse, in your own business, you will have undoubtedly had the pleasure, or displeasure, to deal with employees. No other group of disparate souls can conjure up such celebrated optimism or such heart-wrenching disappointment. This stems from the fact that people must work in order to support themselves and their families, but not everyone is thrilled about it. As we all know, people are different. They have different thoughts and needs, and these differences, when applied to the work ethic, are what lead to such a wide range of results. For years, politicians have been trying to legislate equality, an amusing endeavor at best. In their zeal to sell fairness for votes, they ignore the simple truths that some people are ambitious, and some are lazy, some are motivated and some smoke weed, some are intelligent, and some are less so, some are sober, and some are more fun to hang with, some are open to learning and have an innate sense of humility, and some are Yankee fans. This, *diversity*, to borrow the era's most overwrought, overthought expression, is the culprit that ultimately dooms the scheme—the proverbial turd in the political punchbowl, if you will, that leads to a parade of tortured souls marching into all the newly minted human resource departments to air grievances both genuine and conjured up. New laws designed to protect workers from the wrath of management has resulted in inmate-run asylums and all manner of employee hijinks. You can't reprimand, raise your voice, utter a disparaging comment, swear, dock, punish, or fire a clueless employee, without said employee morphing into F. Lee Bailey. No one knows their job, but everyone knows their rights. I've recently been instructed on my legal obligation to quietly and politely suffer the offenses and that I have no legal standing on employee behavioral issues without two verbal warnings, three formal write-ups, a copy of the employee rights poster, and access to a legal defense fund. Very well, but I *can* write about them

BAIT AND SWITCH

In the early nineties, I was traveling to Miami on a somewhat frequent basis. My purpose for going was twofold. I love the Blue Monster golf course at the Doral Resort and there was a burgeoning food movement going on that they dubbed, *Floribbean Cuisine,* that I found to be interesting as hell. Also, the weather doesn't suck. I would fly down and golf myself silly all day, hit the hottest restaurants at night, and rinse and repeat for three or four days. It was great fun and very inspirational, and I got to know and befriend several of the cutting-edge chefs who were at the forefront of the movement. They were taking techniques and ingredients from the Caribbean, Africa, and South Florida, and creating this New World cuisine. It was a very exciting time to be down there. One night I decided to go to the newest, *it,* restaurant. It was up in Fort Lauderdale, so it was going to be a bit of a hike from Doral, but he was a hot chef at the time and I had eaten in his other restaurant in Miami and loved it. My friend and I made the drive and arrived at about 7:00 p.m. The joint was jumping, as they say, so we had a bit of a wait for our table. The hostess was very nice and apologized profusely that we would probably have to wait an extra half hour for our reserved table. I'm never bothered by waiting even when I have a table reserved. I like being in restaurants, period. If I have to wait an extra hour or some part of it, I see it as an opportunity to have a glass of wine at the bar, do some people watching, and yap with the bartenders, other customers, my friends, or my date. It's just not that important to me what time I sit. I'm always amused by people who completely melt down if their table isn't ready the second they announce their arrival. Aren't you in the company of someone you like? Talk to them and enjoy being with them. Isn't that why you came? Is all the angst and drama necessary for a fifteen-minute wait? I can think of much better things to fret about. Relax, suck down a big white Burgundy, and appreciate the fact that yours is a luxury problem. Also, when a restaurant is busy, like Saturday night on Long Island, can we all be just a little bit happy for the owner before we start negotiating compensation for the chagrin? It means he's doing well and may just be able to stay in business long enough for your next visit. Cut him some slack.

So, there I was, slack cutting at the bar on my second big white, Burgundy when the hostess came up and said, "Sir, your table is ready."

We thanked her, settled the bar bill, and headed for our table. I'm always excited going to a new restaurant and I'm always on high alert, watching the help interact, reading the menu and wine list, and checking out the décor. It's the combination of the prospect of eating something cool and picking up tips on plating, specialty drinks, service techniques, and more, that I find so irresistible.

The waiter approached the table and said, "Hi, guys. I'm John, and I'll be your waiter this evening."

Pass me the pistol.

Did he think we wouldn't know? I'll never, for the life of me, understand why people train their help to say that, and the, *"guys,"* thing is so wrong on so many levels. Maybe I'm a bit presumptuous, but I presume that anyone standing at my table wearing an apron, having a pen and paper in hand, and asking me if I would like something to drink has a better than even chance of being my waiter.

I replied, "Good evening, John."

He continued. "Can I get you anything from the bar? We have great specialty cocktails; you may want to try one."

I said, "You know what, John—can I call you John? I think I'd like to look at the wine list."

He said, "Of course, I'll bring it right over."

I ordered the wine. He brought it out, opened and poured it, and, after reciting a litany of dinner specials, proceeded to take our dinner order. I confess to being a foie gras freak. If any of you object to eating it for whatever reason, that's fine and certainly your prerogative. It just means that there's more available for those of us who love it. I even have a foie gras tattoo, maybe the only one in the world, to show the depth of my affection for the product. I've been known to order three of four foie gras courses at the same meal, to the amusement of more than one dinner date. This was the case that particular evening.

Our waiter, John, took my friend's dinner order and then turned to me and asked, "And you, sir?"

I said, "I'll have the foie appetizer with the orange-scented French toast and for my entrée, I want the tuna with foie gras, mushroom risotto, and the Madeira-flavored demi," which was how it read on the menu.

John said, "You must really like foie gras."

I replied, "You have no idea."

The apps came out and the foie gras was exemplary. I loved every bite. The problem was with the entrée. When I was served the tuna, I couldn't locate the foie gras. I looked under the tuna, inside the risotto, under the risotto, on my friend's scallop dish, and on the floor, but it was MIA. I called the waiter over. "John, I was under the impression that this tuna was served with foie gras."

John said, "It is, sir."

I then asked, "Okay, then. Where is it?"

He said, "I'm sure it's on the plate, sir. Maybe you just missed it."

I told him, "The plate isn't big enough for the foie to get lost, and I'm very familiar with what it looks like, so maybe you want to point it out to me?"

John looked down at the plate in earnest for a minute or so and then said, "Let me take it back to the kitchen and check what's going on."

I said, "Thank you."

Five minutes later, John returned with the same plate and told me, "Yup, I was right. The chef said that the foie gras is on the tuna," and placed the plate in front of me.

Growing annoyed, I asked him, "Okay, John, where exactly on the tuna is it?"

He explained, "The chef told me that they rub the foie gras on the tuna before they sear it."

I echoed, "They rub the tuna with the foie gras before they sear the tuna on the grill?"

John said, "Yes. That's what the chef told me."

"Just so I'm clear. There's no foie gras on the dish; it was just rubbed on to the tuna?"

John replied, "That's the way the chef told me that they prepare it."

I asked John, "What do they do with the foie gras after they're done massaging the tuna with it?"

Looking puzzled, John repeated, "What do they do with the foie gras after they use it on the tuna?"

I said, "Yes, I'd be tickled to find out. Could you ask the chef for me? I have a potentially huge market up in New York for slightly rubbed foie gras, which I had no idea previously existed. If your chef would be good enough to FedEx it up to me, providing he's not using it for other purposes, I'd be thrilled. Would you be kind enough to pass that on for me?"

John nodded and headed for the kitchen. My friend and I were laughing about it when John returned.

I asked, "So, what did the chef say?"

Sheepishly, John said, "He called me an annoying little pain in the ass and told me he was too busy for silly questions. He said that if you don't like the tuna, to order something else."

I said, "Hmm ... Well, John, I'm fine with the tuna. The annoying part is that it's fifteen dollars higher than any other entrée, reflecting what I assumed to be the *vig* for the foie gras. I think the chef ran out of foie and is being a very bad boy."

John then said to me, "Do you want me to get the manager to adjust your bill?"

I said, "John, I'm in the business. I would never ask you to do anything on my bill. I just may quietly make a judgment about returning based on my experience here. I also want you to know that I realize none of this is your fault, so do whatever you're going to do. As far as you and I are concerned, we're good, and I think you're doing a fine job."

He thanked me and went about tending to his other tables. We wound up finishing dinner and having a little more wine, and John, or maybe his manager, bought a glass for me for my troubles. I was never mad, just bewildered, that the chef who was such a big deal in South Florida at the time didn't just eighty-six the dish. I'd much rather be disappointed that I couldn't get the foie gras than think that the chef thought so little of his clientele that he figured he could bullshit his way through the evening. It made me apathetic about going back or trying any of his subsequent restaurants. And apparently his cynicism caught up with him because I received his resume for a chef's position that I'd advertised for recently. Hmm …

TYPHOON LOON

I have a radio show every Sunday morning between 9:00 and 10:00 on WHLI 1100 AM. It's been on for almost twelve years, and I'm proud to say that we are the second highest rated hour on Long Island, on Sundays, right behind Breakfast with the Beatles. It's a food, wine, and lifestyle show, and we talk about all things related to restaurants, food culture, wine, farmers, fishermen, and the like. You never really run out of material because if you think about it, everyone thinks about food at least three times a day and between the ingredients, wines, restaurants, chefs, markets, seafood, and everything else that swirls around the culture of food, the conversation is endless. There are a couple of things that I've learned, now that I've been doing this for twelve years, that are essential if you are going to do a radio show—three, actually. You can't be shy, you need to have a big mouth, and you must possess the ability to keep it running for sixty minutes. It's harder than it sounds. You also need a producer. I happen to have become very friendly with mine. His name is Stu, and he's a great guy. I've handled the content of the show since its inception, and I believe we've been successful because of it. I know a lot about food, restaurant culture and Long Island, so I believe I'm the most qualified of our team to steer the show. Stu, who had has become my cohost as well, agrees with that assessment, and lets me do my thing as far as the content goes. I've been in my own businesses for forty years, so I'm comfortable calling the shots.

One day, in an effort to contribute to the show, Stu approached me and said, "Hey, Tom, I have someone who I think would be very good on the show. I kind of booked him for two weeks from now, but I told him I have to clear it with you first."

I asked, "Who is it?"

Stu said, "It's the chef who is opening a restaurant in Jericho. I talked to one of the partners, and he told me he would bring him in for the interview."

A little background is called for here. This man is a talented Chinese chef who owns several eponymous restaurants across the globe and, through some lapse of reason, decided to open a satellite branch next to a Mobil station right down the block from Coolfish. I'm pretty secure, and although I'm okay with other restaurants moving into the hood, I usually stop short of paying for their advertising.

Stu asked me, "Do you have a problem having them on the show given that they are your competition and they're right down the block?"

I said, "Well, Stu, I appreciate you asking. I really don't, I guess. How do you know this chef?"

Stu said, "I don't. I met his partner and he said he would bring him on the show so I thought that you could talk chef to chef and might enjoy meeting him."

I said, "Sure, no problem. It sounds like fun, and don't even think about the fact that you are assisting me in helping my competition kick my ass. It's feels like suicide by radio."

He laughed and said, "You'll be fine."

The more I thought about it, the more it appealed to me. I really don't worry much about competition because you can't really do anything about it except to concentrate on your own product and make it the best it can be. Control what you can and let the rest go where it will. I also wanted to know some things about the chef and his background, like how he became an international success, and how he handles the world traveling and the pressure. I have a background in Chinese martial arts so his being from China was of interest to me. I prepped what

I thought was a probing and insightful one-hour interview and was looking forward to meeting this force of nature.

The day of the taping arrived and when I got to the studio, Stu pulled me aside. He said, "We have a problem."

I asked, "What's up?"

He said, "The chef may not be able to make it. He was supposed to be flying in from China this morning but there was a typhoon over there, and they're not sure when the plane is going to land."

I said, "Great. Got any ideas for a show? I didn't prepare for a plan B."

Stu said, "Let's wait a half hour or so. His partner said he'd call when he was sure what was happening."

We waited. About forty-five minutes later, his partner, whom I'll call Steve, called to say they were in the car and were on their way. He estimated his time of arrival at a half hour.

Stu and I were sitting in the studio and chatting when an intern came walking in with the chef and his partner, Steve. The chef was a diminutive fellow with a pleasant smile and a firm handshake and Steve was a classic alpha male. Steve did most of the talking for them. He was good enough to tell me what was going to be discussed, what questions I should ask, the points he wanted to make, and when I could bring him coffee. I'm not very good at following orders and I had an hour's worth of material to discuss with the chef. He was the one I was interested in because he was the talent. The money guy doesn't make for interesting food radio. After the introductions we gave them a brief tutorial on the studio, how to use the microphone and the cough button, what we would talk about, and where the bathrooms were. The chef was typically Chinese, very polite, always smiling, nodding occasionally, and saying very little. Steve was in full interview mode, talking up the new venture and telling me how they were going to redefine Chinese food on Long Island. Ho hum. I hushed everyone for the start of the taping.

Stu does all the engineering and after working his magic with the controls, he said to me, "And we're rolling."

I went into my intro. "Good morning, and welcome to, *Playing with Fire*, Long Island's only food wine and lifestyle show, broadcasting to all the food crazed deviants listening today. I'm your host, Tom Schaudel, and I'm here with the cohost, co-deviant, and producer Stu Schrager. Good morning, Stu."

Stu said, "Good morning, Tom, how are you?"

I answered, "I'm well, thanks, and we have some special guests in the green room today that I'm really excited to have here."

Stu asked, "And who are we speaking of?"

I told him, "We have Chef So-and-So and his partner Steve from the restaurant that just opened here in town. He is a world-renowned chef specializing in contemporary Chinese cuisine, and he's brought his special talents to Long Island."

Stu said, "That's great. I can't wait to meet them. Let's take a quick commercial break, and we'll bring them in."

As the commercial played, we got them set in their chairs and set the levels on their microphones.

As the commercial ended, Stu cut in with, "You're listening to Tom Schaudel and Playing with Fire. Tom's guests today are Chef So-and-So and his partner Steve from So-and-So restaurant."

I said, "Good morning to you both, and thanks for coming."

Steve said, "You're welcome. We're glad to be here."

I turned to the chef and said, "Chef, my interest in cooking started in my grandmother's kitchen when I was five years old. Those sights, sounds, and smells were the seminal moments in a career that has spanned almost sixty years. Was it similar for you in China? Was your family into cooking and being around the table, or did you start on a different path?"

Happy with the content of the question and satisfied with its articulation, I sat back and thought, *"I've got this. I'm a regular Charlie Rose."*

Nothing could have prepared me for his answer.

He looked at me, and at seventy-five decibels said "I coookkkk Chineeesssse foooddddddd!" and smiled at me.

What the fuck?

Realizing that I had fifty-five minutes of airtime to fill with a gentleman who didn't speak English, I looked at Stu and mouthed the words, "We're so screwed."

Stu stopped taping, and I told them all that I had to get a glass of water.

I went out into the hallway with Stu and said, "Um, you don't happen to have anyone on your staff who speaks Mandarin, do you?"

Stu said, "What are you talking about?"

I said, "He doesn't speak English."

"How do you know?"

Starting to laugh, I said, "You were sitting right there. I just asked him a four-part question and he screamed at me that he makes Chinese food. That doesn't make for compelling radio."

By this point, we were both laughing.

Stu then said, "I never spoke to him; I only talked to his partner. It never occurred to me to ask." I said, "Okay, well, you're the producer. I suggest you get back in there and produce."

Stu went back in, and we put our heads together and decided that because Steve did speak English and was one of the more confident people I'd ever met, we'd conduct the interview with him. He seemed to understand the chef's inability with the language, so I thought maybe we'd be able to glean a few pearls from him by way of translation. We had one hour of Steve telling us how great the restaurant was and how no one, not even Thomas Keller, could duplicate the chef's peanut sauce. Why Thomas would want to was never really explained. I've come to believe that the chef was a *Rain Man*–like savant. He would sit there quietly smiling, and every once in a while, he'd let one go but you were never sure it was related to the subject at hand.

Steve was talking about his trip to China to research the cuisine, and suddenly, the chef yelled out, "I maaaakkkkeeee crrraaaammmmmssss!"

I was so startled that I almost fell off my chair, which was right about the time Stu and I got the giggles.

I asked Steve, "What did he just say?"

Steve told me, "Oh, he was referring to his new clam recipe inspired by the trip."

I asked Steve, "Could you ask him to keep it down a little? He's scaring the staff."

Steve told me, "He's excited to be here."

A little while later, when Steve was waxing poetic about his peanut sauce, the chef screamed, "I maaakkkkeeeee secrrrrreeetttt sauccceeee!"

I couldn't look at Stu. I was trying to engage Steve because obviously we had a radio show rolling and I was biting my lip so hard I think I drew blood. We finally got to the end of the interview and as we were wrapping it up, Steve was nice enough to invite Stu and me to the restaurant for dinner.

The chef heard this and said, "Youuu commeee and I maaakkkkeeee fruukkkeee!"

Stu asked Steve, "He's going to make us fruit?"

Steve, "No, fluke. It's one of his specialties."

We thanked them for coming and bowed several dozen times on the way out. When they left, we fell back in our chairs and howled. Fifty-five minutes of suppressed laughter needs release. We did go to the restaurant one night and had dinner, and frankly, it was okay. I had the peanut sauce. It was served with a chicken sate that was Miami Vice, electric pink. I'm not sure how you get chicken that color and maybe that was what Steve was saying that was not reproducible. I hope he was right because nothing edible should be that color. The restaurant was gone in less than a year.

TESTING, ONE, TWO, THREE

Some years back, a woman with whom I subsequently became very good friends wandered into Coolfish hoping to sell me some wine. She was extremely green as far as her knowledge went, but what she lacked in savvy, she made up in enthusiasm and she was beautiful. As far as salesmanship goes, beauty and enthusiasm are a powerful combination. Her lack of knowledge was refreshingly endearing after listening to all my salesmen prattling on about the mineral content of the soil, brix levels, and the like, so I decided to take her under my wing and train her as to how to sell to me. What I mean by that is every person who buys wine for his restaurant or store has a different agenda and set of needs based on their wine list, inventory, customer base and personal tastes. And each needs to be sold differently. A good salesperson will recognize that and adjust their technique accordingly. I wanted to do something nice because she was so into her new gig. I decided to buy some wine from her, but I wanted to make sure she knew how to sell to, me. We sat down.

She took some bottles out of her pack, placed them on the table in front of me and said, "Thank you so much for taking the time to see me."

I said, "You're welcome."

She asked, "What kind of wine are you looking to buy?"

It's a silly question and it exposed her inexperience.

I asked her, "What kind of wine are you looking to sell?"

Her response was, "What do you mean?"

I asked her, "What do *you* mean?"

She then said, "I'm trying to find out what kind of wine you like so I know what to show you."

I said, "I like them all, for different reasons."

She looked a little confused and said, "You know, I'm very new at this and you're not giving me much to go on."

I said, "Hmm ... To the contrary, I just told you everything you need to know to sell me wine."

She looked at me and said, "I'm confused. Are you screwing with me?"

I told her, "I am and I'm not. Look, I know you don't know much about wine, and I can tell that you haven't been doing this very long."

"Four days," she interjected.

I said, "But as misguided as your energy is, I've already decided to buy wine from you."

"You have?" she asked.

"Yes," I answered.

"Why?" she asked me.

I said, "Because you're so into it and your approach is so bad that I can't let you out of here to do this to yourself again."

She said, "I have no idea what you're talking about."

"Listen. Here's what you need to do to sell me. It may work on others, or it may not I don't know, but this is what works for me. I buy a lot of wine. I buy wine I love; I buy wine I hate. I don't have to like a wine to buy it; it just has to represent itself well as far as price and quality go. It can be expensive or inexpensive; I don't care. I don't care what grape or year it is, and I don't care who made it, how long it was in oak, or if the winemaker wears boxers or briefs. Ultimately, all I give a shit about is how it tastes because at the end of the day that's all the customer really cares about. All that other stuff is fine, and I find some of it mildly interesting, but as far as I'm concerned, it's nose, flavor, finish, and cost. So, what I'm telling you is that if you want to sell, me, show up often, bring stuff to taste, don't come in the middle of lunch or dinner, and don't tell me why you think I should buy the wine. It's that simple."

"You don't want my opinions?" she asked.

"Nope, I'm good," I answered.

She said, "Don't take this the wrong way, but you're a little … uh … different."

I said, "Yes, I've heard the rumor."

She then asked, "Will you try my wines now?"

I said, "Of course."

I tasted through the six or seven bottles she had brought and to tell you the truth, none really stood out.

When we were through, she asked, "Well, what do you think?"

I said, "They're okay, but nothing's making me sweaty."

"You don't like any of them?"

"Not particularly. I'll give you a small order today as a show of good faith and you can establish Coolfish as an account, but you should come back with some different things next time."

She then asked, "Will you taste one more wine?"

"You have one?" I asked her.

She said, "Yes," and pulled a bottle of red out of her bag. "I haven't even opened it yet because I wanted you to be the first to taste it. It's phenomenal. It's by far the best wine in our portfolio."

I said, "Really?"

She said, "Yes, everyone I taste on this wine goes crazy for it. You're going to love this wine, I promise, and the best part is its only ten dollars a bottle, front line. It's called Excelcius."

I said, "That's quite a name and quite the sales pitch, I may add."

She gushed, "It's an Italian Merlot/Sangiovese blend."

I tasted it and didn't care for it. I thought it was hot and a bit out of balance and told her so.

She said, "How do you not like this? Everyone else who tasted it liked it."

I said, "Sell it to them."

She indignantly said, "I happen to think the wine is very good."

I said, "Then buy a case for yourself. I don't like it."

"You're impossible," she said.

I bought a few cases from her, and we established a good working relationship. A few weeks later she called me and told me that her boss wanted to meet me. I told her that was fine, and we set up a date. She asked me if I would mind doing a working lunch and would I taste a few wines while we were eating. I told her it would be okay, and we met about a week later. After the introductions we sat down to eat. We tasted some of the wines and chatted about Italy and how we both got into the business. It was all very pleasant.

Toward the end of the meal, her boss said, "Tom, do you mind tasting one more wine?"

I said, "Of course not. What do you have?"

He reached under the table, came up with a bottle of wine wrapped in a brown paper bag, poured me a glass, and said, "Tell me what you think of this."

I tasted it, looked at him, and said, "I think it tastes like shit … the same as last time I tasted it."

He had a bottle of Excelcius in the bag and tried to blind-taste me on it hoping I would tell him I liked it. Blind tasting can be a bit tricky so he was obviously thinking I could blow the call. He underestimated my consumption record.

I said, "I think I've just witnessed the worst sales technique ever tried."

He sat there mute.

I then said to him, "Let me just understand this. If I said it was good, you were going to say, *'Ha ha, got you!'* and then hope I would order ten cases? Or did you just want to quietly prove how stupid I was, hoping that as an act of contrition, I would pour it by the glass? Please, help me out here."

He stammered, "I just, ah … I kind of thought … um … that I'd test you."

I said, "Allow me to help you out. You're an imbecile. You've embarrassed yourself, hopefully, providing you're even capable of it and I'm sure you've embarrassed her. But I'm in awe of your stupidity, I really am. I'm in absolute awe. Congratulations. You just closed the account using the best wine in your portfolio. I don't believe that's ever happened before."

COMPREHENSIVE EXAM

I passed my test, but some of my employees … well, not so much. In our constant strive to improve our game, we're always looking for ways to motivate and educate our staff. Anyone who's supervised people knows what a challenge it is. Eighty-five percent of the workforce seems to be trying to slide through the day taking the path of least resistance. It's especially frustrating to me because the restaurant business is such a detail-oriented thing and only a few of my employees seem to care. After answering elementary question after elementary question from the waitstaff about the menu, I hit the wall. They are all told at orientation that we will substitute a vegetable for a vegetable, and a starch for a starch, and we will serve any sauce on the side. The reason we have these three simple procedures is so, on a busy night, they don't have to stop what they're doing to come and ask the question. Jewel is a very large space, and it can take considerable time to do so.

Two hours later, I hear the following.

"Chef, can they have spinach instead of Brussels sprouts?"

"Can I get the sauces on the side on table forty-two?"

"He wants two veggies instead of the veg and potato. Is that cool?"

"A guy on table sixty-three just asked if he can have the cauliflower instead of rice. I told him I had to check with you."

It's excruciating. How many times and ways can you explain something that's so simple, that you feel ridiculous explaining it?

The answer: thousands.

I decided we need to test the staff. My thought was that if they didn't know that they could substitute a veg for a veg, it was probably the tip of the iceberg—a big, fat, glacial iceberg. The results were mixed. Some knew all the material and we sort of knew who they would be. Some were borderline and right at the pass/fail grade, with those on the red side allowed retesting a second time. A few were hopeless and wouldn't be able to pass if the answers were on the board and we had to either reassign them or let them go. But one waiter turned in a test that was so magnificently bungled, it would have had Hermann Rorschach rethinking his career. I can't tell you how many laughs we've had, and continue to have, over his test results. Sometimes I'll pull it out of the file just to gaze at it if I'm having a rough day. It's that good. This is one of those things that you have to see to truly appreciate, and I can't do that here, so I'll give you the questions, some context about them if necessary, the right answer, and then his answers and any relevant comment on the part of yours truly. Drumroll, please.

Question #1: What is Jewel's address?

I really didn't see this as being a head scratcher. I thought everyone would pretty much ace this one considering they all have cell phones and business cards. Not our hero. No, he stumbled right out of the blocks.

Correct answer: 400 Broad Hollow Rd, Melville, NY 11747

My man's answer: *1000 Board* Hollow Rd, *Meville*, NY

Comments: I'm giving him the benefit of the doubt. A little sharpening of numerical and spelling skills would probably rescue this.

Question #2: Describe the octopus appetizer.

This is one of our more popular dishes. We serve hundreds weekly.

Correct answer: Seared octopus with olive, capers, red onion, grapes, fingerling potatoes, and local Merlot vinaigrette.

My man's answer: Octopus, onions, mixed veg, served on long, skinny plate.

Comments: Two out of seven doesn't get you to the Hall of Fame. I'll give extra credit for the plate info.

Question #3: How do we make specialty cocktails?

I can see this being a bit tricky because of the ambiguity.

Correct answer: By carefully measuring each ingredient with a jigger to ensure consistency.

My man's answer: *Wha* do you mean, how?

Comments: There's really no such thing as a silly question, and there's no such word as *Wha*. Really, no really, no, no really ...

Question # 4: I'm ordering the Taleggio pizza. Which wine would I order, and why?

Here, we're looking for a basic knowledge of wine pairing. Taleggio is a pungent cheese, which could use a bigger red to handle it.

Correct answer: A robust red that could stand up to the strength of the cheese.

My man's answer: good question. I have no idea.

Comments: I admire honesty. We look for it when we hire people and hope that the judgment call was correct, and I've never felt more strongly about the honesty of an employee.

Question #5: What French reds do we pour by the glass?

I guess it could be a bit hard for some with the pronunciations and all, but this is required reading for bartenders and servers. All we were looking for were generic names.

Correct answer: A Bourgogne and a Côtes du Rhône.

My man's answer: Pinot Noir. I can't spell the name—starts with the letter *B*.

Here, he combines the honesty of answer #4 with the spelling of answer #1—the perfect storm of menu ignorance.

Question #6: What temperature do we cook our scallops to?

This is relatively easy. We tell our servers to let the customer know that we cook scallops medium rare, but if they want them cooked through, they can certainly get them that way.

Correct answer: Medium rare.

My man's answer: Two hundred degrees Fahrenheit.

I'm not sure what would possess him to guess at a number that randomly, but you have to admire the courage. What the hell, take a shot; it had to be somewhere between sixty-five and four hundred. I'm picturing him with his hand under his chin, looking at the ceiling, and thinking, *"Two hundred, yeah, it's got to be two hundred."*

The next two are my favorites because there were two answers to the same question taken at two different times when he was retested. Check it out.

Question #7: What is Otoro?
All the sushi and sashimi items from Be-Ju had been gone over with the staff. I understand that it's foreign to some but with a little effort, it can be memorized.
Correct answer: Otoro is the fattiest part of the tuna and comes from the belly, so there is very little, and as a result it's highly prized.
My man's answer: Part of a fish called tuna near the ass bone.
I was grateful for the anatomy lesson considering that I had no previous knowledge of a Bluefin Tuna sporting an ass bone. I now look at tuna from a whole new angle.

Question #8 as a redo of question #7: What is Otoro?
How lucky can you get? You have a second shot at the same question. He nailed it.
My man's answer: The name of the head sushi chef.
What can you say? I almost pissed myself and have been calling my sushi chef that ever since. *"Hey, Otoro, great job tonight."*

SCREWY STEWIE THE SCREW

Stew came to work for us some time back. According to Stew, we had never had another waiter quite like him. Truer words were never spoken. No one I'd ever met before possessed Stew's level of confidence. The fact that there was absolutely no reason whatsoever that one could point to as a basis for it had never occurred to him. I believe he was an aspiring lawyer, navigating his way toward a bar exam, and was using the restaurant business as a way of supporting himself while still in school. I admire that but something tells me that Stewie had been on the receiving end of more than one participation trophy in his young life.

"You got the best when you got me," he would remind us, ad nauseam.

"How did we possibly get this lucky?" we would ask.

"Just be grateful," was the response, and then he would go and blow up a table.

Diane was assigned to train him but it's impossible to train someone who knows everything. They aren't listening.

Diane told me, "I'm not sure he's going to work out. He's a great kid and everyone likes him but he's clueless, never shuts up, and refuses to listen."

I said, "Well, then, he's chosen the right profession. He'll make a great lawyer."

Diane said, "That's nice but what the hell do I do with him in the meantime? He keeps telling me he's a great server. He said that he practically ran the last restaurant that he worked in, and no one could keep up with him. It's exhausting."

I laughed and asked, "How is he tableside?"

"He's a disaster. He's going to law school and every time one of his customers talks to him, he chimes in to let them know that he's only waiting tables temporarily. He has no concept of boundaries. I'll have to keep a close eye on him."

Chatty servers irritate me. As I've stated previously, I get all itchy when they announce, *"Hi, I'm Stew, and I'll be your waiter for this evening."* I always think, *Thanks for the heads-up, dude. The apron was a dead giveaway.* Or how about this: *"Would you care for some fresh pepper on that, sir?"* while waving a porn star–sized peppermill over your salad. Nah, how about you bring me some of the stale stuff that's been sitting in the kitchen since you signed the lease? And my favorite: *"That's an excellent choice, sir."* Could you please shut up?

Stew had them all.

Diane told him, "We don't do that here. The owner doesn't like it. Just go to the table, take the order, and be as unobtrusive as you can. They don't care about your name or that you approve of the order. You are there to serve them; you're not the master of ceremonies."

Stew told Diane, "You're killing me. This is my schtick. This is how I work my tables. It's what separates me from all the mediocre servers out there. It's how I make my living, how I roll."

A table of four Japanese businessmen walked in and were seated in Stew's station.

As Stew stepped up to the table, he said, "Hi, I'm Stew. I'll be your server this evening."

Cue the fingernails on the blackboard.

Four heads bowed in unison. He continued. "Can I get anyone something to drink—a cocktail, a glass of wine, craft beer?"

One gentleman said, "I rike-a to see wine-a rist."

Stew said, "Excuse me?"

The gentleman said, "Can I see wine-a rist?"

"I'm sorry, sir, could you repeat that?"

Exasperated, the gentleman made exaggerated hand motions to resemble bringing a glass, or *"grass,"* as the case may be, to his mouth and said, "A-rist with wine, led and a-white, orr of the wine on same a-rist."

Stew said, "Oh, you want a wine list?" Four heads bowed in unison.

Stew came back to the waiter station, and Diane asked, "What was the problem over there, Stewie?"

Stew responded, "The problem over there is that I don't speak Chinese."

Diane looked at the table and then back at Stew and offered, "I wouldn't think they do either."

"What are you talking about?"

Diane informed him, "They're Japanese, Stew, not Chinese."

Stew said, "Same thing. I can't understand them. I thought there was something wrong with his wrist, but it turns out he wanted the wine list."

Diane told him, "Bring it over there and pay attention. I've had them before. They're very nice, and they're good tippers too."

Stew brought the wine list to the table and handed it to the host.

The host perused the list for a minute or two and then told Stew, "I'rr have bottre of Win Lun Pinot Noil."

Stew said, "Woodland Pinot?"

The gentleman, "No, Wind Lun Pinot. W-i-n-d L-u-n Pinot."

"Could you point to it, sir?" Stew asked. He did, and Stew then said, "Oh, Wind Run. Wind Run Pinot. Great choice, I'll get it right away." Four heads bowed in unison.

Stew returned to the bar to retrieve the Wind Run Pinot Noir.

Diane saw him with the bottle and the four wine glasses and asked him, "You want me to open that for you?"

Stew answered, "Are you kidding me? You got the best right here. I'm all over it."

I didn't see this for myself, but I'll attempt to describe this to you as it was described to me. Stew got to the table, put a glass down in front of each customer, grabbed the wine bottle in his left hand, inserted the corkscrew with his right, and began to turn it. If he only would have stopped there. With great ceremony, he struggled to screw the corkscrew in and eventually had it down to the hilt, beads of sweat forming on his brow. He started to pull on the cork, but it wasn't budging. The harder he pulled, the more stubborn the cork became. He slid the lever to the lip of the bottle thinking the added leverage would make the difference. It didn't; the cork held fast. Stew, perspiring at a more elevated rate, executed the plan B move that all inexperienced servers do when faced with a stubborn cork. He placed the bottle squarely between his knees and started yanking on the cork until the veins on his neck resembled a roadmap. Still, it didn't budge. I'm not sure what the Japanese words for, *"Could you please find a waiter who can open a bottle of wine?"* is, but it must have been what they were saying at the table. Stew is nothing if not determined and he wasn't about to let a difficult cork kick his ass. Diane should have, by this point, given him a hand but she was hysterical in the waiter station watching the best waiter on Long Island being humiliated by a two-inch cork. Deciding that brute strength was the only solution, Stew—and I kid you not—placed the wine bottle on the floor, kneeled next to it, summoned every ounce of power his body could muster and, with his gaze fixed on the heavens, gave a final, balls-to-the-wall heave-ho and let out a scream as the corkscrew came flying out of the bottle. As he stood up, Diane looked over through the tears in her eyes and saw blood running from his elevated hand down his arm.

Diane rushed over laughing and asked, "Are you alright?"

Stew said, "I cut myself trying to get this damn cork out, but it won't budge."

Diane said, "Bring that over here." The men at the table were laughing and having a pretty good time at what I believe was Stew's expense.

Stew said, "The damned corkscrew pulled right through the cork. I'm going to have to get them another bottle; there's something wrong with this one."

Diane asked, "How's your hand?"

Stew answered, "It's okay. It's a small puncture. It looks worse than it is."

Diane said to him, "Give me the bottle and follow me."

Stew said, "You should get a fresh bottle. I think that one's corked."

Diane looked at him and said, "It's not corked—it has blood on it. Follow me, player."

Diane walked up to the table with a new bottle and Stew in tow, twisted the screw cap off the bottle, poured it for the host to taste and after he nodded his approval, poured the wine for the other three.

Looking at a stunned and visibly shaken Stewie, Diane said, "Yup Stew, we are one lucky restaurant to have you."

Four heads nodded in unison.

THE BEST-LAID PLANS

In 1987, my partner and I bought a restaurant in East Hampton. I was especially excited because I'd spent a lot of time there and considered it my adopted hometown. It was the year everything went wrong. As we were about to stake our fortunes in the Hamptons, a conspiracy of events took place that would serve to extinguish my euphoria, almost for good. We purchased a beautiful restaurant on the highway that had been shuttered for a few years, but it had parklike grounds, living quarters upstairs, a barn for storage, and enough seats to keep me slinging hash for the length of the lease. It also had quite the East Hampton pedigree because it had been operated for years by the same family, who had nurtured it, and the business, until the father decided to sell the property. I thought we had stumbled on something special. It was special alright. Here are some highlights from the summer of '87. Opening night, it was 106 degrees, and we had invited one hundred people down to experience the new restaurant. About twenty minutes after everyone arrived and had settled in, the lights and the air-conditioning went out. I called the power authority and was informed that they had a huge problem and hoped to get the electricity turned on by the next day. It was Tuesday before we took off the miner's caps. I'm not sure if you're aware but 1987 was, on the Chinese calendar, the year of the tick. Ticks have lived quietly out east on the rear ends of deer and rabbits for centuries and anyone who lives out there is aware and takes certain precautions, but in 1987 they had their coming out party. All you read about was how Lyme disease was spreading like wildfire and how the South Fork of Long Island was the epicenter of the epidemic. There were the usual warning signs with pictures of the offending parasite just to make sure everyone knew to get the hell out of the Hamptons. It was also the year that heroin addicts took up surf fishing. How else to explain the four syringes that washed ashore in Southampton, elevating the pulse rate of the media and dominating the twenty-four-hour news cycle with reports of tons of medical waste on the pristine Hamptons beaches? Stock pictures of needles, diagrams of the currents, and reports on wind patterns all made us aware of the fifty-fifty odds of emerging from the surf with someone else's needle stuck in your ass. Right around the beginning of August a sperm whale with a defective GPS beached itself in Amagansett and became an all-you-can-eat buffet for every shark within a twenty-mile radius. Three weeks of nonstop coverage of the gore and clips from the movie Jaws ensured that all the beaches were deserted for the rest of the summer. Suffice it to say, it was a challenging time.

As the weather turned cooler and fall arrived, I was invited to play in a golf tournament at the Maidstone Club. It was a chance I would never pass up, seeing as how a Brooks Brothers wardrobe and a punched ticket on the original Mayflower voyage were mandatory to just walk the grounds, a testament to high-society exclusivity. It promised to be a bright spot in an otherwise brutal season. The date: October 19, 1987. It's referred to as Black Monday, I seem to recall. The crash began in Hong Kong, traveled through Western Europe, and landed in East Hampton right as I was about to yank yet another four-foot putt left of the cup. We were just coming off the eighteenth green when the rumblings started passing through the club and it became apparent that the world was about to change, and so would all our carefully laid plans. The jumpers outnumbered golfers by the closing bell.

But there was one moment back when we were building the restaurant where I was on the right side of a plan that went haywire and almost made up for all the other heartache. As I said before, we bought the place when it was closed and except for the living quarters, it had been uninhabited for a few years. Nature has a way of reclaiming things that are left unattended, and the place needed a ton of work. The landlord had let his son and some of his friends live upstairs, and they turned the place into Animal House. There was a plumbing break in the main floor men's room and plumbing, being a series of interlocking pipes headed for the same place, the breakage forced excess waste to be deposited on the floor and in the urinals and toilets of the restaurant bathrooms. The boys lived up there for several years and never realized or cared that they were causing quite the accumulation of shit every time they flushed the bowl. They were out of there for about a year when we came in, so the entire men's room was caked in dried, cracked shit. My partner Marty and I walked in, looked, and walked out.

Marty said to me, "Cleaning this is going to suck."

I must tell you that Marty is a world-class do-it-yourselfer; I'm not. In his defense, we had limited funds, but I wasn't about to clean caked, cracked shit out of other people's toilets and I told him so.

He said, "I have a feeling we can rent a power washer and this stuff will come right off and we can just sweep it down the drain."

I said, "You're nuts. I'm out."

He continued, "No really, I've used them before, and they work great. I'll get one this afternoon, I'm telling you, it'll go quick."

I insisted, "I'm out, dude."

Marty rented the power washer that afternoon and, after hooking it up and plugging it in, went upstairs to change into what I assumed was his plumbing uniform. He looked like Ed Norton fresh out of the sewer, goggles and all. The process of hydrolysis does not allow you to spray water at whatever pounds per square inch of pressure onto dried, caked shit without getting any on you, so he covered up as best he could. We were both standing there looking at each other.

I spoke first. "You look ridiculous."

He said, "I don't want to get any on me, so whatever was in the locker room, I put on. You should be thanking me for this instead of breaking my balls, by the way."

"I still think you're out of your mind."

Marty put his goggles on and went into the bathroom. I heard the rumbling of the power washer starting up. He was in there for about ten minutes when I heard the machine shut off.

He came out of the men's room, removed his goggles, and excitedly said, "T, come and look at this."

He led me into the men's room to show me an area of the ceramic tile floor, about six inches by six inches, which was once covered in dried, caked shit, shining like a showroom.

He said, "Do you believe this? It's coming right off."

I said, "I've got to hand it to you, you're the man. It must be comforting to know you have a potential second career if the restaurant doesn't work out."

He then told me, "My only problem is that my goggles get fogged up and wet from the spray, so I can't use them."

I said, "That is certainly *not* your only problem." The toilet bowls and the urinals were the worst, so I asked him, "Would it work on the porcelain toilets, or do you think the water pressure will crack them?"

He said, "I don't know. I guess I could try it, and if worse comes to worst and it cracks, we'll just have to buy new ones."

Let me think. When was the last time worse didn't come to worst?

Marty said to me, "Move the machine closer to the booth and when I ask you to, turn it on."

"Aye-aye, Cap."

He positioned himself in front of the booth, placed one hand on the nozzle for control and the other on the trigger, and pulled it. Are you familiar with the expression, *The shit hit the fan?* Well, now you have a witness. When Marty pulled the trigger, the water shot out under so much pressure that it immediately cleaned the shit off the sides of the bowl. I mean immediately. The problem was there was nowhere for it to go because the toilet was clogged. As Marty was wrestling for control of the nozzle, I stared at him in disbelief. The once dried, caked, and now recently rehydrated shit started to spin furiously inside the bowl. It took only a slight angle shift of about one degree, as Marty was desperately trying to regain control of the nozzle while square dancing on the wet floor for balance, to send five pounds of shit, sixty miles an hour, launching out of the bowl. It looked like a poltergeist. It sent him flying violently back, creating a perfect brown effigy on the wall behind him. He took it right in the puss. Now, I'm as sensitive as the next guy but when your best friend knocks himself out with a power washer and five pounds of flying shit it's nearly impossible to muster the appropriate level of concern. At first, I thought he might be dead. My second thought was if he's not, he'll wish he was. The only thing standing between me and a convulsion, was that he still had his eyes closed but when he started blinking them, the contrast between the whites of his eyes and his newly acquired tan sent me running. It was the kind of laughter that you can't do standing up. Kneeling, sitting, hunched over, or lying down are the only positions suitable for convulsive laughter because you need to be close to the ground.

I said, "I'm going outside."

We had a large piece of property, and I ran out onto the lawn and collapsed.

As I was making my way to the lawn, I could hear him saying, "You'd better run, you fucking asshole."

I mean, really, is that any way to talk to your best friend?

He said, "There's no running water in here. How am I going to get this shit off my face?"

I literally could not breathe. I said, "Try the power washer; it did wonders on the bowl."

"Fuck you."

I think it was the only time I laughed that whole 1987 season but let me tell you, it was one of my all-time, top-three hardest ever. The funny thing is that was 1987, thirty-five years ago. Awhile back, I went to visit him in Amelia Island where he's happily retired. He still doesn't think it was funny.

ALL BETS ARE OFF

My younger brother lives in Las Vegas. For some folks, that would be an issue, as in a blessing or a curse. For me, it's neither. I like to say that I don't gamble, and I don't, unless you consider the restaurant business gambling, which it certainly could be due to its ten percent success rate. I have no problem going on the hook for considerable dollars, win or lose, and I've done both on a restaurant deal, but if I lost ten dollars on a blackjack table I'd be furious for weeks. It's a sort of sickness, I suppose, but I know something about the restaurant business so there's a degree of comfort there. The only thing I know about gambling is that the Bellagio, where I usually stay when I visit, is slightly more well-appointed than my house and Steve Wynn has slightly more disposable cash than I do. That's pretty much all you need to know about your odds in Vegas. When I was fifteen years old, my friend Shorty gave me some sage advice.

He said, "Boy, don't never write no checks wit yo' mouth that your body can't cash and don't never gamble on nuttin' you can't control." Words to live by, I'd say, and I have. But there was one instance where I fell off the gambling wagon, and it was a bet on something I had total control over: World Championship hockey.

In 1982, I was working in a restaurant that had, by my best guess, one of the craziest line cooks I'd ever known, and the last American dishwasher I'd ever worked with. Gino, the line cook was engaged to be married, was dating every waitress in the restaurant, and had an insane sense of humor. Rich, the dishwasher, was a nineteen-year-old who was working while waiting for the results of a civil service test he thought he had aced six months earlier. He was an industrious fellow with a sly sense of humor and the two greatest loves of his life were boxing and hockey. He was not only a fan but also played hockey on a local team and he trained in a gym that taught boxing and martial arts.

Both guys were a lot of fun, and we all became fast restaurant buddies. The 1982 World Hockey Championships were taking place at the time and Rich was glued to them. Rich was a huge Wayne Gretzky fan and was closely following the Canadian team. The competition was being played in Finland and the Soviets were the favored team. Canada was doing very well also on the strength of Gretzky's performances and the showdown between Canada and the Soviet Union was happening the following day, to be aired on NBC.

Rich asked me, "Can I bring a television into the kitchen tomorrow?"

I asked, "What for?"

He said, "Canada is playing Russia in the World Hockey Championships and I'd like to see it."

I don't even allow music to be played in my kitchens, let alone a television, but knowing what a huge Gretzky fan Rich was I said, "Okay, just this once, but keep it in your area and no sound, okay?"

He promised.

I said, "You know, Canada is going to get their asses kicked. Russia has won the last 120 championships, or something like that."

He told me, "Dude, no one had Gretzky before. I have a feeling about this. I think we're going to win."

I said, "I don't know much about hockey, but I know the Russians are impossible to beat, except for that one freak game in the Olympics."

Rich said, "Well then, Chef, would you like to make a little wager?"

I said, "No. I'm not much of a gambler and for me, watching hockey is like watching a bridge rust. I'll pass."

Rich turned to Gino and said, "Hey Gino, a little bet on the game?"

Gino said, "Nah, not into it."

As I said before that year the World Championships were held in Finland, which is seven hours ahead of New York. Apparently, what happened was that the game had already been played by the next morning, ahead of the scheduled broadcast, and I'd heard on the BBC that the Russians had won 6–4. I'm assuming amateur boxers and hockey aficionados who wash dishes for a living don't listen to the BBC because as I arrived at work, Rich had the television all set and ready to go. I didn't have the heart to tell him that I knew that Canada had lost so I went about setting up for dinner. Rich was like a little kid, excited as hell, and couldn't wait for the game to start.

I pulled Gino aside and said, "Don't tell Rich but I heard on BBC that the Russians won 6–4. I don't want to ruin the game for him."

Gino said, "That's for real? They already won?"

I said, "Yup, a done deal."

Gino told me, "Oh man, Rich is going to be crushed. He's so into this."

I said, "I know. Let's not spoil it for him."

Gino said, "Okay Chef, I won't say anything."

And that was when Rich said the words that turned us into what some may refer to as *degenerate* gamblers. "Hey, any of you doubters, there's still time to make a little wager!"

I know it was the wrong thing to do, but really, how can you not? Gino looked at me. I looked at him ... and shrugged.

Gino said, "All right, I'll take the Russians and I'll even spot you one goal. That's just the kind of guy I am."

Rich asked, "Chef, you want in on this?"

I said, "All right, what the hell."

I looked at Gino and burst out laughing. He put his finger to his lips to shush me.

Rich asked, "How much are you two willing to lose?"

Gino said, "How about something interesting? Let's not make it for money. How about this? Whoever loses has to eat one pint of the habanero salsa from El Mexicano."

Rich said, "You're on!"

I was doubled over on the line, and to his credit, somehow Gino kept a straight face. The habanero salsa at El Mexicano was hot—no, I mean hot! I've eaten hot food, and that stuff was hot! It was hysterical watching Rich watch the game. He almost couldn't work. Every shot was life and death for him, all so fast and all so futile.

When it was over, a slumped-shouldered Rich came over and said, "I can't believe they lost. I had this feeling. Do you think Gino is really going to make me eat that stuff?"

I asked him, "Would you have made Gino eat it if he had lost the bet?"

Rich answered, "Honestly, yes."

I said, "Well then, bon appetite, I guess."

He asked, "When?"

Gino chimed in and said, "Let's go there Monday night. Some of the Spanish guys want to watch a Gringo deal with the peppers, and it's their only night off."

The following Monday a bunch of us went to see Rich pay his debt. Like the trooper he was, he dutifully ordered the salsa with a mess of chips and a beer and proceeded to pay up. The first couple of bites didn't hit him. Then it kicked in.

He said, "Yeah, this stuff is hot."

A couple more bites.

Rich said, "This stuff is really hot."

A few more bites.

"Holy shit, this stuff is really, really hot. Holy fuck, this is insanely fucking hot!" His face was bright red, and his nose was running like Usain Bolt. His lips were beginning to swell, and he wasn't even halfway through. As he powered on, I could see his discomfort increasing with every bite, and although he was laughing, the pain was obvious.

At about the three-quarter mark he stopped and said, "I don't know if I can do any more. I feel like a firecracker went off in my mouth."

Gino said, "All right, you want me to let you off?"

Rich looked at him and said, "What do you think? You've eaten this stuff."

Gino said, "Okay, you've made good on the bet as far as I'm concerned. I'll call it off on one condition."

He asked, "What's that?"

Gino said, "That there are absolutely no hard feelings about this going forward."

I couldn't look at either one of them.

Rich said, "No, I lost the bet. No hard feelings."

Then Gino said, "Okay, you're good. Push it away."

He must have had six or seven beers trying to extinguish the burn. We all eventually stopped laughing and left.

Two days later Rich showed up for work. I was still giggling about the salsa.

He said, "Hey, Chef, thanks for letting me off the hook on that salsa."

I said, "Don't thank me. Thank Gino."

Rich went over to Gino and said, "Thanks for letting me out of the bet early. That shit was hot, dude."

Gino said, "It was the least I could do," and he moved away from Rich closer to the door. Gino continued. "Yeah, I knew Russia would win."

Rich said, "Well, Canada played them tough. It was a good game."

Gino said, "But I knew Russia would win."

Rich said, "Oh, now you're the big hockey expert? You got lucky once and now you know about hockey?"

Gino replied, "There was no luck involved. I *knew* Russia would win. Dude, they were playing in Helsinki. There's a seven-hour time difference. Chef told me that afternoon when he came in that he'd heard it on the BBC that Russia had won 6–4. That's why I spotted you the goal. I wanted to make the game exciting for you. You should thank me."

Rich looked at me and asked, "Is that for real? You heard the score before the game started?"

I said, "Yeah, it must have been some kind of tape-delayed broadcast."

I could see the emotion welling up in him. He said to me, "If you weren't my boss, I'd kill you right now but that little shit … I'm going to rip his head off." He ran after Gino, who was already hauling out the door.

Thank God Gino was fast. The two of them ran up and down the block, chasing and hiding around cars, for about twenty minutes until they were both exhausted.

Gino spoke first. "Hey Rich, I know you're pissed, but you have to admit it was a good one."

Rich said, "Fuck you, Gino."

"C'mon, man. You'd have done the same to me."

Rich was quiet for a minute and then it started with a chuckle and broke into side-splitting laughter. I came out looking for them only to find the two of them hysterical on opposite sides of a Lincoln Town Car.

I asked, "You two ladies make up?"

They both said, "Yeah," and we all went back inside and had a real hard laugh.

You've got to hand it to Rich. All said, he took it pretty well. And you've got to admire the diabolical side of Gino. It was brilliant.

When we all settled down, I said to Rich, "Tough night for you, my man. You lost the game, the bet, and three of your five senses."

He said, "Yeah, tough night and an even tougher morning, let me tell you."

Laughing, I said, "Well, I have to give it to you: you took it pretty well. Gino was running for his life before the two of you gassed out and started laughing."

Rich looked at me and said, "Chef, you've got to give it to him: he got me, dude. But he'd better start sleeping with one eye open ..." We cracked up all over again.

I love restaurant people.

SHAKESPEAREAN?

Is there any other emotion more fun than suppressed laughter? Trying to hold in a laugh is hard enough but when I'm in a situation that calls for the utmost in decorum or self-restraint, that's when I'm at my worst. I simply can't control myself. And the more serious the situation, the funnier I find it. My three finest moments have come in a church where a South Korean priest with a speech impediment eulogized my alcoholic uncle, at the Bar Mitzvah of my friend's son where the cantor's voice bore a remarkable resemblance to Tiny Tim's, and at a yearly bowling dinner at an Elks Club that, for reasons that still escape me, my ex-wife insisted I attend. But before you judge me too harshly, you need to know that it's not the people, the afflictions, or the circumstances that I find so funny. It's usually some combination of a comment or gesture and the *"Do not under any circumstances laugh at this moment"* restriction that sends me over the cliff. Or maybe it's just organized religion. I don't really know but because the church and Bar Mitzvah incidents are kind of self-explanatory and I'm sure most of you have been in situations like those and can empathize with my social deficiencies, I'll let you in on the Elks Club debacle.

I need tell you this to set up my customer story so please indulge me for a moment. Thirty-something years ago my beloved ex-wife had a girlfriend who was the president of the Does. For those of you who aren't up to speed on the animal kingdom, a Doe is a girl Elk. Ralph had Alice, Fred had Wilma, and Elks have Does. Who knew? Anyway, Diane's friend was the resident president of her local chapter of the girl Elks with all the assumed responsibilities that the position implied. One of those responsibilities included chairing the oxymoronically titled Fun Committee. I'm under the impression she was operating in good faith when she and her sister Does decided that they would stage a bowling tournament, subjecting their husbands, boyfriends, and significant others to a night of competition, exercise, and spinal realignment, all while wearing other people's shoes. How I became involved is still the subject of some lingering ill will between the ex and me and I had to take off on a Saturday night to attend, so not only was it painful, but it was expensive. Here's how it went.

Diane said, "Arlene is having a bowling party with a dinner afterward at the Elks Club in three weeks. Do you want to go?"

"Yeah, like I want an enema."

Diane said, "We never do anything fun together. You're always working, and we never do what I want to do. We're going."

That pretty much sealed it. The little I knew about marriage at that time was that you had to be able to compromise. If she wanted to go bowling and I wanted to go to work, we compromised and went bowling. So, there I was, three weeks later, throwing a sixteen-pound ball at ten wooden pins, doing and saying all the things real bowlers do and say.

"Good spare."

"High-five."

"Johnny's on a beer frame."

"Jerseeeeyyyyy!"

"Where the hell is the waitress?"

You get the picture. I started to drink Herculean amounts of beer because as you might imagine, the wine list at the bowling alley had a rather curious selection and I figured if I had to be there, I would drink enough beer so that the memory of the evening could be eliminated.

There ain't enough beer.

After three fun-filled hours of trying to figure out how you can throw a ball ten times, potentially knock ten pins down each time, and score three hundred, we set off for a gala reception at the Elks Club. No self-respecting president of the Does and the head of the aforementioned, Fun Committee, could possibly start dinner without a cocktail hour—one where the beer choices were Carling Black Label or Pabst Blue Ribbon *(black and blue)*. Three Feathers rye stood proudly atop the highest shelf and there was a quaint little Elks custom called the cash bar. Men were Elks and women were Does and for all you Honeymooners' fans this was like the Raccoon Lodge on steroids. There were murmurs all during the cocktail hour that it was almost eleven o'clock. I thought maybe that was going to be last call, so I ordered four more Pabst Blue Ribbons to make sure I had enough ammo to get through dinner. Again, I heard it.

"It's almost eleven. It's almost eleven."

I asked the bartender, "Are you closing at eleven?"

He said, "No. Why, you want another beer?"

"No, I have four stashed in my wife's pocketbook. It's just that everyone seems so concerned that it's almost eleven."

This was what a grown man told me with a straight face. "Eleven is the hour of the elk."

"Huh?"

"It's the hour of the elk."

Who knew elks had hours? But they do and boy was I about to find out. We were ushered into a large banquet room where each table was set with eight water glasses, an ashtray, and a cardboard Carling Black Label box, the kind that holds twenty-four cans and comes halfway up to meet the plastic top that protects the can from germs so you can serve it at the Elks Club without a glass. In each box sat a paper bag full of assorted sandwiches, potato salad, and coleslaw that were made in some commissary in New Jersey.

"Diane, would you pass me another beer, sweetheart?"

All of a sudden: "Shh, shh, shhhhhh!"

"What?"

"Shh, its eleven!"

The rest of what I'm about to tell you actually happened, I swear. There was a large wall clock hanging in the banquet room over the stage. It had—I kid you not—antlers on it. At precisely 11:00, the hour of the Elk, the lights dimmed, the clock bonged and flashed eleven times and the band, who looked old enough to be the four founding Elks, playing instruments that resembled an amateur plumbing booboo, struck up *Auld Lang Syne.* Out came a gentleman who I later found out was the *Grand High Exalted Mystical Elk,* wearing a hat adorned with antlers. I'm assuming he's not a hunter. He stepped up to the microphone and, as God is my witness, said, "Wherever an elk may wander … wherever an elk may roam …"

That was as far as I got. When security came to remove me, I was under the table with a napkin stuffed in my mouth, convulsing. Security in the Elks Club isn't all that scary; it was a couple of guys in baseball hats and T-shirts. I convinced my captors to let me collect myself a moment and promised that I would leave peacefully.

I asked if I could use the men's room and they were kind enough to say yes. Just as I managed to regain the slightest bit of control, I asked, "Where is it?"

I believe it was the bartender who said, "Over there. It's the door with the *E* on it."

How much can one take?

Security finally let me leave about a few minutes later and as I was unceremoniously tossed out of my first and only Elks Club with the admonition that I never return, my beloved ex-wife issued the line of the night. She said, "If you didn't want to go bowling, why didn't you just say so?"

I told you that story to tell you this one. A rather peculiar-looking fellow came to dinner one night out east with a party of four. He had on a bow tie. It's a dead giveaway. If you're not involved in a wedding, you can't wear a bow tie and be normal. Aside from the bow tie, he had on a tweed sport jacket, very loud plaid pants, and he had a voice with an interesting and amusing register. You remember when you were a kid and thought you had one over on one of your friends, and you needed to rub it in his face? You would use that annoyingly tinny tone, half through your mouth and half through your nose, and scream, *"Nyah, nyah, nyah, nyah, nyah, nyah!"* That's what he sounded like but with an admittedly better and very proper vocabulary. He was a cross between Thurston Howell on Gilligan's Island and Frasier's little brother, Niles. When he arrived, he turned into one of those furniture shoppers that endlessly amuse us with their inability to find a chair that will appropriately accommodate their ass. Some people, no matter where you put them, just can't sit there. This guy couldn't find a table for the life of him: *"It's too bright, it's too dark, this one wobbles, this one doesn't."* He had the hostess at the end of her rope. He pretty much went through all the inside tables and there are, sadly, only so many, when he decided to give the patio a try. The hostess had been keeping us apprised of his movements with the occasional profane invective during his wanderings. Then presto, he sat down. Not looking entirely comfortable at this new locale, he tried to settle in, only he just … couldn't … get … comfortable. I'll briefly describe the patio for you. It's a patio. There that should do it. It has a floor, an awning, tables, chairs, lights, and three high windows on the wall that separate the patio from the kitchen. Halfway through cocktails, Thurston got itchy. He told the waitress to get the hostess because he couldn't sit at this table. The waitress told the hostess that the guy wanted to change his table, yet again, and she proceeded to the patio to try to figure out just where this guy could possibly park himself. A conversation ensued, nothing got resolved, and the hostess came into the kitchen.

She said, "He's not happy with the table on the patio."

I asked, "What is it now?" The hostess is very bright and has a sharp sense of humor.

She had that look in her eye and said, "You need to hear this."

"Hear what? What did he say?"

"You have *got* to hear this."

"There's a problem with this table too?"

She said, "The man said there most certainly was."

"What's the problem?"

She said, "He stood up, looked me right in the eye, and in all his plaid and tweed-ness, said, "We are *awash* in the glow from the kitchen windows."

"He's a-what in the what?"

"*Awash* … in the glow of the light coming from the kitchen windows."

"What does he want us to do? Shut them off and cook in Braille?"

"I don't know. I only know that he's *awash* in the kitchen light coming through the windows."

I think I said the word *awash* one more time, in the form of a question, before I had to be physically helped from the kitchen to the couch in the parlor. Unlike some very unfriendly Elks, I'm happy to report that members of my staff were able to extract me from the situation without the aid of security. Sorry, but I simply cannot listen to a South Korean priest with a speech disorder talking about a drunken uncle like he was Padre Pio, a falsetto cantor singing in Hebrew like Barry Gibb, in tight underwear, at the top of his lungs, an Elk of either sex sporting a hat with antlers, or a guy with a whiny voice, plaid pants, a tweed jacket, and a bow tie saying the word *awash* without losing control of myself.

I apologize.

ANTONIO'S LUNCH DATE

I thought about saving this for a future book strictly about all the employee situations I've seen and suffered through over the course of the last fifty years, but this is just too good to wait. For the last forty years, there has been a sizable Salvadorian population in Nassau County, and I have been fortunate enough to have some of these wonderful people work at the various restaurants that I've been involved with. The best part about being around people who weren't born here is that you realize that they appreciate what this country is and the possibilities it offers. You never hear whining about entitlements, rights, lawsuits, or hyper-spun political opinions because they don't have time for it—they're working. Working to build a better life for themselves and their families on their own without any help from government agencies, bureaucrats, or some political huckster promising free money for a vote, is something that was at one time an American ideal. I hope it remains so because from where I sit, the entitlement thing doesn't look like it's working out all that well. It's ironic that I've probably learned more about what America is by being around non-Americans, but there are some interesting and subtle changes that sometimes occur in the assimilation and naturalization process. As they become familiar with the information needed to become a citizen, like who Washington and Jefferson were, and what the Constitution and the Declaration of Independence are, they also learn idiosyncratically American lessons that are a direct result of a pop culture that doesn't exist for them back home. In their desire to become Americanized they can, through the process of guilt by association, learn things like if you drink enough Coca-Cola your teeth will fall out, or that a Happy Meal is not necessarily a healthy meal. As I've watched them struggle to strike a balance to preserve the culture of their homeland while trying to adapt to this leviathan that is America, I've had some amusing moments but none better than, *"Antonio's Lunch Date."*

Antonio was born into the Cardoza family which has, the last time I conducted a kitchen census, six brothers. These guys are the nicest, hardest working, honest, stand-up people you could ever hope to hire. All six have worked for me at one time or another and at any given time, you can expect to see three or four kitchen guys with that surname wandering around diligently cooking, slicing, prepping, or chopping ... except for Antonio who seems to prefer the more tropical climate of the dishwashing station. Maybe he's homesick. Every one of his brothers started in the dishwashing station, every one of his brothers couldn't wait to get out, and every one of his brothers became a cook. Not Antonio. No, for Antonio, dishwashing is not a job—it's a calling. Sometimes I'll look over there on a Saturday night and see him peeking over a mountain of dishes, with every busboy yelling for glasses, forks, or doggie bags, and he just looks at me, smiling. His brothers shrug their shoulders and shake their heads as if to say, *"That's Antonio."* He's really one of the nicest and most gentle human beings I know and he's a pleasure to have around except on that rare occasion when he decides that it's time to have a cocktail. He's since reformed but there was a period when he was nipping a little at work. I first became aware of it one night when I was covering for one of my chefs and couldn't find him for three hours. He disappeared. I later discovered after an extremely frustrating conversation in broken Spanish—his, not mine—that he was drunk and had fallen asleep in his car. I love the guy so let him off with a warning. Besides, as any restaurant veteran will tell you, if you have a dishwasher who *wants* to be a dishwasher, you've found yourself the rarest of birds, so I figured that a little flexibility was in order. Antonio apparently thought that flexibility was his new American entitlement because he went on a drinking binge that turned me into Gumby. For about two months, he was a mess. I would send him home and punish him for a few days by not letting him work and I think I even fired him twice, but he would always show up, give me that smile, and promise to stop drinking, so I always forgave him. The guy had more comebacks than Muhammad Ali.

I once asked his brother Rafael, "What's with Antonio and the drinking?"

Rafael told me, "Jeffe, I donno. He like drinky. He like boracho."

I said, "Listen, Ralphy, I like boracho too. I just don't like it when he's working. One more time, and he's out."

Rafael shrugged his shoulders, shook his head, and said, "Okay, Jeffe, I tell hing, but I no teenk he stop."

"Just tell him, Ralphy."

Whatever Rafael said got through because Antonio quit drinking just like that. Did he find God, do twelve steps, or see a video of himself on YouTube? I don't know or care; I just know that he quit … except for one little relapse.

One day, Antonio came into work and announced that he was going to get married.

I asked, "Is she aware of what you do for a living?"

Antonio said, "Si, Jeffe, but we hab amour."

I said, "Amour's great, but you're going to need some money to go with that amour."

"Jeffe, money can no buy all deese tings."

"Antonio, its *Money can't buy everything,* but trust me on this: the only thing that money can't buy is poverty and if you think this through, you may find yourself having a change of heart. Just think about it, okay?"

"Okay, Jeffe, but we hab berry big amour."

"Yeah, well, try paying two months' rent in advance with your berry big amour."

I looked at Rafael, who shrugged his shoulders, shook his head and said, "I teenk, Antonio, he's crazy."

"Yeah, no kidding, Ralphy."

A day later, Antonio said two things to me that I didn't know at the time were connected. First, he proudly announced, "Jeffe, I goying to be a Gringo, a Jankee, American, me."

I said, "That's cool, good luck. I'm proud of you."

The second thing he said was, "Monday, I bringy my novia to eat."

I asked, "You're bringing her here for dinner?"

"No, Jeffe, in dee day. Too much money in dee night."

"Oh, you're coming for lunch?"

"Si."

The following Monday, Antonio came with his novia, had lunch and some cocktails, and passed his Gringo test with flying colors. We had an early warning to his arrival. Apparently, in an attempt to put a little extra special in his special day, Antonio had been marinating in Old Spice cologne for what had to have been several hours. The smell could have knocked a buzzard off a cesspool cover.

I asked Diane, "How the hell are we going to serve wine in there? The whole dining room smells like the fifties."

Diane said, "I can't go in there. He's stinking up the whole dining room."

Diane bravely made her way through the fog to his table. He introduced his novia to Diane in a six-minute treatise of language and barriers and ordered two margaritas.

Diane came into the office and said, "He's so cute. He came for lunch with his girlfriend."

"Yeah, cute and stinky. Is the smell gone yet?"

"I'll go check." Diane returned and said, "Antonio just sent back his margaritas. He said they needed more tequila."

"He's drinking?"

"Yeah, two margaritas with extra tequila."

"He sent them back?"

"Yeah."

By this time, both of us were laughing, and I asked her, "What did the bartender say?"

"He said that Antonio was becoming an American faster than we thought."

We moved out to the bar and the three of us were cracking up at poor Antonio's expense, but it was funny. Then I saw the busboy go out to his table with a basket of bread only to return moments later with the same basket, full.

The busboy came to the bar for water, and we asked him, "Antonio didn't want the bread?"

He said, "No. He sent it back because it wasn't hot enough."

"It wasn't hot enough?"

He got his reheated bread, gave Diane his lunch order, and proceeded to send back nearly everything that came out. The salads both went back for more dressing. He needed less fire on his steak and more fire on her chicken, all while washing it down with copious amounts of double-strength margaritas. Here's a guy who I had never seen eat anything other than rice and black beans carrying on like he was Frank Bruni of the New York Times, and he was related to everyone in the kitchen that he managed to anger. They had three desserts and decided at about 2:15 to go to the bar for an after-lunch drink. I went in the kitchen to talk to Rafael about getting Antonio a ride home.

I said, "Ralphy, Antonio is getting boracho at the bar, and I think we need to get him a ride home."

"No, Jeffe, he no need a ride. We goying to keel hing right here."

Still laughing, I asked him, "He got to you, huh?"

He said, "Jeffe, he sen efryting bock."

"I know. What's with that?"

"I tol' you, Jeffe, he's crazy."

"I believe you. But we still have to get him home."

"No me, Jeffe."

When I returned to the bar, I witnessed a scene that for a fleeting moment made me wish I was blind. Antonio was furiously making out with his novia. The bartender looked like he was going to throw up and Diane was laughing uncontrollably behind the office door. While I was figuring out how to get Casanova out of the tequila bottle and into a more chaste and spiritual mood, they parted lips, sounding like a bathroom plunger clearing a clogged commode, and Antonio headed straight for the john. As he was attending to his business his novia whipped out a pen and a piece of paper and wrote down her name, address and telephone number and, slipped it to the bartender with her forefinger placed provocatively to her lips. Antonio returned, none the wiser, to a more recalcitrant novia, which I'm sure he assumed to be the normal hormonal ebb and flow of a typically healthy female. One who had essentially traded him in for a six-foot-four American citizen who happened to look like a Greek god. But I guess if you're going to get married why not concentrate your efforts on securing yourself the benefits of immediate citizenship with someone who can make a double-strength beverage in a fancy glass, rather than with someone who spends most of his time washing them? I'm just asking. We got them home in one piece, and I'm happy to report that Antonio has seen the error of his drinking ways and has quit for good. The bartender was able to resist the advances of Antonio's now ex-fiancée, as I regretfully report that the wedding is off.

The next day, Antonio told me, "Jeffe, I no get marry now."

I asked him, "What happened?"

As only Antonio can say it, he told me, "Sung tines when my novia drinky, she crazy."

GUYS AND DOLLS

Here's an employee story from Montauk, at The Downtown Grille, but first an observation. There's a Democrat and Republican, mainstream-media, type of double standard that exists when it comes to husbands and wives, wives being the Democrats and husbands the Republicans. I'll give you an example. A Democrat can and has said—on the record, mind you—that Barack Obama is clean and articulate and can speak without a Negro dialect and no one in the press says a word. If a Republican says that President Obama's fiscal policies are hurting small businesses, they scream racism from the top of the Washington Post building. It's hilarious. How does this apply to marriage? Well, anyone who's ever been married knows that, like the Democrat, the wife can say anything she wants about her husband anytime, anyplace. The husband, much like the Republican, must be extremely careful about what he says about his wife because it will eventually blow up in his face. Trust me, I was briefly married, so I'm an expert. We all know that there is very little democracy in marriage when it comes to who's running the show. I'll throw you another example. I went to a friend's house to pick him up early one morning for a golf game. I walked into Normandy Beach. They were in a full marital meltdown complete with high-decibel profanity and hand gestures.

She screamed, "You're not going!"

He screamed back at her, "Yes, I am too going!"

I said "Whoa, dude, we don't have to go. I'm playing like shit anyway."

He said, "We're going!"

She screamed down the stairs, "You're not going anywhere until you finish what you should have been doing yesterday!"

It seemed that she had given him a list of things to do with the express purpose of making sure he didn't enjoy his day off. Maybe she caught him smiling? It was just some simple things, really: cut the grass, clean out the garage, wash the cars and change the oil, spray down the patio furniture, get the grill shined up, replace the roof and the all the windows, bury the oil tank, and move the elm tree from the front of the house to the backyard, and then back to the front.

I said, "This isn't that important to me, so I'll wait in the car until you two figure it out."

Ten minutes later, he jumped in the car and said, "Drive!"

I started to say, "Look, we don't—"

"I said drive!"

He didn't say a word until the fifth hole, and then he finally let it out. He said, "Do you believe that?"

I said, "Do you know what I don't believe? Not being married, I don't believe the list thing. And I don't believe that the shoe is ever on the other foot. Can you imagine your wife's reaction if she were standing at your front door with two of her friends on their way out for a day of shopping, and you screamed, "Oh, no, you're not going anywhere until you finished that list I gave you yesterday. I want the kitchen floor washed, the ironing done, my socks darned, and all the dust bunnies out from under the bed."

It just doesn't happen because of the double standard. Besides, you'd get killed.

Indulge me one more. Diane was waiting on a table of six: three wives, three husbands. One of the wives pulled her aside and asked her, "Could you put a candle in my husband's dessert? It's his birthday."

Diane said, "Sure, which one is your husband?"

The woman answered, "He's the fat, bald one."

Diane looked at the table and made the following observation, "Um ma'am, all three are fat and bald."

The woman laughed and said, "Sorry. He's the one in the blue shirt."

After they sang, *Happy Birthday,* the wife recounted the story at the table, and they all had a good laugh. Now try to picture a man, after singing about his wife being one year older, saying to the table, *"The waitress wasn't sure who the birthday girl was, so I told her that you were the one in the blue moo-moo with the cottage cheese ass, and the swollen ankles."*

Think anyone would be laughing? Men and women: double standard.

But sometimes it works in reverse, and it's wonderful to witness when a woman will compliment her man even though it's an accident.

There's an expression that goes, *"God takes care of drunks and dogs."* I'd like to add ditzy women to the list. And I had the duchess of ditzy women working for me one summer in Montauk. I'll call her Donna. Donna came to apply for a hostess position. She was maybe the sweetest kid I've ever hired … and the ditsiest. She was a very pretty young woman but what the Good Lord gave her in looks he took back in brains. Donna wasn't stupid in the sense of the word; she simply got a lot of things wrong to the point where her screw-ups became not only legendary, but also looked forward to. We would schedule her on busy weekends, at our own peril, just to watch what would transpire.

A customer said, "Hello, we have a reservation for four under the name Jones at 8:00."

Donna, checking the list, said, "Okay, here you are. How many are you?"

The customer said, "Um … that would be four of us."

"Okay, and what time would you like to eat?"

Think I'm kidding? One of my more mischievous cooks once told her, "Chef needs you to push the breast of chicken special tonight."

Donna said, "Okay, how's it prepared?"

The cook told her, "It's made with shallots, an intense chicken jus and foie gras butter, and Chef only uses the left breast because it's the more tender of the two."

Donna, "Why is that?"

The cook told her, "I'm not sure, but I think it has something to do with the birds being mostly right-handed. Chef never really explained it; he just uses the left breasts for the special."

Donna said, "What does he do with the right breasts?"

The cook replied, "He uses them for family meal."

At 10:30 that night as I was talking to a table, I heard her behind me, *"Tonight, the chef has prepared a left breast of chicken with shallots, an intense chicken jus, and foie gras butter. I hear it's fabulous."*

What do you say? But my all-time favorite Donna line had to do with her boyfriend.

I was at the bar late one Saturday night as things were winding down. There were several of us chatting about the night's events when this gentleman came to the bar with Donna. He was in his mid-forties and looked like he'd just arrived from the gym: big chest, big arms, big tan.

Donna pulled me aside, pointed at this fellow, and said, "He would like to meet you."

Assuming he was a customer, I said, "Cool."

She introduced him to the group first and then brought me over and said, "Chef, this is Vinnie. Vinnie, Chef Tom."

I said, "Hi."

He said, "Hi. Nice to meet you."

We chatted briefly and then went our separate ways. The next day I was at the hostess desk checking reservations when Donna came in.

She said, "Hey, Cheffy, what's up?"

"Same stuff, different season."

She then asked, "Oh Chef, what did you think of Vinnie last night? You know, the guy I introduced you to at the bar."

I said, "I don't know. He seemed okay. He just doesn't seem like the Montauk type to me. He doesn't strike me as a surfer."

Donna said, "He doesn't surf, he's, my boyfriend."

You have to love the purity in that. She never got a whiff of the sarcasm.

Shocked, I asked, "He's your boyfriend?"

She said, "Yeah. We've been seeing each other for about a year already."

"How old is he?"

Donna replied, "Forty-four."

I asked, "Donna, how old are you?"

"I'll be twenty-three in October."

I said, "Then I have to ask you a question."

Donna said, "Sure, what?"

"Is he some kind of pedophile?"

I swear she said, "No. He manages a vegetable store."

Yup, he's got the right girl. There's no double standard there that I could possibly envision. Even if one did insult the other, I'm not so sure that the other would notice. I'm rooting for Donna, although I haven't seen her in quite a while, and we've lost touch. I can picture them living happily ever after, though: Vinnie, in the vegetable store polishing his tomatoes, and Donna, running for Congress.

THE BOOBOO

You've got to love lawyers. The United States is essentially run by five hundred or so of the finest unemployed legal minds in the country. Someone—I don't remember who—once said that America was founded by geniuses so idiots could run it. Who ever thought that we'd try so hard to prove it? Watching these guys operate is like watching a poorly acted sitcom sponsored by Hart, Shaffner, and Marx, and written by Larry David. And have you ever noticed the umbilical relationship between politicians and insurance companies?

What a coincidence.

Insurance companies amass huge sums of money which just happens to be the mother's milk of politics. The symbiosis of those two entities makes for some very interesting decisions. Not content to keep the stupidity inside the Beltway, where at least it would be contained, the ripples from the relationship are spreading out across the nation. I present my case.

About two years ago, I had a wonderful young man, aged sixteen, apply for a job in the kitchen. He told me he was going to be a chef, was studying cooking in BOCES, and wanted to go to the Culinary Institute of America when he graduated high school. Hearing that is like hearing a great guitar solo. I was conflicted about hiring him, though. *John* was a tall, very thin young man who looked like he needed to eat a meal more than cooking one. He was a real nice kid from, presumably, a nice family and there was still an innocence of sorts about him. A kitchen can be a very rough environment for the young and although we've improved vastly in that department since I first started, it can still be a jaw dropper for a doe-eyed youth. When I started, I was a streetwise kid and I still got quite an education having precious little to do with cooking, I assure you. Considering that this boy was so motivated, and that I had a great group of guys working with me in the kitchen, I decided to give it a try. I figured that it would be a part-time thing for him a few hours a week, and because we run what we like to call an asshole-free zone in our kitchens, it would be a decent environment for John. It turned out well. The kitchen mafia took him under their wing and taught him the ropes to the point where he was holding down his own station on a Saturday night—at sixteen years of age. That's no small feat, mind you, and he turned into one of our most prized students and valued employees. And he was tough. Remember what I said about kitchens being rough places? I always tell young cooks coming in that they must be careful and aware. Everything in the kitchen is hot, sharp, or slippery, so that can make for some rather exciting moments if you're not paying attention.

One day John cut himself butchering a lamb rack. Cuts and burns are badges of honor in our profession and, if they're severe enough, topics of conversation for years to come. If you work with knives and fire, you are going to get cut and burned, end of story. The good news is it happens less frequently later in your career as you gain more experience, but it does still happen occasionally. My crew and I still laugh over the time I dumped a half gallon of boiling fat into my right Croc, which sent me hopping around the kitchen like a deranged flamingo. That's a story for another time but my point is it can happen anytime to anyone regardless of your experience, so you must pay attention. John wasn't paying attention and he paid the price. We looked at the cut, and it really wasn't bad. Here's where my being a chef gives me a skewed perspective on medical treatment as opposed to, say, a doctor. I've cut myself more than any doctor I know. Here's a partial list for my resume's sake. I've gotten my pinky stuck between the blade and the guard on the slicing machine *(don't ask),* and if not for the nail, I may have lost the tip altogether. I once gashed the base of my thumb while removing a food-processor blade from the cardboard box, exposing two tendons and the bone. I sliced open my thigh wiping a knife on my pants while in a hurry to cut a birthday cake. And in a daze of supermodel distraction, I jammed a recently sharpened oyster knife into a vein in my left forearm, leaving both myself and the supermodel feeling sorry for me, for two completely different reasons. That's the short list but it gives me some juice when it comes to diagnosing a cut. I'm also not beholden to lawyers or insurance companies when making my diagnosis because I'm not paying the latter and am not I afraid of being sued by the former. It makes my diagnosis more realistic because I'm not spending any time or anyone else's money covering my ass. We looked at the cut and could it have maybe used one stitch? Yeah, maybe, but what's really the difference between a stitch and a butterfly? His cut was what I would classify as a booboo. I keep Crazy Glue in the kitchen specifically for those occasions. We simply glue the thing shut and get back on the line. John was a little queasy about my diagnosis and even less enthusiastic about the glue, so we taped him up and asked him if he wanted to go to the hospital. He said he did and being young, called his parents to let them know. He had just gotten a car, so we asked him if he wanted us to take him, but he said he was fine and drove himself. About an hour later he returned with one stitch, a Band-Aid, and some gauze on the finger and like the tough cook he was, he finished his shift. I was duly impressed. A lot of kids would have bagged it and gone home. He showed me something that night. The rule of the jungle is that, if you possibly can, you finish your shift. The other guys are counting on you.

A funny thing happened, though, right after he left for the hospital. Before John could even get to his car, the restaurant phone rang, and it was his dad. He had a couple of questions for us and some concerns about the injury.

"Do you have workers' compensation insurance?"

"What is the policy number?"

"What is the broker's name who sold it to you?"

"Where is he located?"

"How can I get in touch with him?"

"Do you have a private insurance carrier for the building?"

"What is the name of the company and that policy number?"

"I'll need the contact person's name also."

"Do you have his or her phone number?"

"Who was present at the time of the injury?"

"How can I get in touch with them?"

"Were the EMTs called?"

"Has the weapon been secured?"

Man, this guy was out of control.

I'm a little more cynical than the average bear from years of witnessing these scenes and as the manager was mouthing to me what he was asking her on the phone, I couldn't help but say, "Tell him it's a booboo, and they think that with a little luck, he just might pull through."

I'm sure John didn't know anything about what his dad had done, and I didn't have the heart to tell him. He remained the fabulous employee he'd always been before his brush with death, finished up with us, won some school awards and went on to the Culinary Institute of America. A few months after the incident I was looking to save some money in my business to compensate for the downturn that the restaurant business had taken at that time. I called my insurance agent, who is also an old friend, and asked him to shop my policy around to see if I could get a better rate. I heard nothing for about a month. When I called him back, he told me that there wasn't much he could do because of the claim that had been settled. I was surprised when he said a claim had been settled because I knew nothing about it. Most times when there is a claim, I have to go to testify to the slickness of the ladies' room floor that they slid the length of, the height of the step in the dining room that they tripped over, or the angle of the light that shined in the customer's eye seconds before they walked into the brick room divider. None of that had happened. This was totally under the radar.

I said to my friend, "What claim are you talking about? We never had a claim."

He told me, "I don't know. I assumed you would know. They said it was a substantial claim."

I said, "Can't be. I would know if there was a claim. Find out what the hell is going on, please."

He said, "All right, I'll see what I can do."

A week or so later, he called and said, "Did you have a cook there named John So-and-So?"

I said "Yeah. He worked here months ago. Why?"

He said, "He's your claimant."

I asked, "What are you talking about?"

He told me, "The medical report says he was treated at North Shore hospital for a knife wound."

I said, "A knife wound? A fucking knife wound? It was a booboo! A fucking knife wound? He got one stitch. The only reason they sewed the thing up was to justify the doctor dragging his ass off the golf course, or maybe some practice time for the intern. It was a booboo! We offered to glue it shut and save him the trip, but he was a little shaky about it. Hell, one of the cooks offered to kiss it and make it better. That's how unimpressive a cut it was. I know cuts and I'm telling you it was a booboo!"

The insurance broker, who's as even keeled as I am not, said, "Well, I'm not sure what the insurance company thought but whatever it was they decided to settle with him on the cut. Who knows why they do what they do? Sometimes they give it to the lawyers and the lawyers, for whatever reason, advise them to settle. That's what probably happened. Maybe the kid had a lawyer saying he could never flip the bird again and, as a result, would have to live with the frustration the rest of his life and the insurance company decided it wasn't worth fighting it. Who knows?"

I said, "Don't tell me they gave this kid money for that cut and that's what's preventing me from getting a better rate."

"Yup, that's pretty much what happened."

"How much money could they possibly dole out for a booboo for God's sake?"

He said, "Well, they settled for seventy thousand dollars."

I lost it. "They gave him seventy fucking, thousand fucking dollars? For a fucking booboo?"

He said, "Yeah, I'm afraid so."

I said, "Seventy thousand dollars?"

"Yup."

"For a booboo."

"I'm afraid so."

I said to one of my cooks when I returned to the kitchen, "That's it. Where's a knife? I'm opening a vein. Right now, I'm opening a fucking vein. I'll be living in Maui by the weekend. I've cut myself worse shaving than he did that night. Give me that knife there. Give it to me, damn it!"

Laughing, he said, "Calm down. You're scaring me."

"I'll calm down. That fucking booboo paid his entire college tuition. One fucking stitch! I've had hundreds! I should be debt free, driving a Ferrari, and living on the ocean. Seventy fucking thousand fucking dollars and I can't shop my policy because of a fucking booboo!"

The cook said, "God bless America."

I'm still not sure if I'm fully recovered from the trauma of it all because every time I hear the term *insurance*, health or otherwise, I react like Lou Costello to Niagara Falls. I shudder to think of where we're headed as a people with minds like these flying the plane. The one bright spot is that I'm creeping up on retirement age and suddenly there's a plan B. I have considerable knife skills, and I can do twelve stitches standing on my head.

LAUGHING IN THE FACE OF DEATH

Here's a story from many years ago that always makes me smile and shows you what a nutty place a restaurant kitchen can be. When I was a kid, all I wanted to do was cook. I was mesmerized by the gleaming fish, the fresh vegetables and the sounds and smells of the kitchen. I couldn't wait to go to work and was mad when I had to leave. I was lucky enough to meet Sandy when I was eighteen years old. Sandy was working weekends in a restaurant owned by a friend of his, moonlighting from his nine-to-five job in Howard Johnson's research kitchens. Sandy had been Pierre Franey's sous-chef at Le Pavillon restaurant in New York City, and had stayed friends with Pierre, eventually following him to Howard Johnson's research kitchen. He was enjoying his semi-retirement, but cooking was in his blood, and he was feeding that beast on Friday and Saturday nights working the line for his friend. I came to work there and met Sandy who became my mentor and lifelong friend—actually, more of a father figure really, as Sandy is twenty-five years my senior. From that day forward we worked together for well over thirty years, six days a week, and I truly missed seeing him on his day off. We worked together at first, and then he bought into the restaurant so I, technically, worked for him. Then we opened a restaurant together and finally as he was winding down, he worked for me. We had quite a run. As a kid I was enthralled with Sandy's stories about the high-end restaurants in New York in the 1950s. He had worked them all and with a broad range of characters; Pierre Franey, Henri Soulé, Roger Fessaguet, Paul Keiffer, and Jacques Pepin among them. He was extremely well trained, as patient a teacher as you could ask for, and maybe the kindest human being I've ever known. In the fifty years I've known him, he's never said a bad word about anyone ever … except Jacques Pepin. You could mention John Wayne Gacy, and Sandy would say something like, *"You never know what his childhood was like, Thomas. It was probably horrible."* Joseph Stalin: *"He was certainly misguided, but he had exceptional leadership abilities."* O. J. Simpson: *"I'm sure he did it, but people can't help themselves when it comes to crimes of passion. Remember that."* But Jacques Pepin? He would go off like a Roman candle. Don't ask me why Jacques set him off so—he would never tell me, which was totally in character while he was acting out of character. He wanted me to know how he felt but still wouldn't gossip or disparage another human being. That was just who he was, a lovely guy, and atypical of whom you would meet on the line in restaurant kitchens especially back in the early seventies when this kind of work didn't carry the cachet it does today.

After about six months Sandy and I worked the three-man line by ourselves. That was for two very important reasons. Number one, we were two extremely strong line cooks, if I do say so myself, and number two, his partner was a disaster in the kitchen: great guy, terrible line cook. As the restaurant got busier and busier, it became apparent to both of us that, macho aside, we needed to get some help and his partner wasn't the answer. We hired a guy, whom I'll call, *Jim,* to work with us. Sandy and I had a routine and anyone who's worked a restaurant kitchen knows that there are some cooks you just click with. We were that way. He would move this and way, I'd instinctively move that way. He'd grab a plate; I'd grab a garnish. He'd sniffle; I'd sneeze. That kind of choreography is difficult to cut in on when you're new, but Jim was trying very hard, and he had reasonable skills. When we had downtime, I would bug Sandy for recipes or stories from the Sherry-Netherland Hotel days and Jim, trying to be one of the boys, started telling us stories about his days cooking in the service. It seems he served in the army … and the navy … and the air force … and, yes, the marines. I never felt safer in a kitchen.

One day after a particularly tall tale and betraying my youth, I said to Sandy, "You know he's full of shit, right?"

Looking back, I'm sure he wanted to roll his eyes, but he didn't. He looked at me, and in that patient tone asked, "Thomas, did you enjoy that story?"

I said, "It was a funny story, but it wasn't true."

Sandy asked me, "When you watch a movie do you ever wonder if the story is true? You watch it for the entertainment value. How much does it cost to see a movie? Maybe eight dollars?"

I said, "Yeah, I guess so."

Sandy then said, "Congratulations, you just saved eight dollars. It doesn't matter if it's true or not; it matters that it's a good story. That's what counts, Thomas. Enjoy it for the quality of the story. The other stuff doesn't matter."

I had a different outlook after that and never really forgot it. In his own way he was telling me to give people some room. Don't judge them lest you be judged. Sandy taught me much more about life than anyone I've ever met and more than I could ever convey here but that was one of his more important lessons … Jacques Pepin notwithstanding.

Jim died suddenly shortly after that. We were shocked, as you can imagine. Back then if you worked in a restaurant, you worked ten to twelve hours a day, six days a week and you wouldn't dare ask for a day off. To lend perspective to young cooks who prefer to work by appointment, I worked the day my dad passed away, the two days of his wake and the day of his funeral after the services because I had a seasonal business, little help, and no disposable income. That's just how it was and I'm telling you this to explain that we just couldn't shut down the restaurant and go to the wake; we had to pick our spot. Jim had only been with us a month or so when he passed so we really didn't know all that much about him other than the fact that he was America's busiest guy during the war. We didn't even know if he was married or had children because almost everything he told us was made up.

I asked Sandy, "Do you think we should go to the wake?"

He said, "We probably should go, Thomas."

I asked, "When do you want to go?"

"Well, I guess we'll have to go tomorrow between lunch and dinner."

I said, "That's like the first day. Isn't that for the family?"

Sandy said, "Yeah, but it's the only time we have. Let's just go, pay our respects, and get back here. It's the right thing to do."

There's a thing about death and the finality of it, the emotional aspect, and all that builds up and needs release. The Irish have it down to a party; the Italians use food. As kind as Sandy is he has a mischievous sense of humor. We could always make each other laugh; hard. We had been walking around all day with our heads down, feeling terrible.

I started it. I said, "Sandy."

"What, Thomas?"

"You think he's really dead?"

I know he didn't want to laugh but suppressing it is hopeless.

He asked, trying to stifle a laugh, "Do I think … hee … hee … he's dead?"

"Yeah. You know, he could be bullshitting us. Maybe he's working at another restaurant."

Sandy, losing it, said, "Maybe he joined the French Foreign Legion. It's the only branch he missed."

We were a mess.

Sandy's partner came into the kitchen, saw us, and said, "All right, you two idiots can just knock it off right now."

We couldn't look at each other the rest of the night. The next day we left the restaurant to go to the wake. When we got there, they were just opening the doors and letting in the family. His mother was at the front of the queue, and she was a disaster. The worst karma you can have, as any parent will attest, is to outlive your child. We were led in but hung back in the lobby because of the commotion inside. The mother, consumed with grief, was trying to hug the corpse and was fighting attempts to calm her down. It was truly heart-wrenching.

When things cooled down, Sandy said, "Okay, let's go in, pay our respects, leave these people their privacy and get back to the store."

In we went.

Sandy went up to the casket first, kneeled, said a little prayer and broke down. I saw him as he got up, he was more upset, crying quietly into his hands as he was walking back to where I was standing.

As he came up to me, I went to console him and said, "Are you alright?"

He moved one hand from his eye and said, "Thomas, wait until you see his hair."

Are you kidding? Who says this to someone who is about to kneel over the dead? Frankly, I might have missed it. It seemed that when all the fuss was going on over the coffin, his mother did a Vidal Sassoon on Jim's doo, making him into a dead ringer for a forty-year-old Alfalfa from The Little Rascals. It was sticking straight up in the back and cocked to one side. I covered my face as Sandy had done and walked the length of the funeral home to where he was standing in back and the two of us were uncontrollably hysterical—in the funeral home, with the family. The only thing that saved us, sort of, was that the sound of laughter and the sound of crying are strikingly similar. As we were trying to figure out what to do, Jim's mother came over to console us. Could it get any worse?

We were standing there with our faces buried in our hands, stomachs cramped, and Mom said, "You must have loved my son."

The two of us simultaneously shook our heads. "We ... we ... did."

Mom said, "He said he enjoyed working with you."

"We ... weee ... weee did too."

I said, "Excuse us," and we ran down the stairs to the men's room.

You can only imagine what happened when we got there. I don't know if you've ever laughed to the point where no sound comes out but that's what happened. I really thought I was going to faint. We had been down there for about a half hour when the first search party came down to see if we were all right. And we almost were until he got there and asked us. We went right back to the face-in-the-hands position.

After we assured him that we'd eventually be okay, sometime that spring, he left and Sandy said, "Thomas, we have to get out of here. Don't look at me, don't say anything; just walk up the stairs and out the door. Not one word, Thomas. Not one word."

It took about five attempts to get from the urinal to the bathroom door. We just couldn't get it together. Finally, the thought of getting caught set in so the plan was that the guy in front, Sandy, had a responsibility to not have his shoulders go up and down no matter how hard he was laughing. My responsibility was to not make any small animal sounds through my nose, that would set his shoulders jiggling, which in turn would set off a chain reaction and collapse the plan. We ascended the steps, Sandy looking straight ahead and me, at my shoes. We got to the top, made the left out of the building, and ran for the car.

His partner was waiting for us outside and said, "I don't think I've ever met two bigger assholes in my life."

We laughed all the way back to the restaurant and it wasn't out of any disrespect for Jim. It was letting go of all that tension and emotion.

SIDNEY FELDSTEIN, RIP

It would take a month of Sundays and more adjectives than I'm familiar with to duly describe Sidney Feldstein. Any of you who have read my writings over the years know that I never out my customers and I have named only one person in the twelve or so years that I've been telling these tales, and that was a coworker and dear friend who to the relief of more than a few folks who knew him, is no longer with us. I named Sidney for three reasons. Number one, because he was one of the most cantankerous, complaining, annoying, demanding, condescending, miserable, grouchy old bastards I had ever known. Number two, he recently passed away and he can't yell at me anymore. And number three, he was singly the most fun, most loved, most missed, hysterical, and most loyal pain in the ass any restaurant owner could ever hope to endure. I opened Coolfish on July 24, 2000. Two weeks after that, we began lunch service. Sid was our first customer. I know you are going to think I'm exaggerating but except for the occasional overnight hospital stay he ate lunch with us five days a week, every week, until the fall of 2012 when he passed away. He never missed a day, and he never once had a good meal. He spent so much time with us that we considered him family, which is why he made the employee chapter. You could set your watch by Sidney's arrival every day around 11:55. He'd come in and say hello, waving his hand at no one in particular. Then he would walk right by the hostess, completely ignoring her, and proceed to his usual table in the back left corner. That was the only pleasant thing he would say until, waving his hand on his way out the door again at no one in particular, he said, "Goodbye, see you all tomorrow." In between hello and goodbye, there was nothing but trouble. I must have served Sidney one thousand bowls of soup in those twelve or so years, and not once was the soup hot enough.

"I don't understand why I can't get a hot bowl of soup in this place," he would shout for the whole room to hear. "Twelve years I've been coming here, and I can't get a hot bowl of soup. You would think, in twelve years, he would even accidentally serve a hot bowl of soup, but no, not him."

The funny thing about being with Sidney all those years is that you began to understand that he meant no harm and wasn't really mad at you; it's just that he believed it was the best way to get what he wanted. It's sort of like the metaphor *"The squeaky wheel gets the oil."* But I must tell you that between the crankiness, and the Catskills comedian-like delivery, he had us in stitches almost every day. About five years into our relationship Sidney pulled a no-show. We realized at about 12:15 that he wasn't at his table. Sid was about eighty at the time and his health was on the back nine, so to speak. We were trying not to think the worst.

Diane asked, "Should we call the cops to see if there was an accident, or maybe the hospital to see if he was admitted? I tried his house, and there was no answer."

We weren't sure what to do.

Fifteen minutes later, Diane called his house again, and he answered. "Hello."

Diane said, "Hi, Sidney, it's Diane from Coolfish."

"What do you want?"

Diane said, "When you didn't come for lunch, we were worried that something may have happened to you. You never miss lunch and then I tried calling but you didn't pick up."

Sid replied, "I was in the *terlet*, for God's sake. Besides, it's snowing and I'm afraid to drive."

Diane asked him, "Sid, do you want me to come get you? I'll come and get you, and I'll drive you back home when you're done eating."

"Really? You'll come and drive me?"

"Of course. Lunch isn't the same without you. How long will it take you to get ready?"

Sid said, "Not long. Okay, here are the directions ..."

From that day forward, every time there was a weather event—and I'm including partly cloudy as a weather event—someone from the restaurant had to go pick up Sidney. We'd get the call around 11:30 and ask for a volunteer and you know what? Everyone wanted to go. As he got older, he was more and more worried about driving. He was pretty good to and from in straight lines but the more nuanced maneuvers, like parking, were presenting their share of challenges. Sidney's solution was pure Sidney. He'd walk in at 11:55, wave hello, and instead of ignoring the hostess he would hand her his keys and say, "Could you park it for me? I left it out front." It would be half in and half out of the space and he would just give up and come inside. From that day on every time he came in we parked his car and backed it out. He would nod his head to whomever was there, saying, "I left it running."

I was sitting in the office one day doing menus and lost in thought about the economics of the restaurant business. It's something that I constantly must think about but never get any better at for some inexplicable reason.

Lenny, the chef, came in and said, "What's up?"

I said, "Nothing, just menu stuff. I have to raise some prices and frankly, I'm worried about bumping the burger at lunch. I need go up two dollars."

Lenny said, "You worried about people paying two more dollars for a burger? I don't think they'll notice."

I said, "Sidney likes hamburgers."

He said, "Oh, yeah. You're toast, dude."

"No kidding."

Lenny then asked, "You really think he'll notice?"

I said, "I'm willing to bet that Sidney still has the financial records from his first paper route. Yeah, he'll notice."

The following Monday, Sidney came in and ordered a bowl of soup.

Diane brought it out to him and before it hit the table, Sidney said, "Take it back—it's ice cold."

Diane said, "Sid, you haven't even put the spoon in it yet and you're complaining. How do you know it's cold?"

Sidney said, "How do I know it's cold? Ten years I've been eating lunch here. Ten years I've been ordering soup. Ten years the soup is cold. What, today he decided to serve hot soup? He always serves cold soup. That's how I know. Take it back."

We were doubled over in the kitchen upon hearing Diane recite the diatribe. Sidney ordered a hamburger, which he did frequently, and after redoing it three or four times, he ate it and asked for the check. Watching Sidney peruse a check is like waiting for the results of your colonoscopy, praying for good news while expecting the worst. Bam—he locked in on the increase.

"Is he kidding me? Diane, come here. Is he kidding me? Twelve dollars for a hamburger? Is he kidding? A chef who can't serve hot soup, twelve dollars? I'm not paying it. I'm not!"

Diane came into the kitchen laughing. "Sidney's very upset with you."

I said, "Oh, yeah? The burger?"

"Yup, and he says he's not paying the increase. He says you're trying to get rich all in one day, the prices here are like the stock market, and your soup is always cold. What do you want me to do?"

I said, "What can you do? Give it to him for ten. I'm not going to fight with him. He's like, one hundred years old."

From that day forward we had a menu, and a menu with prices for Sidney.

Some years ago, someone decided that the only thing missing in Sidney's life was an iPhone, and they gave him one for his birthday. It was an act of profound cruelty. Watching Sidney trying to work an iPhone was like watching a monkey trying to open a coconut.

Sidney said, "They tell me I can access the information highway; it'll find my car keys when I lose them, and I can even launch missile strikes against Iran … if I could only turn it on, I could do all that!"

We tried to show him how to work it, but the technology was tripping him up. After weeks of fumbling with it—and this is exactly how my luck runs—he stumbled upon a twenty-year retrospective of Rosemary Clooney's greatest hits. What are the chances? From that day forward, Sidney would walk in at 11:55, wave at no one in particular, say, "Hello, turn off the music," ignore the hostess and walk to his table. For the last two years of his life, we heard every song Rosemary Clooney ever sang wafting through the dining room, from 11:59 until somewhere around 3:00.

Have you ever sat through, *"Come On-a-My House"*?

The last year of his life was a struggle for Sidney. We could see his health was failing and it was getting harder and harder for him. He would come in with his friend Jack, also a widower, and they would play Rosemary Clooney songs while looking at pictures of their wives, reminiscing and sometimes crying. It was hard to watch the fight sap out of such a feisty guy. And just when you thought he was about to give up his family hired a live-in nurse whom, for reasons unbeknownst to the rest of us, he grew to hate. I think it was the discipline she was doling out, and he was having none of it. When she was around, he was like a petulant child. She made him take his medicine, watch what he ate, and had him on a restful schedule. He hated her for it in a funny, Sidney kind of way but I think that the emotional charge extended his life.

The first day we met her he walked in, waved, and said hello but before walking to his table he pulled Diane aside and said, "I have a nurse. She'll be in shortly. She's out parking the car. You'll know her right away—she's colored. Put her lunch on my check." Then he proceeded to his table.

In came Jack, his buddy, who joined him at the table for the Rosemary Clooney Hour and two minutes later, in walked the nurse.

Sidney got up and we thought he was going to pull the chair out for her. Instead, he walked over to her and said, "Here, you sit at this table," and sat her at a table across from him and Jack.

Now between the *colored* comment and the separate table you could misconstrue Sidney's motives. I assure you he didn't have a racist bone in his body. He just hated to be told what to do, and the *colored* thing was strictly generational. He headed back over to Jack and then stopped, turned around, and went back to the table.

He looked at the nurse and said, "Have anything you like for lunch, if it's ten dollars or less. I suggest the hamburger. The soup is always cold and I'm not paying for alcohol so have a soda if you'd like."

He then went back to Jack and Rosemary, had lunch, and eventually left. It was the last time we saw Sidney. A few days later we got word that he'd been admitted to the hospital. About a week after that his family contacted us to tell us that Sidney had passed away. They thanked us for being so kind and patient with him and told us how much he loved us all. It was a rough day at Coolfish, to say the least. Sidney was family and we loved him as one of our own. I'm glad he didn't suffer or linger on, and they said that he died quietly in his sleep. I'm not buying it. Sidney never did anything quietly and I don't think he'd have started there. I'm sure inside he was as feisty as ever and if there's a heaven or Valhalla, he'll have the place straightened out in short order. And if there's a restaurant up there, they'd better get the menu prices right and their soup hot or they'll be in for a rough couple of weeks. We all miss Sidney very much and I know it's a cliché, but Coolfish isn't quite the same without him. As much as he'd fuss and fight with you, he always had envelopes for the waitstaff and the bartenders on the holidays and a kind word for you ... if you weren't waiting on him at the time or heating his soup. Sidney wasn't a good customer—he was a great customer and if I had two hundred more like him, I'd close and make it a private club. He was a loyal and faithful patron, a generous soul, and one hell of a character. He's a part of the very fabric of Coolfish, and the best pain in the ass I could have ever hoped to have had the pleasure to reheat soup for. We all loved you, Sidney. Goodbye, friend.

PULL-IT SURPRISE

Sometimes I get to star in my own stories, and it is in the interest of fairness that I tell you this. Occasionally, someone will issue a statement, misuse a word, or confuse a thought that will drop you where you stand. In my previous book, *Playing with Fire*, I've named these little hiccups, Pull-It Surprises. It's obviously a naked take-off on the Pulitzer Prize, with the difference being that instead of recognizing tremendous accomplishments and contributions to mankind, it memorializes someone's ability to massacre the English language by *pulling* a word out of their ass that is so close to the real McCoy, that it *surprises* you with a literary contribution to your own personal laugh track. That's the criteria for qualification. I have a friend who is the author of so many of these priceless gems that I swear he's creating a new dictionary. I'm to the point where I write them down because at some point in the future they have to be published. It wouldn't be right not to have his unique talents go unheralded. Here are some examples of what I'm talking about, and this is word for word, I promise you.

I once asked him after not seeing him for a while, "Hey, how's your father doing?"

My friend said, "Not so good. He's in the hospital."

Me, "What happened?"

"It's a long story. He was reading the newspaper and saw an old friend's name in the *barbituary* column. He wanted to pay his respects and go to the funeral, but he doesn't drive anymore so I took him in my car. While we were following the *Hertz* to the cemetery, he became lightheaded and very anxious. He said that he felt like he was going to faint. I thought it was psycho-*semantic*, but he insisted on going to the emergency room and it's a good thing we did because when they checked him out, they found a blood *clog* in his neck."

Nowhere in that soliloquy is there a spot where you can say something funny and relieve yourself. You've got to stand there, take it like a man, and thank your lucky stars you haven't had a beer in the last couple of hours. I know you think I'm making this up, but I have witnesses to corroborate. Check this one out.

I once asked him, "What did you do last night?"

He answered, "We went to dinner with my wife's friends."

Always interested in restaurants, I asked, "Where'd you go?"

He said, "I don't remember the name. It was by their house. It was alright but my wife's friend is a pain in the ass. She's *lactose intolerable* and can't eat anything. So, her husband, who happens to be *anal attentive* and needs to control everything, in his *infidelity of wisdom*, chose some *food-to-table* place that does the local thing. Let me tell you, it was a long night."

You don't know what long is, my friend. Try to sit through that without snickering. I've developed some serious acting chops over the years. Don't get the wrong idea; I'm not picking on my buddy or looking down my nose. I generally don't get the words wrong all that often because of my interest in writing and the editing process, which is both humbling and educational, but

I've done my share of wrecking a moment by saying something stupid and my timing seems to be flawless. Watch this.

Sometime back, I was asked to do a cooking show on one of the local channels. I didn't want to do it, but I didn't want to seem like a diva and say no.

I called Lenny, the chef at Coolfish, and said, "Hey man, you want to be on television?"

Lenny is one of the nicest people I know so of course he said, "Sure. Where and when?"

I told him the details and then called the producer and told her that Lenny would do the show.

The producer thanked me and then asked, "You'll be coming with him, I'm assuming?"

I said, "No, Lenny will be fine. He's very personable and a strong cook."

The producer then said, "We usually have two guests seated at the table on the set to sample and comment on the food and the host was hoping that you would come. He was looking forward to meeting you."

What can you do? This was Telecare, the Catholic channel, and the host is a priest and a very nice man. Because I'm trying to atone for the years between 1965 and 1978, this looked like a golden opportunity for some time reduced for good behavior. I went. It turned out to be a fun gig but whenever I'm put into any religious situation, however light it may be, I revert to a nine-year-old child being scolded by a nun, feeling guilty while wondering what I did wrong. I'm always thinking that I'm going to say or do something wrong and isn't that always when you tend to screw up? I do, and man, did I ever.

After the show was over, I was talking to the host and he told me, "You guys were great, and thank you for coming."

I said, "You're welcome, Father. It was a lot of fun."

He said, "I know. I enjoy doing the show, but it's hard to find guests."

Surprised, I said, "Really? I would think chefs would love to come on and cook with you."

He told me, "Yeah, you would think that, but a lot of people will book a date with us and then either cancel right before they're due to be here or not show at all."

"Welcome to my world, Father. I deal with it all the time." Adding to that, I said, "If you have a problem getting someone in a pinch, call me. I have several restaurants in the area and if I can help you out, I will."

He took my number, thanked me and we said our goodbyes. I felt pretty good about my standing in the universe by giving the offer on the way out when I proceeded to smash my elbow on the metal door handle, while making a less-than-graceful exit with the cooler. There is absolutely nothing funny about that bone and in case you haven't noticed, I'm comfortable with profanity. It's a response that I haven't the ability to control. It happens on its own and the shortest measure of time is that little slice between the banging of the elbow and the f-word that follows—at the Catholic channel, in front of the religious icons and statues, and in earshot of a priest. As Lenny's eyes opened wide, he started laughing, put his finger over his mouth, and shushed me at the very moment I put the cherry on the sundae with, "Jesus, that fucking hurt. God damn it!" I thought Lenny would piss himself.

He said, "Chef, we gotta get out of here."

I said, "Yeah, before they send an exorcist."

A week later the producer called me and asked if I could do a show in two days. Seeing as how I told Father I would, I said, "Of course."

So off I went that morning to scour the walk-in to find what I wanted to cook. It was spring and I wanted to show off the season with some of my favorite spring items: asparagus, morels, spring peas, and Girl Scout cookies. The asparagus hadn't arrived yet, morels weren't on the menu, and Tag-Alongs fare better without the application of heat. I grabbed the peas.

While looking around I saw that we had pea shoots so I thought that the best way to highlight them would be to make the peas the focus of the dish. I was going to use penne pasta with a little sliced shallot, fresh peas, pea puree, pea shoots, lemon zest, and Evo—very simple, very spring, and very cool. I assembled everything and off I went. I arrived on time, fully prepared, and tried not to look any of the holy pictures in the eye. As I was setting up my ingredients and we were getting ready to tape, the host came in and we started to chat. He told me how the show was going to go, what he wanted me to do, and what we would talk about. I told him what dishes I was going to make and assured him that I was a seasoned television guy and was sure it would be a snap. Five, four, three, two, one … and we're rolling. Father opened the show, introduced me, and we were off to a brilliant start. I had each ingredient laid out before me in the order in which I would use them, my pan had been preheated, and the shallots were pre-sliced.

Emeril, watch your ass.

As I was assembling the pasta dish, I noticed Father eating some of the pea shoots which I intended to use as part of the prep and for the garnish.

I was afraid I wouldn't have enough if he kept eating them, so I tried to distract him by saying, "Do you like the pea shoots?"

He asked, "Is that what these are, pea shoots?"

I said, "Yes, they're the young, tender shoots of the plant and we're going to use them in the cooking of the dish and also for the garnish."

Father then said, "You know, I didn't know what they were but when I tasted one, I thought it tasted like peas. That's amazing. Are these local?"

I told him, "Yeah, we get them from Satur Farm out east."

He asked, "You do a lot of local foods, no?"

I said, "Yes, we try to do as much as possible to support the homies. There are seasonal realities to it all, but we hang with Long Island as much as we can."

He said, "That's great. It supports the region and it's also environmentally beneficial as well, cutting out transportation and fuel and all."

I said, "Yeah, it all makes good sense."

Then he said, "So tell me about this pasta dish you're making. What are you doing there?"

I said, "Well, I wanted to showcase a seasonal ingredient. We had these beautiful peas at the restaurant, so I decided to do pasta which everyone likes and is easy to make, to show them off. I'm using a little sautéed shallot and then I'm making a pea puree for under the pasta which will act as a sauce. The peas and the shoots will be cooked into the main body of the dish, and we'll use more shoots for the garnish."

Father commented, "That's great. It's simple and flavorful. That's the essence of Italian cooking, no?"

That would have been a great time to shut up and cook but I couldn't keep my mouth shut if I had a gun to my head, and that was precisely when I pulled the Pull-It Surprise for the ages.

I said, "Exactly. Here you have the silkiness of the puree, the toothsome quality and the sweetness of the peas themselves, and the freshness of the pea shoots. This dish is the essence of pea-ness."

Houston, we have a problem. No matter how you spell it, *pea-ness* sounds remarkably like *penis* when it's spoken and I just spoke it to a priest, on the Catholic channel, in front of the religious icons and statues. I was afraid to look up. I assumed Father heard me. He was about fourteen inches away from me when I decided to turn Telecare into the Playboy channel and the cameramen who were fourteen feet away were all on their knees with their heads bowed. I'd like to believe they were praying. He never blinked, said a word, or cracked a smile. He powered right through the rest of the taping like nothing happened, as pleasant and jovial as he ever was. I'm sure they cut it because although I've never seen the episode, friends have, and they've never mentioned it. It must be getting easier to book guests these days because they haven't called me back to fill in. And fill in I would because I've never worked with a finer actor.

SUPER TURD

This story is not for everyone. If potty humor isn't your thing you may want to stop right here. This is not for the squeamish, fainthearted, or easily offended. I'm going to attempt to convey this story in as tasteful a manner as possible but I'm telling you, it's probably futile. Consider yourselves warned so I don't want to hear it if you decide to go further. After all, we're adults and are responsible for ourselves. I'm telling you this to show you the lengths that we go to and the things we must suffer for our art, things the instructors at the Culinary Institute of America had to know about but never told us. You'll never hear this on the Food Network, on Martha Stewart Living Radio, or from Arthur Schwartz. You'll never see this in a food blog, on Restaurant Impossible, or on Hell's Kitchen. You're about to get a dose of restaurant reality, a problem that we in the business deal with on a regular basis but rarely talk about. Call me a voice in the wilderness, a renegade, or a moron but I'm hoping that relaying this story will make at least one person pause before dropping a bomb like the one dropped on me in 1972. It's a men's room tale you're not likely to forget anytime soon; it's been about fifty years and I still have the nightmares. It's a little ironic because almost all my bathroom tales are about the ladies room. The level of wreckage between the men's and ladies room isn't even close in almost all cases. And it's ironic because left to our own devices at home, women tend to be neater and better housekeepers than men. I'm sure there are exceptions to the rule but I'm comfortable with the statement in its generality. I don't know what happens when women enter a bathroom that they're not responsible for cleaning. Is it rebellion, latent anger, acting out, or a deep-seated desire to punish or get even? I don't pretend to know, but I have to believe it's a complete reversal of how they behave at home. Women have systematically destroyed every ladies bathroom, in every restaurant I've ever worked in or owned, and it usually happens within the first fifteen minutes that you're open. It's an amazing accomplishment. Ask any commercial plumber, and he'll tell you it's ten to one for ladies to men's rooms on emergency calls. Most of it is paper related because there isn't one woman, I know, who will sit on a public toilet seat, but the curious thing is that it doesn't preclude them from shrink-wrapping the seat with reams of toilet paper before hovering over it like a UFO. And women are the most fearless flushers among us. You can't imagine the things I've seen plumbers pull out of my pipes over the years. They'll clean out a pocketbook and flush what they no longer want or need. How else can you explain my plumber having retrieved, lipstick, used makeup compacts, address books, a telephone bill, all manner of women's products, watches, rings, a pair of thong panties, and more than one cell phone?

Years ago, I attempted to outsmart my female clientele and I really should have known better. In about 1983, someone came to me with a new type of toilet seat. It was a regular type of seat, but it had a motor that was attached to a mechanism that wrapped the seat in new plastic with just the touch of a button. It would pull the used plastic into the housing onto a spool as the new plastic fed out to cover the seat. It was kind of cool and I figured that I could pay for the thing in a week with reduced paper and plumbing fees. What a great idea, almost. What I hadn't accounted for was the fact that the girls didn't trust that the already sat on, or hovered over, plastic was being totally returned to the housing so they would hit the button four or five times, just to be sure. This exercise was problematic because instead of getting the *hundreds of heinies* per roll as promised by the salesman, we were averaging about four. I think the first night we had the thing installed we used twenty-two rolls. We were told two hundred uses per roll. I promise you we didn't do eighty-eight hundred dinners that night, assuming each of the 4,400 women came with a date. My partner yanked it out that night after service. I thought it was a good idea for the restaurant, my bottom line, and the rain forest, but the girls would prove me wrong. The first time I saw a rest room in Europe that had just a hole in the floor, I thought, *"Man, what barbarians."* I've since been shaken out of my naiveté by flooded bathroom floors, broken pipes, and endless plumbing bills and I have a newfound respect for Europeans. It's not barbarism that led them to open the floor, it was enlightenment, and it sure could have come in handy that fateful day in 1972.

Okay, here goes. This is your last chance to turn back.

I was prepping in the kitchen on a sweltering summer day and decided to take a men's room break. I'd been drinking gallons of seltzer and being as hot as it was, you reach a bursting point. As I walked into the men's room an odor hit me like a punch in the face. You all know the deal, so I won't elaborate but it was awful and because I was the only one in the building at that point, the source of the odor had apparently been there overnight. I gagged and left. As I was trying to get my breath back one of the other cooks came in to work.

I walked into the kitchen, and he said, "Hey, what's up."

I said, "I think there's a dead body in the men's room."

He asked, "A dead body?"

Me, "There's a dead something. You can't believe the stink in there. The toilet must be clogged or something. It's wretched."

"Come on, grow up. Just plunge the thing and open the door."

I said, "I don't think you understand the severity of the problem."

He said, "Come on, tough guy. I'll help you."

We went to the men's room and when he walked in, he said, "Oh, my god, I thought you were exaggerating. That is ripe."

"I tried to warn you. It's got to be coming from the booth but I'm afraid to open the door."

He told me, "I have to get out of here for a minute or I'm going to heave."

Seeing an opening, I said, "Take a break there, tough guy. I'll wait for you here."

He asked, "Are you really going to stay in here?"

"Are you out of your mind, I was kidding."

He laughed. "Man, I had no idea how bad it was."

I giggled. "Told you."

My buddy was always the responsible one and thank God he was there, or I might have kicked the can down the road, so to speak, and waited for a porter to come in. And as much as that was the preferred plan, we decided that we just couldn't do that to anyone else.

I said, "I've been holding in three quarts of seltzer for ten minutes so I'm going to the ladies room. When I get out, let's do this and get it over with."

He said, "Okay, I'll find the plunger."

When I got back, he was standing there at the door, plunger in hand, taking very deep breaths. He said, "I'm going to hold my breath. I suggest you do the same. Let's just run in, do it, and get out. We can leave the rest for Juan when he gets in."

I said, "Alright, General. I'm right behind you."

He said, "Okay, on the count of three, we go. One … two …"

We each took two deep breaths and, on the count of three, burst through the door and began our assault on the booth. He pushed me aside and threw open the booth door. He immediately stepped back, turned and looked at me with eyes as wide as golf balls and involuntarily uttered the most prosaic phrase one could possibly hope for under the circumstances, "Holy SHIT!" Then he ran out of the room. I followed him like a frightened schoolchild.

When I got outside, he was laughing uncontrollably, sitting on the floor in the hallway, and saying, "Did you see it? Did you see it?"

We were both sitting on the floor laughing hysterically only I wasn't sure what I was laughing at. I said, "No, I ran out when you did. What the hell is in there?"

He said, "You have to go in there and look. You've never seen anything like it. Trust me."

"What the hell is it?

"Just take a breath and go back in."

Which was exactly what I did. I took a deep breath, entered again, opened the booth door, gasped, ran back out and collapsed on the floor next to my friend. I don't think we stopped laughing for ten minutes. From that day on, I believed in monsters. You had to see it.

In all my writings over the years, I've never attempted to describe a turd before so please bear with me. I'll give it to you as gently as I can.

My first fleeting thought was that it was an anaconda. It was that big. The thing had the circumference of a beer can. Half of it was on dry land and the other half—or third, or tenth—disappeared into the hole so you really couldn't quite get a grip on the length; you just knew it was a whopper. I'll venture a conservative guess at two and a half feet. I'm serious.

When we finally stopped laughing, we looked at each other, and he said, "Do you believe the size of that thing?"

"No. We need to get a camera. This has got to be a world record. You can't even describe it; it has to be experienced. You ever see anything that big before?"

He said, "Maybe at the Bronx Zoo?"

I said, "At first I thought it was breathing."

We lost it all over again and we were already about a half hour into the plunging detail.

He said, "Do you remember seeing a reservation for a Sasquatch party last night?"

Laughing again, I said, "I can't believe I'm even mildly curious about this, but you can't even tell how big it is because it disappeared into the hole. That thing deserves a weigh-in. It's magnificent."

My friend, real serious-like, said, "You know, I don't even think it began to taper as it got to the hole so there's no telling the true size. How the hell did he get that out?"

I said, "It must have been tapered, otherwise you would have heard his sphincter slam shut all the way in Hoboken when that baby came sailing through. You think he could have had a Lamaze coach? You'd have to have your breathing right to give birth to something like that. He could have been in labor for hours."

That was it for me. I was crying. Every time we tried to get it back one of us said something stupid that continued to fuel the hilarity.

Fifteen minutes later, he said, "Look, as funny as this is, we have to get rid of that thing and get some work done. I'm going to go in and flush it."

I said, "Can I sing, *Born Free,* as it goes down?"

Ten more minutes of stupidity. We finally settled down enough to deal with Super Turd. As disgusting as it was and as ridiculous as this sounds, we both wanted to see it one more time, so in we went holding our breath. I reached the booth, opened the door, and pushed the flush lever. It's not like I was expecting a twenty-one-gun salute, but I expected *something* to happen. The turd didn't move—not an inch. The toilet flushed and refilled, but it never moved. The two of us looked at each other and ran out of the room back onto the hallway floor. Neither of us could speak for few minutes.

Finally, he said, "No one is going to believe this, you know."

"I know."

"All kidding aside, we have to get rid of that thing."

I said, "Any ideas? It won't flush."

He said, "It has to. Let's give it another shot."

Attempt number two, pun intended, was the same as number one. The thing didn't budge. Remember, every time we went at it, we had to hold our breath and it was making me light-headed. That's the only explanation I can think of for the following statement.

I said, "Let's go find a stick and break it up."

Brilliant, no? That's probably why I'm still a cook fifty something years later.

He said, "I'm out, dude. You are on your own. You're actually going to break the seal on that? Good luck. I'm going back to work. I've had all the fun I could stand for one day."

"Thanks. I'd consider giving Juan a hundred dollars to deal with this, but he's smart enough to hold out for a lot more. I'll find a stick. If I'm not back in the kitchen in fifteen minutes, send a hazmat team."

I went out back and picked the longest stick I could find. He was crying when he saw me parade through the kitchen with the stick. He said, "A regular Don Quixote."

I said, "Yeah, large brown windmills."

I almost didn't make it back to the john. When I got there, I held my breath, went in, pushed open the booth door, flushed, and parried furiously. As I was turning blue, I could see my worst-case scenario, one I was totally unprepared for, unfolding before my eyes. The water in the bowl started to rise at an alarming rate and I remember thinking, *If this thing winds up on the floor, I'm moving out of state*. Mercifully, whatever happened in the pipes happened and just as the water was about to spill over the bowl, something down there let go and everything went down. I ran out just as I was about to faint. Juan eventually got the john back together again and life resumed its normal pace. I've dealt with a thousand bathroom issues since then, but none with the size and scope of Super Turd. In a perverse way, I'm glad I saw it. Much like watching Segovia play guitar, Ali box, or Nureyev dance, it's special to see people at the top of their game. This fella, in my judgement, was the Prince of the Porcelain, the Monarch of the Movement, the veritable King of the Can, and he deserves all the credit I can give him for a uniquely unmatched effort. It is with great respect and humility that I congratulate you, sir, whomever you may be. It was the best I've ever seen.

BACHELOR #1

I've concluded that you can go broke being charitable. It's not a martyr's sentiment; it's simply that there are so many charities and so many functions that if you agreed to give to or do every one that's asked of you, you would need one with your own name on it to buy you out of the hole. For that reason, I've limited what we give or work with, to Long Island–based organizations involving the needs of children. Homegrown and child-based—that's it. Diane, whom I consider to be my right-hand woman, has been working for me for what seems to be forever; it's at least twenty-five years. She is clean and sober but some years back Diane would have the occasional cocktail. We all do it but some of us do it better than others. I think it has to do with the production, or lack thereof, of enzymes but whatever the reason, giving Diane the occasional cocktail back then was like giving a three-year-old a blowtorch. She had a tendency to become a one-woman, whirling dervish, of adolescent mischief. Diane has a wild sense of humor and is very intelligent—a deadly combination when it comes to pranking and pranking is something she is expert at and has taken, at times, to unparalleled heights. Several years ago, I was hanging at the bar after work. Diane came to me and said, "Hey, Chef, the ladies at the Pediatric Cancer Center, where I volunteer, asked me if I could get you to help them out with something."

I had done some fundraising for them in the past, so it wasn't an unusual request. I said, "Sure, what?"

She continued. "It seems that they are having a bachelor auction to raise money for the center, and they asked if you would participate."

I asked, "What do they need? Some food?"

She said, "No, they want you to be in the auction."

I said, "Are you out of your mind? Do they know how old I am?"

"Yeah, they know but there will be all different age groups of women there. C'mon, it'll be fun, and you'll be helping the kids."

I said, "I don't think that the expression, *you're not getting older, you're getting better,* has ever been shouted at a bachelor auction."

Diane said, "Could you just do it this one time? I told them I could get you to help out."

I said, "All right, what the hell."

The simple fact is that the ego is involved in ninety nine percent of terrible decisions, at least mine anyway. All it takes is a little flattery and you veer right off the path. I've also never heard a bad idea after a bottle of Pinot Noir. That said, if you take the fact that I have an ego, it was being stroked after too much wine, you'll forgive me for making a stupid decision. Combine that with Diane, who was still cocktailing back then, being the point person and you can pretty much rest assured that this was going to blow up. And it did.

The next day I was in the shower when it dawned on me that I'd made an extremely bad call. I phoned Diane right away and said, "I can't do the auction."

She said, "What do you mean, you can't do it?"

I said, "I can't *do* it. I'm too old for this shit. I can't do it. It's ludicrous."

She said, "You have to do it. I already told them you would. You were the last one on board and they are going to press today. You can't back out now. I'll look ridiculous."

"What will look ridiculous is a forty-nine-year-old bachelor parading his ass around a dance floor in front of five hundred overserved women in their twenties. That's ridiculous!"

Diane said, "You're looking at this the wrong way. What's the worst that can happen? You'll have to spend a couple of hours with someone having dinner, or something. Is that going to kill you? And think of the kids."

I said, "I know what's going to happen. A train wreck, that's what. What if no one picks me? I'll never hear the end of it."

Diane said, "Chef, you're getting crazy over nothing. It'll be fine. Besides, someone will pick you. You're catnip for the over-seventy chicks."

I said, "That's comforting. I'll finally get to go on my dream date with a frisky septuagenarian waving her social security check and screaming, *take it off, take it off!* I'm not doing it!"

"Will you please get over yourself? You are doing it, and that's the end of it. Just relax and think of the kids."

As the weeks wore on, I forgot about it and was less stressed when I did think about it because it really wasn't a big deal in the scheme of things and the money—providing that the shameful peddling of my wares would produce some—would benefit sick children. That goes a long way in softening the blow of making an ass of yourself in public. As the big day got closer all the dread came back and I tried to back out the night before, but Diane wouldn't let me. She started bringing up the kids again, appealing to my latent Catholic guilt, so I gave up.

She asked, "What are you wearing tomorrow?"

I said, "How about a yellow Speedo? What the hell, I couldn't possibly be any more humiliated. We might as well give them a good laugh for the money."

Diane said, "Stop being an asshole. Just make sure you show up presentable. You're not exactly what anyone would call fashion conscious."

I asked, "Are you coming to this debacle tomorrow?"

Diane, now hysterical, replied, "Are you kidding? There's no way I'm missing this."

I told her, "I hope you're enjoying yourself. If you bring a camera you're fired."

The next day was an angst-ridden nightmare. I got to Coolfish about 5:00 for the 7:00 trip to the auction. Diane and a few of the waitstaff who weren't working that night met me at the restaurant and I'm sure it was to make certain that I'd follow through. Truth be told, I had considered bailing out. I took Diane in the office and sat her down.

I said, "I could kill you right now for getting me into this. Volunteer work doesn't mean you volunteer someone else."

Diane said, "I wouldn't be worth much in a bachelor auction. Besides, we'll have fun. We'll get to party when it's over."

I said, "Yeah, I've got a feeling I'll need a drink when it's over. Listen to me. Here is what we're going to do." I handed her fifteen hundred dollars in cash and said, "Take this money and buy a round of drinks for the staff when we get there."

She said, "That's a lot of money for a round of drinks."

I said, "Yeah, no shit. I want you to behave yourself until I'm up and then I want you, *paying attention,* to the bidding, okay? And if it looks like it isn't going well, I want you to bid me up."

Diane asked, "You want me to bid on you?"

"Yeah."

"With your own money?"

"Yes."

She said, "You know, Chef, it really doesn't matter about the amount of money you raise. It's all about helping these kids."

I said, "They're going to get what they get. I understand the concept here but right now it's not about them, it's about me. If I can help it, I'd like to prevent five hundred drunken, screaming women from laughing at my expense! And since it was your bright idea that got me into this fiasco you are going to make sure I get out of this with, at least, a shred of dignity. So, behave yourself, pay attention, and bid me up if I'm tanking."

When we arrived, my worst fears were confirmed. I was the oldest bachelor by a minimum of fifteen years. The others were probably wondering whether I was the official date chaperone. There must have been ten or twelve of us and all the others were about twenty-five to thirty-five years old, in shape, and magazine handsome. I come rolling in, staring fifty in the face and looking like a cross between an aging hippie, an outlaw biker, and Charlie Manson. After a couple of hellos and a glass of wine, they started the auction. They took the first victim out and you could have heard the roar in Cincinnati. I'm guessing there were three hundred or more women out there, whistling, catcalling, shouting all kinds of obscenities and making lewd offers. Things were beginning to look up.

"Can I get a hundred? Two hundred? How about two …? I got two, can I get three? Three hundred … Four … Five … going once, going twice … Sold for five hundred dollars!" And so it went. Most of the guys sold for between five and seven hundred except for a young, handsome doctor who scored $950.

Right this way, Tom.

I walked into a bright spotlight and a sea of people. There was a huge dance floor in the middle of the room that had been cleared and all the girls were on the perimeter, laughing and shouting.

The guy who brought me out told me, "Walk all the way around the dance floor and keep doing laps until the bidding is over."

I said, "You're kidding me, right?"

"No, that's what everyone had to do."

I was looking for Diane but couldn't find her in the sea of humanity. I started to panic, thinking she had gotten bored and left, or gotten drunk and forgot. As I started walking the gauntlet, I realized why women avoid construction sites. I was the last to go, so by the time I got out there, the ladies were very well oiled and making some interesting comments. I just wanted to get it over with and desperately wanted not to be the lowest number.

"Can I get one hundred? One … Can I get two? Two hundred dollars. Can I …? Two … I have two. Can I get three …?" And on it went. I was sweating out every hundred dollars, hoping to surpass some of the other bids. When I finally got to the low bid of four or five hundred dollars, there was a great sense of relief, and I was hoping it would come to an end and that I could get off the dance floor … but it kept going.

"Six hundred … Can I get six hundred? Can I get seven? Can I get seven hundred?"

Suddenly, my spirits were lifted, my gait became confident, and my attitude improved considerably.

"I have seven hundred. Can I get eight? I need eight … Can I get eight hundred dollars? Eight hundred dollars from the woman in the back. I have eight hundred dollars … Can I get nine?" It was the number nine that cut through my euphoria and set me to wondering what kind of date I could come up with that could possibly justify the expense, but I figured I'd work that out later and enjoy the moment. I was even starting to like Diane again, whom I still couldn't find in the crowd.

"Nine hundred … I have nine hundred. Can I get one thousand, a new record? One thousand … I'm looking for one thousand dollars."

Just when I thought that this couldn't have possibly gone any better if I'd scripted it myself, this twenty-six-year-old, Taylor Swift lookalike, came to the front and yelled out, "One thousand dollars!"

And that was when I found Diane.

It was precisely at the one thousand dollar mark that Diane awoke from her mojito coma and shouted, "Eleven hundred dollars!"

You can't be serious.

I saw her in the back of the room, teetering on one of my waiter's shoulders and having the time of her life. I looked over and gave her the *knife across the throat* sign several times in rapid succession but to no avail.

Taylor Swift yelled out, "Twelve hundred!"

Diane, at the top of her lungs, screamed, "Thirteen thousand! Thirt …" Then she bent slightly, listening to the waiter whose shoulders she was perched on. "Oh, what? Sorry … oops. I'm … oh … Oh, shit!" Then she said to the auctioneer, "Thirteen hundred. Yeah, thirteen hundred. I meant hundred, not thousand. Hundred!"

I yelled out, "You're fired!"

Taylor yelled, "Fourteen hundred!"

Thankfully, someone in my crew tackled them and placed Diane on a chair with his hand over her mouth for the duration of, *"Going once, going twice … sold!"*

I went over there immediately and asked her, "What the hell is wrong with you?"

Diane said, "What??"

"What? What were you thinking?"

Diane said, "You told me to bid you up."

I said, "I was up, damn it. I wanted you to bid me up if I was down. And another thing: did you see whom you were bidding against? She's drop-dead gorgeous. I knew this was a bad idea."

Diane said, "What was?"

"Putting you in charge of rigging the bidding."

Diane said, "What are you complaining about? Look at all the money we made. You would have been stuck at a thousand dollars without me. You should be thanking me."

I couldn't help but laugh. Diane gets me like that. I can't stay mad at her no matter what she pulls, and she has pulled some corkers over the years. Diane can be a little crazy but she's crazy like a fox. I truly believe, after having thought about it for a while, that she had orchestrated the result from the very beginning. I stated before that she was very intelligent and a master prankster and used both those talents, and me, to get as much money for those children as she possibly could. That's a big-hearted woman right there.

I'm glad to say, if only for my own sake, she's done with mojitos but continues to give of herself in the cause of sick children and I'm extremely proud of her on both counts. And in case you were wondering, I never did go on the date. Taylor Swift asked me what I would like to do, and I told her that the only thing I was good at was going out to dinner. She told me that she would be down for that, so we set up a telephone date to set the details. I called her several times and didn't get an answer, so I finally left a message. She called back and told me that her boyfriend was struggling with the idea and that she had better not go. Thank God we didn't. I accidentally bumped into them out together one night, some months later, and after seeing him I was glad she didn't press the issue. He was the size of Texas.

(It was for the kids ... for the kids ... I swear it was for the kids!)

LOUIS ELLIS III

It's only fitting that I should finish this book the way it began— full circle, if you will. As you can imagine after reading this far, there have been quite a cast of characters who have passed through the many kitchens and dining rooms I've been involved in, but there was no one who was more pathologically screwed up, more dangerous, funnier at his own expense without ever realizing it, or more unforgettable than Shorty. I use his real name because even though I haven't seen him since 1972, I'm cocksure there's no way he could possibly be alive. And I need you to know that my friend Shorty existed. I could do an entire book on the man, as I said in the introduction, and although our time together totaled only three years, Shorty packed so much action into so little time that to not document his existence would be truly unfortunate. Shorty's real name was Louis Ellis

III. Upon learning his name, a year and a half after I met him, all I could say was that I was having quite a time imagining how numbers I and II managed to turn out who would become number III. Apparently, it takes a village to raise a lunatic. In my eyes he was Louis Ellis the Only. I've never met anyone quite like him and believe me I don't make that statement lightly. I offer you some vital statistics: Shorty was an African American man of about thirty-five to forty years of age when I met him. He gave a different number every time he was asked, so I'm forced to speculate. He was a stocky, heavily muscled man who was very intimidating, in a Joe Frazier kind of way, until you got to know him. I'm not sure where he grew up or under what circumstances because he would never tell me.

I once asked him before I got to know him well, but he just gave me that Shorty badass face and said, "Why you gots to know all that shit, boy? Mind yo' own bidnez."

I always suspected there was a wound he was protecting, and I felt sorry for him because of it. Shorty always called me, *"Boy."* Only once in the three years we were together did he call me by, what he believed to be, my given name, *"Tommy James Shondell,"* because at that moment he was describing to me, in detail at two hundred decibels, how he was planning to end my life and I'm assuming that because he was ossified, he didn't want to forget whom he was going to kill. He hadn't had much of an education, and I found out because he insisted on the waitresses calling out all their orders instead of writing them down. He was brilliant on the rare occasions he was sober, expediting hundreds of dinners without ever seeing a dupe, and I had learned later that he developed the talent because he was unable to read. Shorty always said he was five foot four, hence the moniker, which I think was a rather optimistic assessment of his stature. Suspecting he was full of shit, I once asked him to prove it by showing me his driver's license but in a rare display of governmental wisdom, the State of New York had revoked it.

Now, I'll offer you the qualities that endear me to him to this day. Shorty always wore a hat—always. His lid of choice was his beloved derby. The only time I ever saw him without one was when I unexpectedly caught him coming out of the shower, in the motel where he lived, when he panicked and scrambled around, losing his towel, while trying to get it back on his head. A dripping, naked Shorty, with a crushed derby leaning sideways over his ear is a vision I suffer to this day. It was then that I understood him never being without it; his head was the shape of a peeled onion and a bit too small for his frame. He had an infectious laugh that would cause his shoulders to scrunch up over his ears, which made him appear even shorter than he was, and he had a missing front tooth that made it impossible to not chuckle at him while laughing with him. He could consume more cheap vodka than any man on the planet, annihilate the English language like George Bush on crack, and use the word, *motherfucker,* as a noun, a verb, an adjective, an adverb, and a dangling participle. He was subjected to severe leg cramps that caused him to suddenly fall down, writhing in pain and screaming, possessed the emotional stability of a two-year-old, and had a penchant for carrying unlicensed firearms. That combo platter was irresistible to a sixteen-year-old street kid. Whom could be more fun to hang out with? And hang out we did because I was the only friend Shorty had. We were together day and night for the three years that I knew him and here's a glimpse of some of the situations I found myself in as a result of my friendship with this maniac.

1) I was beaten over the head with a pool cue by a seriously troubled Vietnam vet, whom Shorty somehow convinced that I, and not he, was the source of his agitation.

2) After agreeing to be his best man, he left me, *standing at the altar,* dressed like one of the Pips, while pulling a no-show at his wedding.

3) He fractured two of my ribs in a fight we had over the proper color of medium rare.

4) He chased me for a mile down Old Country Road and once again threatened my life, while clutching his bloody nose, after I smashed it with a roasting pan in response to example three, nine months after the original assault.

5) He threw his last pint bottle of Smirnoff vodka at my head due to my inability to control my laughter at his use of the word, *tempitude* (Shorty for the word *temperature*), and then asking me to borrow the money to replace it.

6) He locked me in his residency motel room with a six-foot, four-inch, three-hundred-pound guy who happened to live next door to him, and thankfully was in on the *joke,* after telling him I called him the n-word, just to see how I would react.

7) I reacted by duct-taping him to the chair he was passed out on one week later in the middle of dinner service, replacing his derby with a two-gallon coffee filter. Then I pulled him out into the main kitchen to take a few photos with an Instamatic camera and left him there with explicit instructions to not cut him loose until I was at least a half an hour out of the building.

8) He had me red-lining my 1963 Volkswagen Beetle driving away from a pursuing mob after Shorty, in a moment of drunken chivalry, intervened in a barroom domestic dispute by pulling out his gun and a plastic badge and proclaiming at the top of his lungs, "I am the po-lice!" I immediately thought, *'And I'm the fuck outta here!'*

9) He made me the incredulous offer—at three in the morning, after approximately two quarts of vodka and salami on rye—to get out of the taxi, come into my house, wake up my father, and explain to him why he shouldn't be so hard on me for underage drinking.

10) He pulled his switchblade on me no fewer than ten times while, thankfully, managing to open it only twice and nearly filleting the both of us when I tried to show him how to close the damn thing after he had finally calmed down.

11) He tried his damnedest to kill me and three hundred unsuspected patrons one Thanksgiving Day by seriously undercooking Grandma Ellis's Secret, Down Home, Giblet Gravy using what were clearly not sushi-grade giblets and introducing the lot of us to the weight-loss miracle known as salmonella.

12) We spent two and a half hours retracing his steps from the night before, going to no less than six different bars in two different counties and paying off four separate bar tabs because Shorty had misplaced his derby, and in his words, "I looks ridiculous in a fedora, boy! I needs to find my derby. It's one of my *idiocracies*" (Shorty for *idiosyncrasies*).

I could go on for days, but I'll leave it to your imaginations for now and I guarantee you that you couldn't conjure up, in your wildest dreams, what a typical Saturday evening with Shorty was like. I'll go into further details of our adventures at some other time but here is a fourteen-carat gold Shorty story that has to be my all-time favorite.

One Saturday night in 1970, Shorty and I were fighting all throughout dinner service. He was on his second bottle of vodka and was becoming impossible, yelling and cursing at me and abusing the waitstaff. After four hours of this bullshit, it dawned on him that he didn't have any money to go out. There was no way that Shorty wasn't going to go out on a Saturday because he believed it to be the best night for him to get lucky. His reasoning was that because Sunday was a relatively easy day at the restaurant, he could come in late, which would afford him some extra time on Saturday night to work his magic on the ladies. On Sundays, he would drag what was left of him into work and sleep off most of the shift anyway. He reasoned that since he had his own personal Cinderella, I would pick up his end of the workload. Sundays turned out to be the easiest day for Shorty and, subsequently, the hardest day for me. So that was the reason he was trying to make up with me, thinking that if he turned it around, I'd fund him. I wasn't buying it.

Besides, in the shape he was in, he couldn't have bought a conjugal visit in an all-girl penitentiary with a winning lotto ticket, as they say.

Shorty, "Come on, boy. I didn't means nothing by calling you a shit-ball little honkey. It was just in the heat of the moment."

I said, "Shorty, I really don't care what you call me and I'm too tired to be offended. I'm just sick of you drinking yourself stupid before we get the dinners out. You're killing me back there."

Shorty said, "Come on, let's go out and get *emutilated* [Shorty for inebriated]. Everybody's going to Pepi's."

I said, "I'm not going anywhere with you. You're *emutilated* already and nothing good happens to me when you're *emutilated*. Besides, you just want to go with me so I can pay for your sorry ass."

Indignantly, he said, "What? You think I needs your pilanthery [Shorty for *philanthropy*]?"

I said, "Yeah, I do. And speaking of that, your *pilanthery* bill is running into the hundreds."

Shorty then said, "I should charge yo' ass for all the teachin' I do ya'."

Refer, if you will, to examples 1 through 12.

The truth is I was softening a little and really could never stay mad at him for very long but no one in the crew heading to Pepi's wanted to deal with him, so I came up with what I thought was a win-win solution. There was another bar called the Sulky that was five or six blocks west of Pepi's where we also used to hang out. I told Shorty that I wouldn't give him any money but that I'd give the bartender at the Sulky ten dollars to run a tab for him for the night.

Shorty said, "You ain't stayin' and *dranking* with me, boy?"

I said, "Nope, not tonight."

Shorty said, "Can you make it fifteen? I gots to leave a *grannuity* [Shorty for *gratuity*]."

I gave in. "All right, but that's it. I'm done with you tonight."

I took him to the Sulky and gave the bartender fifteen dollars for Shorty's tab. Fifteen dollars bought a lot of pouring vodka in 1970 and not being known as an overly generous tipper, Shorty made good use of it. Sometime, in the course of the evening, someone or something pissed him off and he pulled out his gun and popped three caps into the ceiling, hitting a water line, flooding the bar area, and earning himself a uniformed escort to the pokey. I found out the next day when I got to work. Our furious boss had gotten the one call that the law allowed Shorty to make, and he decided that because it was Sunday and we were going into the slow part of the week, he was going to leave Shorty in jail for a few days to teach him a lesson. That following Thursday he arranged for Shorty's bail, but he was still so mad that he wouldn't drive him back to the restaurant, so he sent me to pick him up. I knew Shorty well, and I knew he was a little shaken, but he put on the tough-guy act and told me how everyone in jail was scared to death of him.

I said, "Tough week, eh?"

Shorty replied, "Boy, you thinks a little *incanceration* [Shorty for *incarceration*] is gonna bother Louis Ellis III? I showed them motherfuckers some shit!"

I couldn't help but laugh.

He said, "Boy, this is some serious shit right here. You gots to help me out. You da only one I can turns to."

I said while giggling, "Shorty, I'm the only one who even likes you. You're a disaster. Who does a shooting in front of forty-seven witnesses and on a bar ceiling no less? And while you were *incancerated*, did you mention to your fellow inmates that you were there for murdering an air-conditioning unit?"

Shorty, with the *bad-ass* face said, "Boy, don't fuck with me now. I ain't in the mood." He went quiet for a moment and then said, "Boy, I did it this time. I fucked up good. You know, I gots what they call priors."

I said, "How come I'm not surprised? What did you do? Kill a washing machine and a couple of microwaves?"

He looked at me with big, wide eyes and said, "One mo' motherfucking word outta you, and I'm gonna kill yo' little honkey ass."

He looked like he was going to strangle me and even though he needed my help, I thought I'd better shut my mouth. I'm not suicidal.

Then he said, "Listen, boy. You gots to help me get out uh dis shit."

I asked him, "What do you want me to do? I'm seventeen."

He said, "I was thinkin' 'bout it when I was *incancerated*. I needs you to make a phone call for me."

I said, "Alright, who do you want me to call?"

I realize you're about to become skeptical, but I swear to you the following was word for word.

He looked at me and said with a straight face, "I needs you to call Perry Mason."

I admit it's a rather perplexing request.

All I could come up with was, "Huh?"

Losing his patience, he said, "Perry Mason, boy, Perry Mason! I needs you to call him. He's the only motherfucker that can get me out uh dis shit. That motherfucker ain't never lost in a law court, not one motherfucking time. You thinks he'll take my case?"

I can't begin to imagine, and would love to have had a picture of, the look on my face when I asked him, "Do I think he'll take your case? You're asking me if I think Perry Mason will take your case?"

Shorty, "Yeah, boy, dat's what I'm *axeing* you!"

Incredulous, I said, "Um, no, Shorty, I don't think Perry Mason will take your case."

He asked, "Why? 'Cause I'm black?"

I said, "No, 'cause you're an idiot. He's not a real lawyer—he's a TV character."

He said, "He's on TV but those are real cases. Y'all seventeen boy; you don't know shit. Just call his ass, all right? I think he's in California someplace 'cause I always sees palm trees by his headquarters."

I said, "Thanks for the heads-up."

I drove him back to the restaurant pleading with him to keep the conversation between the two of us, but he wasn't listening. When we got there, he asked me to ask the owner of the restaurant to call Perry for him because he still wasn't speaking to Shorty. I said I would and did. You can imagine how that went and the two of us were doubled over for about ten minutes before we could even go back out and look at him, never mind explain it to him. When we were finally able to come out of the office, we saw Shorty sitting in one of the booths talking to one of the waitresses who was lying in the seat across from him with her face buried in a napkin.

Apparently, Shorty had taken matters into his own hands.

Still worried about Perry Mason's potential racism, he looks sheepishly up at the boss and me and asked, "Did you call him?"

I said, "Yeah. He wasn't in, so I left a message with Della Street, and she said that he'd get back to us. He's probably out to lunch with Paul."

Shorty said, "Okay, good. Did you tell her I was black?"

What can you say? After a brief recovery period it took the boss, the waitress and me a good fifteen minutes to finally convince Shorty that Perry Mason was a figment of Earl Stanley Gardiner's imagination. To this day, one of my clearest memories of him is when he finally realized that Perry wouldn't be returning the call. He placed his head on the table, clutched his derby with both hands, and wailed, "I'm so fucked. I am sooo motherfucked. They gonna *incancerate my ass good* [Shorty for lock him up and throw away the key]."

Sadly, when I went off to cooking school, we lost touch. The last time I came back to visit him, as I often did, he was gone from the restaurant, and no one knew where he went. I don't know what became of him after 1972. I'm pretty sure he did some time for his indiscretion. He was roughly forty years old back then, which would make him north of ninety today. Do the math. Two or three bottles of vodka a day for sixty years is not a proper recipe for a centennial birthday cake, so I'm reasonably certain he's passed. I'm assuming the undertaker waived the embalming fee because Shorty would have surely been, by the time he was called, fully pickled. I had three special years with him and wouldn't trade them for anything. He did teach me quite a bit and most of it was what *not* to do, but there was tremendous value in that, nonetheless. It was a very unlikely friendship for 1968 when we had first met: a forty-year-old African American man and a sixteen-year-old white kid but for that period we were inseparable. We had a ton of fun, got in a world of trouble, cooked a lot of steaks, smoked a lot of cigarettes, had some insane fights with each other, shared a lot of cabs, and drank a cellar full of vodka. It was a friendship that I will always cherish. I miss him to this day and never a week goes by that I don't think of him, his antics, and what ultimately became of him. As much of a nightmare as he could be at times, and he was, he had the redeeming qualities of a big heart, an infectious laugh, and he could cook eight hundred steaks without one coming back. I loved the guy. God bless you, Shorty. Oh, and God, you may want to hide the vodka.

ONE FOR THE ROAD

M y daughter has a master's degree in forensic psychology, and I've spoken to her on occasion about our shared interest in how and why the human brain can, on the one hand, create masterpieces of art and music, bridges and skyscrapers, rockets and satellites, and solve the mysteries of the universe, and on the other hand, manufacture a John Wayne Gacy, a Pol Pot, a Mao, or the woman I'm about to describe. It boggles the mind trying to contemplate the causes that send the brain off the rails, resulting in behaviors in people that are impossible to understand for the unfortunate souls who cross their paths. And although this woman obviously could never achieve the levels of mayhem wrought by John, Pol, or the Chairman himself, it wasn't for lack of trying.

On one of my many lucky days, this woman walked into the restaurant with three friends—or attendants, as the case may be—and proceeded to sit at the fifth table offered. After her friends—or attendants, as the case may be—gave the server their drink orders, she said, "I'll have a glass of water. Is it filtered?"

The server responded, "No."

The woman then asked, "Can you filter it for me?"

The server again said, "No, but I can get you a bottle of water. I think they're filtered."

The woman, "No, I'd like a glass. Why can't you just filter it?"

The server, "Because we don't have a filter, nor do we filter glasses of water. That's why we serve bottled water, for those who are squeamish about tap water."

The woman said, "Do you know what's in tap water—the chemicals and all?"

The server said, "No, I try not to think about it."

"Well, let me tell you." The woman told her, and then recited fifteen to twenty of Monsanto's favorite chemicals to an enthralled group of tablemates and a thoroughly bewildered server.

The server delivered the drinks and began to take the dinner orders. One by one, the tablemates—or attendants, as the case may be—gave the server their orders without so much as a hint of an allergy, a gluten issue, vivid descriptions of gastrointestinal events, a pharmacological diatribe, or dietary no-nos. Optimism is a fleeting thing.

The server turned to our girl and said, "And you, ma'am?"

The woman looked the server in the eye and said—word for word, I swear— "I am a keto-practicing vegan, I'm allergic to gluten, and I'm dairy intolerant. Make the kitchen aware of that, please." Then she said, "I'll have the lobster roll."

Realigning misfiring synapses takes several seconds.

The suddenly dumbstruck server said, "I thought you were a vegan, ma'am,"

The woman answered, "I am."

"And you want a lobster roll?"

"Yes."

The server said, "I don't think you can eat that."

The woman, "I'm well aware of what I can and cannot eat, miss. I'll have the lobster roll."

Again, I ask, what could possibly go wrong?

The server came into the kitchen with the order and said, "There's a woman out there who says that she's a keto-practicing vegan with gluten issues and dairy problems and she just ordered a lobster roll. Should I put that through the computer?"

I said, "Uh, could you repeat that?"

The server said, "The woman said she's a keto vegan, whatever that means; she can't have gluten or dairy and she just ordered a lobster roll. What should I do?"

Processing insanity requires one to eliminate all peripheral thought, clear the mind, slow the respiration rate, and bear down on the problem, with your mouth slightly ajar. I stared at her blankly. As the fog lifted and what she told me came slowly into focus, I asked the first of several probing questions. "Are you fucking serious?"

The server said, "Yup. I said that I thought she couldn't eat that, but she assured me she could and made sure to tell me that she wanted the kitchen to know that she has dairy and gluten issues."

My second probing question: "She's fucking serious?"

"Yes, she's serious. What would you like me to do?"

"I'm assuming she's aware that a lobster isn't a vegetable. It has a face, a mother, a heartbeat, a respiratory system of sorts—all the things that should strike terror into the heart of a vegan."

"I would think so."

"You clearly heard her say *vegan*, correct?"

"Yup, it was the first thing she told me. She said she was a keto-practicing vegan. What is keto, anyway?"

"It's the latest restaurant torture manual for bored housewives."

The server said, "Okay, what would you like me to do?"

Laughing, I said, "Put it through. I'm pretty sure I know how this will end but the material could be priceless."

The server put the order through to the kitchen.

The menu read, *"New England Style Lobster Roll/Top Split Bun/ Lemon-Tarragon Aioli/Petite Herb Salad/Sweet Potato Fries,"* and that was what we made. The order went to the table.

Our girl picked up her lobster roll, inspected it from no less than five angles, put it back down on the plate and lost her shit. "Where's the waitress!?"

The server rushed to the table. "What's the matter, ma'am?"

"What's the matter? I told you I was dairy intolerant! This has eggs in it!"

The server was looking back and forth between the woman and the lobster roll and trying to decide who was responsible for the screw-up, the kitchen or her parents. She finally said, "I don't think there are any eggs in the lobster roll, ma'am."

Her tablemates—or attendants, as the case may be—were trying to calm her down, but it was futile. She was on a roll—a gluten-free roll, I assume—and whether this was drama for attention's sake, or an accidental DNA leak we'll never know. Much smarter people than we have been trying to explain crazy for centuries, and to my knowledge no one's completely nailed it. I'm sure there are myriad reasons that send these folks to the asylum, so to speak, and on the whole I'm sympathetic but sympathy has a way of evaporating when the craziness starts heating up.

The woman yelled, "I don't care what you think! There are eggs in it! Are you people trying to kill me?"

I'm reasonably sure there has never been, in the history of coroners, one document that has listed the cause of death as lobster roll. There's also a better than even chance that if we did kill her, it would take the police forever to shrink the suspect list down to a few thousand folks, leaving us plenty of time to accept our Nobel Prize.

She yelled, "I want to see the manager!"

This was destiny at its purest. Diane was working the floor. As I said before, Diane is as nuts as anyone I know but in an extremely funny and mischievous way, with a razor-sharp wit and a killer sense of humor. This was shaping up to be King Kong versus Godzilla, and I almost felt sorry for the woman. Diane headed to the table, briefed in advance about the egg crisis.

Diane asked, "Hi, what's the problem?"

The woman answered, "What's the problem? What's the fucking problem? The problem is there's mayonnaise in the lobster roll! I told your waitress that I was allergic to dairy!"

Diane then asked, "Do you mean the aioli?"

"I don't give a shit what you call it. It's mayonnaise and there are eggs in it! I told her that I was allergic to dairy and still you served me this with eggs in it! Are you trying to kill me?"

A rhetorical question, I'm sure.

Diane—with a completely straight face, mind you—said, "No, ma'am. That would be tragic."

I believe the expression is, *Brevity is the soul of wit.*

At that moment, the woman should have picked up on the fact that she was severely outgunned dealing with Diane. She did not. We've dealt with more affected people than this woman has dealt with restaurant managers, so it was sort of unfair. It's like trying to heckle a comedian. Do you really think you're going to win? Do you really think you're the first drunken asshole he's had to deal with? You're paying to see him. If you were that witty, you could stay home, crack yourself up, and save the fifty dollars. I'm amused by the fact that these knuckleheads never consider that the comedians are there because they are truly funny, sharp-witted, and intelligent, and they have an arsenal of comebacks built over years of dealing with unruly patrons. It somehow never occurs to them. I digress, but this was a parallel situation.

Diane said, "Yes, ma'am, there are eggs in the aioli, but—"

The woman interjected, "I told her!"—pointing at the server—"That I was allergic to dairy!"

Diane readied the kill shot and calmly explained. "As I was saying before you interrupted me, there are eggs in the aioli."

"Mayonnaise!"

"Okay, there are eggs in the mayonnaise, but lucky for you, they're not cow eggs."

"What?"

"They're not cow eggs. We never use cow eggs in our mayonnaise. They're way too big. It would throw off the recipe. We use chicken eggs, which aren't dairy. They're sold in the dairy section but luckily are not a dairy product. Cow eggs would be dairy and if we used them, I could see you having a problem but like I said, those babies were chicken eggs, so it looks to me like we're good here. Can I get you anything else?"

"Uh …. uh … um."

Diane is one of the best I've ever seen. Game, set, and match.

ABOUT THE AUTHOR

After working in restaurants since the age of fifteen, graduating from the Culinary Institute of America in 1973, and training under accomplished chefs, Tom opened his first restaurant, Panama Hatties, in 1983. Since then, he has been the driving force behind such acclaimed Long Island restaurants as Spring Close House (East Hampton), Downtown Grille (Montauk), 107 Forest Avenue (Locust Valley), Lemongrass and Tease (Roslyn), Coolfish (Syosset), Passionfish (Westhampton Beach), Starfish (Merrick), Kingfish (Westbury), Thom Thom (Wantagh), Jedediah Hawkins Inn (Jamesport), Amano (Mattituck), Alure (Southold), Jewel and Beju (Melville), and Plated Simply Events and Catering (Mattituck).

Growing up on Long Island and living on the East End has seriously influenced his culinary sensibilities and his style was once described by Michael Todd of Grapezine magazine as, *"Atlantic Rim."* His current lineup of restaurants includes Amano, Alure, Mill River Country Club, and Tom Schaudel Catering and Event Planning. He has his own line of wines, made here on Long Island, under the Tom Schaudel Reserve label, which are sold at his restaurants and at the Paumanok Vineyards. He has been featured on such television shows as Gordon Elliot's *Door Knock Dinners* on Food Network, and *Chef's Night Out* on Metro Channel, and he has been a frequent guest chef on Long Island's own Channels 12 and 21, Telecare, the James Beard House, MAX 103.1's *Morning Show with Jim Douglas*, and *Ed Lowe's Morning Show*. Tom wrote a previous book, *Playing with Fire*, highlighting his one hundred wackiest customers and he also hosts a food, wine, and lifestyle radio show of the same name on Sunday mornings from 9:00 to 10:00 on WHLI AM 1100 and WHLI FM 104.7.

His band, Hurricane, featuring James Benard, Mike LeClerc, Brian LeClerc, Klyph Black, and Mike Dorio, has been rocking Long Island for thirty years and is still blowing hard enough to avoid being downgraded to a tropical depression. Check social media for gig dates and locations.

Printed in the United States
by Baker & Taylor Publisher Services